MONEY
DOES
GROW
ON
TREES

Editors: Kenneth Kales, Maggie Cramer, Ann Bartz
Copy Editing: Ann Bartz
Cover Design: Danijel Trstenjak
Text Design: Aykut Ogut, Benjamin Cziller
Illustrations: Danijel Trstenjak
Special thanks to David Woghan and Author Imprint for guidance.

ENVIRONMENTAL BENEFITS STATEMENT

AYRA saved the following resources by printing the pages of this book on chlorine free paper made with 100% post-consumer waste.

TREES	WATER	ENERGY	SOLID WASTE	GREENHOUSE GASES
66	5,300	28	230	28,700
FULLY GROWN	GALLONS	MILLION BTUs	POUNDS	POUNDS

Environmental impact estimates were made using the Environmental Paper Network Paper Calculator 4.0. For more information visit www.papercalculator.org.

MONEY DOES GROW ON TREES

The Myths We Create and Live By

Esra Banguoglu Ogut

AYRA Corp

I dedicate this book to my mentor, Darel Rutherford. You are like the sun, forever lighting up all that was in the shadows.

And to all the children, the way-showers of the future, who will keep on lighting the path in new, interesting, and ever-growing ways.

CONTENTS

FOREWORD

As a psychologist, I read a lot and have continued throughout my career to take a variety of courses and attend educational programs about psychology. However, although there is a lot of valuable material out there, I would always feel as if there were a missing piece, especially in handling adult cases.

That missing link I found in the teachings of Ike and Esra, especially because they teach and coach in a manner that is so practical and applicable to daily life.

First . . .

I used everything I learned from Ike and Esra on myself and started experiencing shifts and incredible changes in my own life.

After that . . .

I began to use what I learned on my clients, both children and adults.

Now . . .

I hold space for my clients by helping them discover their self-imposed limitations, their own dreams, and how they can reach toward and become their next desired version of themselves.

I started connecting with my clients not just on a mental level, but also more deeply with the core of who they really are.

Most importantly, I transformed from a psychologist who sees clients as people who have problems that need to be fixed to a psychologist who recognizes my clients' power to discover their own self-imposed limitations and find their own solutions, which empowers them.

I learned from Esra the best version of the "Inner Child" work I have ever come across. It changed my life deeply and in applying it to my clients now, I witness every day how effective it is.

On a personal and business level, I learned what it means to smile at my Ego, to raise my vibration, to own my inner power.

In the process of applying the teachings, I . . .

Found the perfect house
Set up my own business
Increased my income threefold
Created a relationship beyond my wildest dreams

AND got married . . .

I learned to love myself more deeply and experienced freeing myself from my own limitations many times over. But what I treasure the most is that I transformed into a psychologist who has so much more to give to her clients now.

Esra Banguoglu Ogut teaches, above all, by who she is and how she walks her path, and I thank my dear mentor for helping me advance in my career and set up a life that I love. I am forever grateful.

I have no doubt that with this precious book she will enable many more to awaken to their power.

— **Melis Ozmen Bilgin,** *developmental psychologist, MA*

I love, love, love this book! Esra Banguoglu Ogut is a mystic so ancient in wisdom and yet so young at heart. I feel her here in her "Earth self" as well as the other Esra who lives in another place full of light and life, and she shares how we can all do it.

In this read, Esra can reach everyone, and I mean everyone.

Esra is talking and walking with the reader.

She never feels that she is above anyone, and is not talking at anyone.

She is just standing by the reader's side, saying,

"You can do it. I know you can. Let's get going!"

My prayer is that this breath-of-fresh-air book becomes a bestseller.

— **Gurmukh Kaur Khalsa,** *author, Kundalini Yoga instructor, business owner, and the pioneer of prenatal yoga*

The Universe speaks with us, whether that is through a person, a course, or a book. When we are ready, the messages start coming. The book you are holding in your hands is full of such messages.

You will receive as much as you are ready to receive. But I can guarantee this much: When you are done with this book, nothing will be the same in your life.

Are you ready to open the doors to your new life, to your new self?

— **Secil Ozcan,** *clinical psychologist*

I have been working on myself for years as part of an international peer counseling community, making great strides in leadership and antiracism and recovering from loss. But I am still far from where I'd like to be in the areas of love and money.

I was just starting to think that I might be unknowingly sabotaging myself when this book came along. Just reading through it, not even doing the exercises yet, has allowed me to see clearly where I've been holding myself back and to get to work breaking down the early decisions I made.

I can't wait to sit down with Esra and this book and really make some sparks fly!

— **Ann Bartz,** *writer, editor*

TESTIMONIALS

I intended to earn a quarter of a million dollars in my business. This was my "crazy, just for fun" goal I set in the transformational coaching certification program. I let go of trying to figure out the how and I chose to believe it was 100% possible.

Today I am holding that check in my hand.

— **Duygu B.,** *business owner*

So much changed with transformational coaching, I don't know where to start. It's as if the neurons in my brain changed—the way I think changed, how I apply myself in the world changed, and with that everything else changed. I went from being someone who worked really hard and hardly made any money to someone who hardly works and makes profits easily—and on levels I could not have even imagined as possible before.

— **Sibel Ulutas,** *business owner*

I had been waiting to be promoted for a year and a half. Usually the promotions happen in November in my company. I set my intention, became clear about what I felt I deserved to get paid, discovered and cleaned up my limiting beliefs around prosperity, and decided to fall in love with my worst-case scenario.

The day my attachment was broken my boss called me to give me the good news. I had been promoted and I was offered exactly the amount I had envisioned. This happened in March—

not only nine months early, not only a very high amount that I had only dreamt of, but also at a time when the company never made such decisions.

— **Seran E. Macmillan,** *financial planner*

I think I just cried from happiness for the first time in my life.

For eleven years I have been applying for the green card lottery hoping one day I would win. This year in the transformational coaching certification program, I applied the techniques we were learning to this issue. First, I made my worst-case scenario all right. I said to myself, "If I don't win, I am moving to England instead." I let go of my attachment to residing in the US. Simultaneously I visualized, with passion, not only a home in Los Angeles but also a position that would pay me what I wanted. Two hours ago, I received the news that I finally won the green card and that the position I am applying for pays $250K a year.

Secondly, I manifested an amazing relationship.

It is new, and we will see how the dance goes, but the important thing is: I feel as if the old Busra has died. My perception of the world is different, the way I breathe is different, the way I let life in is different. This is what truly matters.

— **Busra Deler,** *physicist*

After understanding what it means to take back my personal power as a result of being in the transformational coaching certification program, I confronted a family member about a longstanding issue. It was difficult and I felt a lot of pain, but I did it anyway.

I used Esra's technique of asking the pain a question: "Pain, what are you there for?" There was just one very clear answer: "To free you!" The pain was showing me the way to my freedom by sitting there and hurting me until I chose out of my self-imposed limitation.

— **Ipek Tiryaki,** *business owner, yoga teacher*

TESTIMONIALS

I have a 7-year-old son who was very social, outgoing, and talkative, but only when we were around. He didn't like being anywhere without us and cried a lot in our absence.

He loved his swimming classes but stopped going since we could not be there all the time. Same thing happened with basketball. I had been trying to solve his attachment to us for years.

One day, I remembered how traumatized he was when we first took him to kindergarten as a 3-year-old. He had cried for hours, thinking we had abandoned him, and I realized from my own Inner Child work that he was still watching that same movie.
So I guided him with the technique and asked him to talk to his 3-year-old self. I asked him to remind his little self that we always returned to pick him up, that we were never going to desert him, and that he didn't have to feel alone and scared.

His eyes widened and he looked into my eyes deeply. I asked him to hug the 3-year-old and say all of the above. He did. It was so amazing. All of a sudden his posture changed, his looks changed, and now he goes happily to play basketball or do other things without needing us to be there.

What wasn't solved in years was solved in two minutes with the Inner Child work.

— **Burcu Korkut,** *teacher, life coach*

I go to that poplar tree, where the lonely boy, ashamed by something that happened, leans against it. This was a long time ago, but that visual would come up every time I felt lonely.

However, it's not the same child anymore because now I spend time with him. We sit together, we talk to each other, sometimes we play a game and wait for the school bells to ring together. A philosopher once said, "The motherland is one's childhood"; this is where I dwell lately, and with each dwelling and journey, I love myself more.

Thank you for the Inner Child work.

— **Cakir Aksit,** *lawyer*

THANK YOU

Special thanks to the love of my life, Ike Aykut Ogut,
a part of my soul. The joy you are, the jokester you are,
the deep seer you are, and the love you give continue to
inspire me every day. This life is a miracle and an
adventure with you. The space you held for the birth of
this book has been incredible.

To Gurmukh Kaur Khalsa for your healing touch and the
way it has opened my heart.

To Diane Opal for holding my hand as I wrote this book.
We discovered so much more together.

Thank you to all the special people above, and to all
my other precious teachers and mentors along my
path who have helped me continuously go toward the
beyond.

— Esra B. Ogut

Know Thyself

— The Temple of Apollo

INTRODUCTION

A PERSONAL STORY

Many years ago, when I was in the middle of experiencing financial limitations of my own, if somebody had walked up to me and said:

— You know, you are experiencing these difficulties because of what you choose to believe.

My response would have been:

— Come again?

I wouldn't have known what to think.

This book is not only about prosperity consciousness and ways to connect with it, but also about how we set up our own realities and limitations. It's not just about exploring the reality we would prefer to be living in, but also how exactly we create unwanted experiences.

- What are the beliefs we have?
- What are the limitations we successfully set ourselves up to experience?
- How are we setting them up?

- Why don't we let go of limitations easily?
- What is the benefit, or the gain, in holding on to them?

For more than a decade, from my 20s to my 30s, I enrolled in many courses of all kinds to discover more about myself, to learn how to have a better life and how to reach my dreams.

I guess deep inside I always felt the discrepancy between who I was taught and conditioned to be versus who I truly am at the very core of my being. While the courses were worthwhile journeys, the shift I experienced from Darel Rutherford's coaching was a turning point on all levels.

Although I always knew that we create our own reality, because life had demonstrated this to me at various times ever since I could remember, through Darel's coaching I got it on an entirely different and tangible level. With this discovery, the level of empowerment that came through was nothing less than life changing.

In the journey of self-discovery, self-help, self-actualization, or whatever one chooses to label it, I had a very black-and-white attitude. I lived with a constant undercurrent of "it will either be my freedom or my death," as for me nothing in between seemed good enough to settle for.

By freedom I meant freedom from pain, wounds, hurts, self-judgements, society's expectations, shadows, other people's authority, financial restrictions, dysfunctional relationships, all of it.

The freedom to soar toward one's potential and beyond seemed like everyone's birthright to me. What was the point, if this was not the journey?

This belief had been such a relentless driving force since my youth that I was prepared to do or relinquish anything for its sake, in large part because the sense of feeling caged inside my psyche had created feelings of not wanting to live at times. So much so that I almost got exactly what I asked for.

At 16 years of age I had a near-death experience. Having almost drowned, I went to the other side; I clearly saw my body left behind as I watched it from above. The amount of information downloaded in what must have been a couple of minutes under the water was many lifetimes' worth. Finally, the answer to my burning questions had arrived:

- Who am I really?
- Who are we really?

Perhaps I will share more details of this incident in another book, but for right now, suffice to say that when we are truly sincere in the seeking, the doors really do open, sometimes in the most mysterious and unexpected ways. I chose to stay even though I was nearly on my way out. I was slammed back into my body, carried in by a wave, and parked near the shore where I swam for my life, like a cartoon figure almost walking on water, the rest of the way.

I thought I was golden and invincible due to the knowledge, or rather the remembrance, I had acquired through the experience— not realizing at the time that knowing something is not necessarily the same thing as being able to live by it. I have since come to understand that knowledge is vastly different from the actual acquired consciousness of it. Just because we have read about how to operate a car doesn't mean we can go out into traffic and drive all of a sudden.

So my life didn't change as I assumed it would after the experience. I had remembered who I was, who we were all truly in our essence, but I didn't know yet how to apply that remembrance to life. The incident was so out there, and with no one to process it with or believe me fully, I had to catalog it as an unknown in the library of my mind for a long time. I had no reference point to ground it. At one point, I even justified it away as maybe some sort of a dream I had as I passed out under the water. Yet part of me always knew it was more real than anything else I had ever experienced.

It goes without saying that this experience guided me through much of my life after it.

In retrospect, I realize my quest for freedom began as a 5-year-old as a result of something seemingly inconsequential, yet it was indeed a very profound point that defined so much else to follow later. I see now how the patterns and themes set up that day have been major influences on how I have chosen to walk my path.

We arrive at specific conclusions about various subjects at an early age and these conclusions or beliefs we carry around become our self-concepts and the beliefs that create our individual relationships to money, to marriage, to success, to failure, to love, or to whatever the subject matter might be.

We may forget what we chose to believe but those beliefs don't forget themselves. They have a life of their own and overshadow our choices, decisions, dreams, our darkness and light throughout our lives. Those beliefs keep us on a certain track until something happens and we awaken from our own setup and make a different choice that changes everything.

It is like a train ride.

As long as we are on a specific track going straight, the stations we are going to stop at are predetermined by what we have chosen to believe. Once we make a different choice, however, it is as if a new juncture is created, and through the crisscrossing rails we jump onto another track.

Now all the stations, or we can look at them as realities, are different and changed both forward and backward. Things will have transformed both in terms of potential future experiences and how we come to see our past.

As a brand-new 5-year-old, I wanted to dance in the rain. I typically did what the grown-ups wanted me to do, but according to me, a birthday was someone's special day and I had the right to do whatever I wanted to do that day. So I demanded to go outside and dance in the rain.

We were living in Bulgaria at the time. The energy of the country was so oppressive under the communist regime. The buildings were dark, the weather rainy, the people unhappy, and the sense of lack and not being allowed seemed to permeate everything. As a child, I sometimes thought of countries as colors. For me back then, Bulgaria was grey.

On that day, the one that was supposed to be my special day, I wanted to dance, to celebrate, to create some sort of fun and joy on my own, but I wasn't allowed because the grown-ups didn't want me to catch a cold. I demanded, I cried. It meant so much to me, but not having the words yet to express what was really going on inside of me and how much it all meant from my perspective as a child, it came out as a tantrum and did not go down well. It was really a crying out for the right to be myself. The grown-ups were angry with me and they expressed it in no uncertain terms.

Either in that incident or a little later, I declared to my parents that I wanted to die and even refused to eat for a bit.

— If this was how life was meant to be, I didn't want life.

Now, you may say:

— So what? It's no big deal.

It is a big deal and not a big deal at the same time.

It's not so much about whether what happened was really dramatic or can be seen as inconsequential. It's also not so much about whether the event was a misunderstanding on our part or somebody's actual fault. What makes it a big deal is our own conclusions about the event, either positive or negative, that we arrive at through these kinds of happenings. Those become the very belief systems that set up our realities in very specific ways.

I am so grateful for that day, as it created a wound but it also created a desire and a commitment to go beyond my perceived limitations no matter what it took. Often the imprints, the limited perceptions, the wounds we acquire that create our shadows become our gifts in the transformation of them.

They are precious.

Initially, I tried to find that freedom by rebelling as a teenager, by moving to the US in my mid-20s, by experimenting with drugs, by trying to earn my own living and stand on my own two feet, only to eventually realize I was looking for freedom in all the wrong places.

Freedom wasn't about what I was doing, it was about who I was being. I wasn't going to find it in drugs or by moving to faraway places. It was inside of me. I was so attached to freedom that I was far away from it.

Now, you might be asking:

— What does all of this have to do with money or prosperity?

It has everything to do with it. Most people want prosperity so they can be free from something or other, not realizing it is not the lack of money that keeps them bound.

How many people do you know:

- Who are very rich and very caged in by their wealth
- Who are very poor and very caged in by their scarcity
- Who are rich yet happy and free
- Who are poor and yet happy and free

There are plenty of examples from each category (though your belief systems might make it seem as if only one category is true).

The common denominator of whether you are happy or sad, feeling free or caged in is not money. It is the beliefs you have developed around the subject.

Darel Rutherford started coaching in the early 1950s, before coaching was a thing, and began coaching Ike and me in 2005. I set myself free with his help as soon as he shed some light on my thinking. I was having financial problems . . .

Not because money was hard to earn
Not because I wasn't an American citizen at the time
Not because of whatever other reason there seemed to be

But because—without realizing it—I chose to.

— What???

In a million years I couldn't have imagined that I was the successful creator of my own limitations around prosperity because of what I chose to believe for such a long time. And I also couldn't believe how fast the illusion I had set myself up for crumbled once I became aware of it. My perception shifted from feeling like a failure to realizing how powerful I am, even in successfully creating limitations.

By virtue of what we choose to believe, we live—whether we end up liking the results or not.

Time and again, I have seen in myself, in Ike's life, and in the lives of the many clients we have coached over the last decade, that when one takes true responsibility for having created a problem, one also gains the power to solve it. Taking responsibility isn't accepting blame, and it isn't finding fault with oneself whatsoever. Rather, it is about tapping into the unlimited true power lying at the core of each and every one of us.

That is what this book is about, with an emphasis on prosperity.

After that turning point, my life started to become more and more like a dream. This doesn't mean I don't have new challenges, new paths to walk down and understandings to gain, or other shadows to overcome, but I do have an incredible life that has been one big, adventurous ride.

- I have a career I love, that I wake up to with joy every day.
- I have a work life that inspires me all the time.
- I'm surrounded by clients finding their own power and light, and ever-growing prosperity.
- We have our own successful business we operate as husband and wife.
- We have a beautiful home we bought in Hawaii, a place that was a long-time dream to go to, even just for vacation.

But the most magical of all is my relationship with Ike. We work together, we journey together, we help one another grow, and we laugh a lot from sunrise to sunset.

Freedom has a very different meaning for me now. It's knowing that all we dream of, whether personally or collectively or whether for our own lives or for the world, is possible.

Freedom is also about loving the limitations in life and in myself that do exist, as there is no journey to be had without them. Indeed, chasing freedom or perfection is the biggest trap. Once we graduate from a certain set of limitations, a whole new and different set comes to play with us, helping us to expand even more.

I intend for this book to shed light and help you transform some limitations you might be experiencing, whether financial or otherwise, as the principles are the same for all subjects.

Included in the book are those certain principles, examples from clients, personal stories with Ike, easy and very basic exercises and questions meant for self-exploration and reflection, and simple practices and habits you can integrate into your daily life.

There is also the deliberate use of repetition, since the book is meant to help you acquire certain tools to travel with on your own, and I find repetition is a must for learning.

Not everybody has the time, the desire, or the current finances to take a course, and I know so well what that feels like. I wanted to create a book that gives as much information as possible but that also requires active participation from you.

Remember, everything you are searching for is in your own backyard.

Money DOES grow on trees.

Myths
which are believed in
tend to become true.

— George Orwell

THE MYTHS
WE CREATE
AND
LIVE BY

We create our myths. In return, our myths create us.

In this sense, everybody is a stellar author. We write fantastic scenarios, and then life becomes the perfect stage on which they are played out by perfect actors amidst perfect décor. The good news is we are as free as a bird to rewrite our story and change our own life experience whenever we choose.

Let's look at two examples:

Rebecca wanted to solve her problem with her living situation. She had been stuck for six years paying rent in a place she hated. It was a room in somebody's house. Though she was super intelligent and capable, her life was not moving forward. The outward reasons for her being stuck seemed to be that she didn't have money saved up for a deposit, the rental prices in the area she preferred were over her budget, and the process of finding a new place was a nightmare, as her credit score wasn't very good. More importantly, she had tried many times without any success. However, a house was just a small example, a symbol, of a much larger pattern that was keeping her from moving forward in general.

She claimed she wanted more income, though she resisted more prosperity. She claimed she wanted a relationship, but she hadn't had one in a long time. She claimed she wanted a better living situation—a nicer, larger, airier place to live—but she'd let six years pass without manifesting a new home.

Why was she resisting a better life?

If we aren't living the reality we dream of, it's because there is a part of us that doesn't actually want to claim that dream. Hence the game of yearning on the one hand and not allowing ourselves on the other hand persists.

I asked her to picture herself in a lovely relationship, in a rental home she loves and with an increase in income, and asked her to get in touch with how she was really feeling in having this dream life.

— What is the resistance here? What comes up?

To her own great surprise:

— Pain and loss. What's the point? It's all going to come crashing down in the end anyway.

— Why do you feel that way about having more?
— I don't know!

And on the superficial, surface level, she was right! She didn't know. We don't know. But if we go down the rabbit hole, we can find out. The information isn't sitting on the other side of the planet hidden in some secret locked treasure box buried at the bottom of the sea and guarded by sharks.

It's much closer to home than that.

When we looked at her earliest memories around money, the scenes that kept coming up were her parents at each other's throats most of the time. And their fights always revolved around money.

As a little girl watching her parents argue, she came to certain conclusions about money:

Money is the cause of unhappiness and pain.

Eventually her father left the house due to all the fighting.

Money brings pain and loss.

For Rebecca, money had various painful emotions associated with it. The fights had been traumatic and any happiness or peace in the household was short-lived. Whenever her mother gave her money or bought her something new, she would end up paying dearly for it.

To receive even a good thing usually ended up as an emotionally painful experience for her. Either her mother would expect Rebecca to appease her in return or she would go on and on about the sacrifices she made for the family, causing Rebecca to feel guilty for accepting anything.

Nothing good lasts forever!
To have more will cost me dearly in the end.

These were her specific decisions around money from childhood that tied into the whole idea of why she was not allowing herself to receive more as an adult.

"Having more" translated to:
* Pain
* Inevitable loss
* Unhappiness
* Having to pay an emotional price

Why would she allow herself to manifest more?

If more of a good thing—a partner, more abundance, or better living conditions—meant pain and loss, she would unconsciously be protecting herself from expansion in those departments. Which was exactly what was going on.

Once she could see that her own limiting beliefs were the real restrictions, she was able to choose to get out of her box, in this case literally, and move into a better house.

That week she looked for a new home and immediately found one, in her first attempt.

It was the perfect new space: in a better neighborhood, a lighter and brighter home. Neither did the landlady care for any of the usual paperwork, nor did she require a credit check. The price was perfect. And what hadn't happened for six years happened in an hour.

Just by becoming aware of how she was limiting herself based on her past, she was able to take a step forward.

Whether it is a lighter and brighter new apartment or a lighter and brighter new future, once we rediscover our own inherent power of choice, the illusion of restriction begins to melt away.

Many of us have experienced that magical moment when something turns around—a problem is solved, we get out of the box, we claim our victory, our body feels light and free, we feel empowered and amazing, as if we have reached the final pinnacle—only to go right back to how we were living before.

Why do we slip back into the old patterns so quickly, when the new can feel so good?

There are two main reasons why we can so easily go back to our old patterns and old ways of being, even after we have seen clear evidence that something more is possible.

1. We haven't made a real new BEING choice.
2. We don't understand the EGO's natural resistance.

Both of the above will be explained in further detail in the upcoming chapters.

For now, I'll briefly say the EGO's job is to maintain our habitual reality. Even if we are living in a situation we dislike, it is going to maintain that reality. That is why the simple act of moving can take six years. That is why finding a simple solution to a problem might seem impossible.

The EGO's job can be summarized as follows:

Getting you back into your box.

It's one thing to get out of our box, a certain reality we have been living in and that we have come to really dislike, but quite another to actually remain outside of that box for the rest of our lives. One of the ways in which the EGO achieves its goal of getting us back inside our box is to erase from our awareness any victories we had outside of it.

The EGO is there to provide amnesia, so we stay put and don't rock the boat too much.

Obviously, in the example of Rebecca, she is not going to go back to her old shoebox living situation. However, does that mean she is going to allow herself to have a better life in general?

Not if she forgets.

At this point, it is so important to learn how to manage the EGO so as to not get caught up in its natural resistance to change. Otherwise the EGO succeeds in putting us back into the box very quickly.

To change a single outcome of a general pattern, such as finding a new home, is one thing, but to shift an entire pattern that touches so many areas of our life is another thing altogether.

Another client of ours, Ipek, worked on herself for 14 months in our certification course and learned very well how to manage her EGO.

— We sold the company we created with my sister. We put in $30,000 to start the business and sold it for over $200,000. I came to Ike and Esra's certification program to learn to create prosperity, but even I wasn't expecting this much. Besides the sale of the business, my monthly income went up as well. When I calculated everything, my total income increased eightfold in just over a year. It is the first time in my life I have had this kind of money. The treatment I got at the bank when I went to deposit it was incredible. It was a lot of fun and very empowering to experience such a reality so quickly.

Ipek, just like Rebecca, had negative associations with money, a myth that was not serving her prosperity.

— I remembered that once when I was a little girl my parents were talking about money in the living room as I watched television. They were conversing about an acquaintance who had recently come into a substantial amount of money and how it had ruined the man. He had started looking at other women, so the relationship with his wife had been ruined; he had stopped talking to his old friends; and his whole life had turned upside down.

As a little girl listening in, she had decided that besides the required amount to live on, money wasn't a very good thing to have.

Money and being rich drives people crazy.

By discovering her original belief around money, she came to understand what was holding her back from allowing more abundance in. She had been unconsciously protecting herself from prosperity.

Ipek chose out of her old belief about money and made a new "BEING choice," as we call it, a term coined by Darel Rutherford.

She decided to become abundant on her own terms. She realized that the story and example of that man did not have to become her own life story and baggage to carry around. It was not a doing process that caused her to jump so high but a change in who she was BEING in relationship to money that created the increase in her income.

In essence, it can be this simple and quick to turn things around:

1. Have a goal, a vision, a dream.
2. Discover what belief separates you from the goal, vision, or dream.
3. See how ridiculous the belief is, where it comes from, and laugh out loud.
4. Make a new BEING choice to belong to what you are asking for.

A new BEING choice is a decision that changes our entire perception of and relationship to whatever the subject matter is. It is not just a new choice, but also a total new decision to BE different in relationship to a subject.

A BEING choice is like a champagne bottle that pops its cork and begins to spray out after you have shaken it a good bit. You pop out of the illusion of your restrictions and become your own little genie granting wishes one by one to yourself.

It usually follows an *aha* moment of realization, like an awakening of sorts, and is not a logical, linear, intellectual process. What looked impossible previously now magically feels possible and accessible, and therefore is possible and accessible. It's a shift in your total state of BEING, bringing equally a shift in your reality.

We make BEING choices throughout our lives many times over without realizing it. But when we can understand the concept tangibly, and consciously place it in our magical hats as a tool to pull out and use whenever needed, then we can move and shake things, solve problems, and shift stuff around at the speed of light.

It really is like being introduced to the fairy godmother or the wizard inside each and every one of us.

Going back to Ipek's story:

She couldn't have created such an increase in income had she not changed her relationship to money. Even if she temporarily created an increase, she wouldn't have been able to sustain the change without knowing that the new fears and restrictive inner dialogues coming up were only her EGO trying to protect her from losing it based on her personal myth about prosperity.

She had to retrain her EGO by giving it a new message to uphold, and let the EGO know and understand it's okay and safe to allow more abundance in.

So far, she hasn't gone crazy and her prosperity is on an ongoing trajectory toward even more expansion.

I would repeatedly have a version of this conversation with my mentor:

— How does one make a new BEING choice?
— How does one jump into a pool?
— One just does.
— Exactly! There is no how to it!
— Huh??

We will dive much more deeply into the EGO and the BEING choice later in the book. Don't worry too much about understanding these concepts just yet. In the meantime, I would like to invite you to consider abundance to be like oxygen.

In reality it is readily and equally available to all of us.

The question is: How deeply are you allowing yourself to breathe in the abundance? And if there are restrictions, the question becomes . . .

Why?

Take some notes. See if any memories around money are begining to emerge for you.

NOTES _____

_____

_____

_____

_____

_____

_____

_____

_____

Mirror, mirror,
on the wall,
who in this land is
the fairest of all?

— Snow White, *Grimm's Fairy Tales*

THE MAGIC MIRROR

Many years ago I found a letter I'd written to my grandmother. When I was a little girl, she accused me of not loving her because I wouldn't behave in the way she wanted me to.

My counter argument was that I loved her very much, but if she did not have the eyes to see how much, it was her problem not mine. I wasn't going to change my behavior to appease her.

I concluded the letter with the sentence below. In reading it back a zillion years later, I smiled to myself.

Life is like a mirror,
the way you look at it is the way
it shall reveal itself to you.

After a huge detour in life, after having completely forgotten what I knew back then, I ended up not only living life from this understanding, it also eventually morphed into my career. When we can clearly see how we create our unwanted reality, then we can clearly see how nothing happens in it by chance. This allows us to take our power back from wherever or whomever we have given it up to.

Whether that be Hollywood, the producers, the fame, the money, the government, the boyfriend, the mother, the past, the need to fulfill other people's expectations or keep up appearances, the list goes on and on indefinitely. Unfortunately, the word "power" may have negative connotations, as we see so many examples of the abuse of power in politics, business, and society today.

Manipulating or forcing people through will, power or status, through wealth or fear, is not what I am talking about here. That is actually another form of being powerless; it just seems like power to some.

What I am referring to rather is the recognition of our true inner power: recognizing that in essence nothing and nobody can hold us back from anything in life other than the people and the concepts to which we knowingly or unknowingly have given up our power.

No matter what the challenge is, there is always a choice of becoming the victim or the victor each and every time.

Darel Rutherford puts it so beautifully:

> You create your own problems.
> You have the solutions, and in the journey in between,
> you get to discover who you really are.[1]

In the morning when we get up and look gloomily at the mirror, we don't expect it to reflect back a smile. If this were to happen we would probably run out the front door naked and check ourselves in to the very first insane asylum we could find. We don't look in the mirror all disheveled, makeup running down our faces, with dark circles under our eyes from being perhaps too stressed out to sleep, and expect the mirror to say:

— You are the fairest of them all!

Yet in life we expect this as if it is the most natural thing. We expect life to reflect back to us something we are not BEING. How can we expect life to bring us happiness when we haven't made a BEING choice to BE happy?

If your belief is:

- Money is filthy.
- Nobody loves me.
- Happy people are dumb.
- Too much money is a bad thing.
- Honest people live humble lives.
- I can't be happy when others are not.
- I can have money only if I work hard.
- I can't become super rich and remain honest at the same time.

How can the mirror of life reflect back to you something different from what you believe?

I ran into someone I had not seen for a super long time. We invited him and his wife to our home in Bel Air. He was shocked as he walked in:

— You can afford this????

He knew my past; he knew the 500-square-foot apartment that was falling apart, the consistent money problems, not even being able to go out to dinner with him and his wife at times.

He asked us:

— So, what are you guys doing to have all of this?
— We are transformation coaches.
— Tell me, where are you finding all the filthy rich people you are fooling?

I wasn't offended by his comment. I had been there myself in the past, so who was I to judge? Being disgusted by and prejudiced against those I perceived as rich had been my thing too. Smiling, we continued walking, but I thought to myself as we headed out into the garden:

— This kind of judgment is exactly what keeps people limited financially.

I also found it amusing that prejudice against the wealthy has not been added to the long list of prejudices discussed out in the world. I knew from experience that you can't have something you judge. I also knew he wasn't getting out of his money problems anytime soon. On the contrary, things were probably going to get worse for him unless his relationship to money changed. Of course he didn't ask and I didn't say anything. It was not my place to do so.

If someone says "filthy" and "rich" in the same sentence, it is obvious they do not have a good relationship with money.

No one becomes rich with real, honest hard work.

Or,

Rich people are bad.

I'd bet my life he had a belief along these lines.

The big joke is that we experience our limiting beliefs as reality. Of course, we have beliefs that serve us greatly, and those areas of our lives happen to work out wonderfully. Let's also look at an example of when something we have concluded can be of great benefit.

When my husband Ike was in middle school, the other children would not let him play soccer. They just kind of let him hang around but that was about it. On one specific day, the team knew

Ike was going in for surgery the next morning, so to be kind they let him have a go at a penalty shot, feeling sure that he wouldn't be able to score. Ike was up against the best goalie, so nobody had any expectations. He scored with one effortless and effective shot. There was a silence and then everyone cheered him on like a hero.

That day he could have decided:

If people feel sorry for me, I will get my way.

That decision right there could have set up a pattern of being a victim to try to get what he wanted in life. It could have been a very plausible conclusion to arrive at under the circumstances, but he didn't choose that. Instead he chose to believe:

I excel at whatever I do.

If we truly believe something, it has to manifest.

When Ike was in his early 20s, a radio station in Ankara, Turkey, gave him an opportunity to do his own show. Minutes before he was to go on air, they handed him his script. It was an awful script—a total rip-off of a famous comedian back then. So all of a sudden, he started making fun of the script instead of following it.

Next he threw the entire script away and just started to improvise. The whole radio team, now inside the glass studio with their mouths gaping open, wondered what on earth was going on. Who was this guy? What was he doing?

Ike had no prior experience but still became an overnight radio phenomenon. The show was famous for years, as nothing like it had ever been done before. He excelled in his first attempt and named the show "The Crazy Man of the Radio."

Much later, after we met and got married, he wrote a book for the first time in his life. Let me tell you this: Ike is not exactly a bookworm; he has never taken a single writing course in his life, and he has the worst grammar and is terrible at spelling. But the book became a national bestseller in Turkey, selling a million copies. He never even allowed the publishing house to edit his book. Not only that, but the book was assigned in some Turkish schools as an example of how good writing is just good writing, even when the language used doesn't follow proper grammar or punctuation rules.

— I mean, really? Come on!

You might say:

— He must be a genius!

I would be the first to agree that he is, but that is not the point here. The point is: He made a BEING choice, a choice to be someone who excelled in whatever he did. There are many geniuses sitting in their garages, twiddling their thumbs, looking at their ceiling and wondering how they are going to pay rent. Potential is fine, but how we choose to relate to that potential is what counts and becomes real.

For example, we are often taught:

DO – HAVE – BE

Get a job / Work hard / Be rich.
Get on a diet / Eat little / Be skinny.
Get an education / Earn a diploma / Be successful.

However, anyone who has ever gone to school or held a job or been on a diet forever knows that the act of doing by itself doesn't necessarily cut it. You can do until the cows come home and still not get your desired result.

It reminds me of a very frustrating time in Los Angeles when I sent out, on average, a hundred resumés a day for weeks and nothing came of it. Absolutely nothing! I completed my BA at the best university in Turkey, Bosphorus University. On top of that, I studied for four years in the film certification program at UCLA. And yet I simply could not get a job to make ends meet. I had done everything right, but all my efforts weren't yielding even a single result.

If you look in the mirror every morning and see a failure, no amount of doing by itself is ever going to get you to feel like a success. Even after tons of diplomas and certifications, it is your self-concept and the BEING choice that needs to change first before the actions themselves can yield new and effective results.

Who would I be BEING if I were already successful?

If you look in the mirror in the mornings and see fat, no amount of dieting is going to produce lasting results. You will keep finding that fat girl or boy as long as this is your identified and default self-image setting.

> Whether you think you can
> or you think you can't,
> you're right.[2]
> — Henry Ford

I am not talking about what we:

- Think we believe
- Hope we believe

- Try to prove we believe
- Really want to believe
- Thought we believed

Often, we don't even know the difference.

One of the ways in which the gap between what we think we believe and what we actually believe expresses itself is through disappointment. This is a feeling we can fear or dislike; however, it is such a great measurement and reality check for our gaps. The proof of what we truly believe as opposed to what we think we believe, on the other hand, is evidenced by our manifestations.

If you want a life of prosperity, for example, if that is your choice, it is wise to ask yourself:

— Who would I be BEING if I were already prosperous?

Are you waking up like that?
Looking in the mirror like that?
Feeling and acting like that?
Thinking that way?

Are you embodying the answer to the above question?

You have to choose to belong to what you are asking for before you can actually have it.

The formula is **NOT**: DO – HAVE – BE

The formula **IS**: BE – DO – HAVE

It takes a journey of self-discovery to unmask the self to the self. No matter what, under the layers and layers of all those masks, beliefs, emotions, and thoughts we all carry around, only love remains. I believe this is our true nature, no matter who it is each one of us may have become through life.

Once when I was a young teenager, my family and I were invited to a party at this incredibly rich man's house. People gossiped that he was up to some shady stuff, but nobody knew for sure as there was no proof or evidence to say either yes or no.

The house was filled spectacularly with super expensive antiques, but people talked specifically about a beautiful mirror in the bathroom. So I went to the bathroom, curious to check it out. It was a big, hefty mirror. I don't know what compelled me, but I decided to take a look behind it.

I guess, in a spirit of adventure, I wanted to figure out if there was a secret passage or a hidden safe the mirror was covering. As I pulled at it to peer behind, the whole antique mirror came crashing down and broke into a zillion pieces on the floor. Thank goodness I got out of the way in time; otherwise it would have landed on my head.

Hot, red, and sweating with embarrassment, I could not even begin to imagine how much it cost and the amount of trouble I was in. I so wished that the floor would crack open and I would just disappear, even though there was no question in my mind that I was responsible and needed to own it. Still, I remained in the bathroom panting and sweating, preparing myself to face the shame.

Eventually I went downstairs, found the rich guy who owned the house, and asked him to come up to the bathroom with me. Upon arriving, with my back to him and pointing to the pieces shattered on the floor, I apologized profusely for breaking something he loved and had obviously spent so much money on. But when I turned around, to my utter shock, I saw he was not mad at all. Instead he had invisible tears running down his face.

— Oh shit! Did this super expensive mirror belong to his dead grandmother or something?

The whole situation felt like it was getting worse by the second. I flashed another fifty shades of red, going from pink to crimson.

In the softest voice, almost shaking, he said, completely unexpectedly:

— The mirror doesn't matter one bit. I thank you so much for being so honest with me.

— What???

In the brief silence we shared, it dawned on me slowly that this rich man did not believe—had never believed—anybody could ever be honest. Not even a teenager like me. In that moment, he was out of his box, out of his regular, habitual belief. Otherwise why would this rich, haughty, older, know-it-all, "everybody is bullshit" guy shed tears from his soul? It was as if a boyish version of himself was standing in front of me, somehow surprised, grateful, and pained all at the same time to witness simple and ordinary honesty.

I just knew in my gut right then and there that the gossip about his shadiness was true. He had never allowed himself to believe that the game of life could be played honestly.

If everybody and everything was bullshit, he had to make sure he was on top by being the best at the game, while at the same time resenting the rest of the world for it. This was why honesty was so outside his box and so shocking.

His story was easy to read in the lines of pain sweeping across his face. We both stared at the loss of his innocence a long time ago. I choked back my own tears as my throat locked in understanding, and I lowered my gaze, hoping to hide my face, as I saw him so clearly now. Looking down at the many broken pieces of glass on the floor, all I could think of was the irony of the décor.

This man is such a perfect contrast to our friend who visited us in our Bel Air home. Wouldn't it be funny if the two actually came to a party together? Silently seething at each other.

The mirror guy:

— You're one of the idiots! For not being wealthy.

Our friend:

— You're one of the filthy rich! For being wealthy.

In this case, our friend would have been right about the dishonest part of the mirror guy.

They would probably hate one another, each seeing the other as the total opposite of what they represent and stand for—never realizing they are playing out the exact same belief through opposite roles in the exact same story.

This is a very common pattern of belief around money:

Money is filthy. Wealth can't be made with honesty.

One had given up abundance to keep his honesty and "goodness" intact; the other had given up his honesty for money. What if both knew that money is not anything more or less than what we individually project onto it?

- Who would they be BEING then?
- What are your beliefs, stories, and myths around money?

Exercise #1: Self-Discovery

1) Who was the main breadwinner in your family?

2) What was his/her/their relationship to money?

3) How did your parents' relationship to money make you feel as a child?

4) What is your earliest memory around money? What were some of the things you kept hearing about money? Observed about it? Experienced because of it?

5) What is a pleasant memory you have about money?

6) What is the most unpleasant memory you have about money?

7) What conclusions about money did you arrive at?

8) Do you see correlations between your financial life now and the conclusions and myths around money you formed as a child or young adult?

9) If you were to come up with your own authentic, current, and updated definition of prosperity, what would it be?

10) What would your life look like with your new definition of prosperity? Describe in detail.

You are so free
that you can
choose bondage.

— Abraham-Hicks

WHAT IS
THE GAIN?

What is the hidden benefit of the problem you are having?

This is one of the most powerful questions I have come to know in my personal journey and in walking paths with thousands of clients. It's a hard question to answer unless you have some sort of understanding that you create your own reality, whether you like the results or not.

Let's say you want to be experiencing something, but somehow no matter how much you want it or how hard you have tried, it hasn't happened.

What is a common immediate response?

— I'm a failure.
— I can't.
— I'm a loser.
— It's over.
— It's too late.
— It's not easy.
— I don't know how.

None of us are failures. We are way too powerful to be! Here is why:

If we claim there's something we want, like . . .

Marriage . . . Wealth . . . Fitness . . . Love . . . Peace . . . Happiness
. . . Success

. . . and it is NOT happening, it is because a part of us has a
GAIN from the state of its lack.

All of us have experienced how hard it can be to change. It can
be frustrating and disempowering, not to mention utterly scary,
pushing oneself into a state of possible hopelessness and eventual
resignation. But what if the seeming inability or failure to change
does not come from an inherent weakness or perceived inability,
but rather from the strength of our choices?

What if it is not a self-sabotage at all but rather a perfect setup?

You may immediately say:

— Well, that doesn't make any sense!

— I'm not crazy. Why would I or anyone else have a gain in
experiencing something negative?

— Why would I have a gain in not having what I want?

— That is absurd!

Yes, I admit it does sound like a riddle from the Sphinx.

However, like those riddles, it takes a bit of reflection to make
sense of it.

In the last chapter, we discussed that we create our own belief
systems. Our beliefs are like the construction of a house, and
they stand tall in our own minds. Once constructed, all the other

thoughts that come must pass through the filter of a specific belief we've built around a subject.

For example:

If we believe we are a failure, we are not going to get out of our comfort zone and try anything new. That way, we can avoid, at all costs, the possibility of the pain of more failure.

— I can't.
— It's too hard.
— It's impossible.
— Forget it.
— It's too late anyway.

OR

Even if we try and succeed, maybe we have a short sense of victory and the thoughts eventually fall back to:

— It wasn't good enough.
— It was no big deal anyway.
— It was a fluke.
— Who am I kidding?

We can always move out of our house if we don't like the neighborhood and go live somewhere else. In the same manner, we are free to change those belief constructions. After all, many of our beliefs are on lease anyway; we have picked them up and borrowed them from other people as we've grown up.

For example:

Money is the root of all evil.

Really? Is that the case? Are there no people around who are doing amazing stuff with their prosperity?

We can change what we choose to believe, especially if we can see how we arrived at those beliefs and conclusions to begin with and wake up to how silly they possibly might be.

We don't really want a 5-, 6-, 7-, or 12-year-old's conclusions about life and money to run the game of our adult lives unless those beliefs are working for us and are aligned with the way we choose to live now.

Even though we don't remember many of the conclusions we arrived at as children, those very beliefs have a charge and a life of their own after we give birth to them, and they don't necessarily disappear by themselves, especially if we aren't even conscious of their existence to begin with. They become the stories and myths by which we live.

Since we are NOT crazy when we originally buy into the belief systems of others or form a conclusion based on what happened around us, mostly as children, this buy-in comes with a certain kind of benefit. There is a perceived gain in the belief. Otherwise, why on earth would we have chosen it in the first place?

For instance, people who have grown up in family situations with verbal or physical abuse have heightened patterns of fear. Their fear in these cases served as protection at the time.

A child *should* be afraid when their father comes home drunk. There could be drama, and it is a good idea to hide to stay out of possible trouble. And if, for example, this child gets a physical beating, they had better shut down their capacity to feel too much; otherwise it is possible they won't survive the pain. But once the circumstances have changed, does it still serve them to keep carrying heightened patterns of fear or being emotionally shut down? Or has it become an obstruction?

Try to look at it like computer programming: Whatever you input naturally is going to have a very specific output.

Recall Rebecca's story from the first chapter. What was her conclusion about money?

Money brings unhappiness, pain, and loss.

If this is how she programmed money in her mind, what would you say her GAIN is in blocking abundance?

"Safety from emotional pain!"

Now think about Ipek's story. What was her conclusion about money?

Too much money makes a person crazy and out of control.

If this is her programming, what can her GAIN be in keeping herself financially small?

"Protection from becoming an out-of-control person."

If your beliefs do not change, you will experience exactly what you believe, not because it has to be that way, but because it is what you have chosen to believe. The EGO protects us from getting out of the box to keep us safe.

Each time we want to change or transform in some way and it just doesn't happen, it is not because any of us are morons to begin with; it is because there is an opposing belief creating conflict and keeping us from where we want to go.

The EGO's GAIN is the benefit we have from things not changing.

Ipek was able to leave behind the little girl running her financial life, and that's what cleared the way for more prosperity to enter her life. She realized it's crazy to believe that all people who become prosperous "lose it" and therefore she no longer needs to protect herself from abundance.

She let her GAIN go as she became aware.

Before continuing, just STOP for a second. Please find a coin.

Now, put it down on a table or flat surface.

Can you please try to pick up the coin?

(Waiting) . . .

Did you?

— But wait a minute! I did not ask you to pick up the coin!

I said try to pick it up! How come you picked it up?

— Confused?

This is really just a silly exercise to drive home the point that there is no state of trying. There are only states of BEING. There are simply two choices: to pick up the coin or to not pick up the coin.

— I am trying.

Is another way of saying

— I am avoiding making a choice.

When there is a GAIN in not choosing, let's say to pick up the coin, we don't. It's that simple. We just call it trying.

When I was in high school I hated calculus with a passion, and no matter how many hours I pored over those thick books, I simply was not getting it. I failed back to back while really, really trying hard not to.

— Trying, but I caaaan't!

The failing grades brought down my general average. According to the rules of the school, we could quit the class if the teacher let us off the hook by sympathizing with our problem. We only had a month and a half left before the end of the semester, therefore I asked my teacher to let me quit, arguing that it was ruining my grade point average in general. He said:

— I don't ever see you becoming more than a C student, but I really believe that you can at least pass the class. So, my answer is going to be no!

What kind of an insult was that? Right then and there I decided:

— I will show you who you are dancing with!

It was the same old books, the same old class, and the same old teacher. Everything was the same but me. This time, I pored over the books in a different state. After he distributed the final exams on the last day of class, he didn't return my exam and instead called me to his office to see me privately. I went not knowing what to expect and not caring what I got as a grade because I had really given the class my best and it was good enough for me. He threw my final exam on my lap almost as if he were mad at me.

— Oh! Shit! (I think I actually said that out loud.)

— You are the only one in the class who got a hundred percent on the final. Congratulations!

I was thrilled and had no idea how this miracle had manifested except for being aware of how different I had felt after his confrontation. Now, looking back, I can clearly see that his confrontation caused me to give up my GAIN to fail by realizing there was no way out of the class even if I was performing poorly. His insult had spurred me into making a new BEING choice to succeed.

I had decided to really BE the one who gets it, instead of just trying.

- We cannot BE overweight and skinny at the same time
- We cannot BE prosperous and poor at the same time
- We cannot BE succeeding and failing at the same time

A solution is always available, but do we really want the solution? Often, we think we really do, and yet there is a part of us that absolutely doesn't.

Now might be a good time to ask yourself:

- What is my GAIN in not creating more prosperity?
- What is my resistance to allowing more to come in?
- What am I really afraid of?
- What am I trying to prove?

Please first reflect on your answers and then write them down before proceeding.

When we find the GAIN in keeping a seemingly unpleasant reality in place, three things happen all at the same time. We discover:

1. THE BELIEF

The belief behind the current reality we are experiencing.

2. THE POWER TO CHOOSE OUT

Once we take responsibility for what is going on in our lives, we also gain the power to change it.

All responsibility, or response-ability, really means is our mature and cultivated ability to respond to life.

3. THE FREEDOM

In finding the GAIN, we are freed up from a sense of feeling helpless and like a victim in the face of our problem.

Let's look at some examples:

Meryem came to take sessions claiming she wanted a more successful life. She was married, and her husband had signed her up for all kinds of courses: an English course, a driving course, personal coaching sessions with me, and more, and all at the same time.

— I want to stand on my two feet and make a living.

Now, it is not like this was entirely untrue. Who wouldn't want to expand their talents?

Initially I found it interesting that her husband was so attached to her bettering herself, and I was curious to find out more. After a couple of sessions and exercises, I could clearly see she was defending the problem, and didn't truly desire to become independent.

— I am trying, but I can't.

Whenever someone is defending a problem with vigor, you can be sure they don't really want a solution for it.

— I'm trying, but I can't.

— Yes, but . . .

— I didn't have time to do the exercises!

— It's hard!

— I don't think I am capable of earning my own living!

— I'm not smart enough.

— I don't think I can manage.

— I'm such a failure.

The desire for change always has to be greater than the GAIN of remaining the same for transformation to take place.

What does defending the problem look like?

Exactly like the above.

1. When the person gives more energy to the problem than to the solution.
2. When the person tries to convince themselves, as well as you, that their specific case is hopeless.
3. When the person whines and complains.
4. When the person is being a victim.

5. When the person is really invested in advertising their
   problem.

There is always an undercurrent of GAIN, a benefit from
experiencing the problem that needs to be brought to awareness
before a person can really be willing to transform.

When we do any of the following in relationship to our problem:

1. Feel sorry for ourselves because of the problem.
2. Blame others or ourselves for the problem.
3. Speak of the problem as if there isn't a solution.

We assume the role of victim and create a state of BEING in which
it is simply not possible to BELONG to a solution anytime soon.
We either BELONG to the problem or to the solution. We cannot
belong to both at the same time.

Why was Meryem defending the problem?

I got her to imagine herself in a picture of ultimate success, one
in which everything she wanted had already been accomplished:
She spoke English perfectly, drove herself around, found a job, and
made enough money to stand on her own two feet.

— What would happen if this were your life now?
— It would be great!

There was hesitancy and discomfort in her voice.

— What would happen?
— It would be really good!

(This is exactly how the EGO defends the status quo.)

— If it would be all good, really, you would be experiencing the solution by now and we wouldn't be having a session about it. Why don't you want to be successful?

She burst into tears.

— If I am successful, then my husband will leave me for sure!

She was shocked at what came flying out of her mouth.

It became obvious that her husband had wanted to get out of the marriage for a while now, but he felt guilty about leaving her before he felt sure she was in a place to be able to take care of herself. Her GAIN in not moving toward her own independence and success was to keep her husband from leaving her. She was using his guilt to keep him at home for as long as she possibly could.

She got it. She wasn't a failure. She was just acting like one and wearing that costume because she had a huge GAIN in keeping herself from success and independence.

— I can't coach you toward holding on to your husband in the marriage when that is clearly what he doesn't want. You have to choose: your independence and willingness to succeed, or keeping your husband around by playing the victim. What do you want?

She chose to remain with her husband for as long as she could. Of course a couple of months later her husband walked out on her anyway.

This is exactly how it works. For us to get out of our own boxes, the active fire of the desire to go beyond the limitation has to be stronger than the active GAIN in staying within the limitation.

There are various reasons why we reject our own power. But whether we get out of our box or not, at the very least, finding the GAIN wakes us up from victim mode.

Finding the GAIN is instant empowerment, because even if you still end up choosing your limitation, you know you are staying in bondage out of your own will. In deeming the GAIN too sweet to give up, you no longer have to waste your energy on:

1. Blame
2. Complaint
3. Defense

Having been the queen of victim psychology myself in the past, I know it like the back of my hand. I know what it looks like, feels like, how it smells, the pain, the naïveté of believing there is no way out, the yearning for someone or something to be my savior or at the very least to give me some understanding, the total disappointment in humanity, the utter abandonment, and the story just goes on and on without a solution.

The problem with the victim psychology is that as long as we are in that space, we are unable to get in touch with the real power that exists inside of us. That is the cost and trade-off in staying in the victim mode.

Finding the GAIN is like finding the hidden puzzle piece within the matrix of our consciousness—our little selves playing hide and seek with the larger-than-life beings we actually are.

Let's look at another example that shows how incredibly healing and empowering finding just the GAIN by itself can be.

Jeremy, a young man with a stutter, came to a session with one big problem: He couldn't say no.

He was a people pleaser.

He always ended up doing what others wanted or deemed appropriate instead of what he really wanted to do or believed in. Even at his job, people would dump all their work on him and because he could not say no, he would take it on with a smile while silently resenting them. He wanted out of his box, but how?

— What would happen if you said no?
— Nothing!
— What did you have for lunch yesterday?
— What?
— Lunch, yesterday?
— Let me think . . .
— Even that simple answer took you a while to reflect on, you see?

Responding so swiftly is the part of you trying to protect yourself from seeing the problem. Don't let the answer be just a knee-jerk reaction. What would happen if you just said "no" to something you didn't want to do? What if pleasing yourself and giving value and support to your own needs becomes as important as running around trying to please everyone else first?

Silence . . . Silence . . . Silence . . .

— I would stick out like a sore thumb and nobody would love me!

Everybody knew him as the nice guy, and it became apparent he did not want to rock that image, so he had chosen to be a people pleaser.

— It's not that I can't say no, I choose not to. Wow!

This pattern looks like the person is such a giver when in fact they are not. A true giver knows very well the balanced way to give and receive. Just as with the breath, we can't live only inhaling nor can we live only exhaling. Even our basic act of breathing requires a balance of give and take. He was giving to others at the cost of not fulfilling his own needs, so as to gain their love and approval.

He was a taker too, but he was just packaged as a giver. Seeing how he set himself up for people to just dump on him and his GAIN in playing that role and the reason for it was an utterly shocking realization for him.

Finding the GAIN was so empowering for him that by our next session, his stutter had disappeared almost entirely. Now it was my turn to be in shock.

The 5th chakra is the energy center in the throat. It rules the consciousness of understanding the power of our spoken word, both in terms of realizing how our words weave our reality, as they are representatives of what we choose to believe, and also in terms of the importance of being able to speak our own truth. When we can't speak our own truth, the energy flow at the throat chakra gets blocked and can even affect our speech patterns.

An awareness of why he was not letting the word NO live in his vocabulary, and a realization it was his choice because of the GAIN he had, was enough to heal his stutter.

Once again, it makes a huge difference to know on a personal level that "I can't" is a lie we tell ourselves. I choose or I don't choose is the truth.

Let's look at another example of GAIN, this time related to restricting financial flow.

I was sitting with a friend in a café in Istanbul, sipping our coffees and watching the boats pass by on the Bosphorus.

Sibel made a moderate amount of money at the time, but she was experiencing financial limitations and so never had enough to live the life she truly desired. She had been working on herself for a very long time, trying to figure out what the problem was.

— I just don't understand why I always manifest finances on a level that is comfortable, but never more than that. I've tried everything. I discovered my beliefs around it but this issue has been a lifelong story. No matter what I do, I just can't seem to break through.

— What if you are getting exactly what you want?
— What? Huh!?
— What if you have a GAIN from holding yourself financially limited?
— Gain? What do you mean?
— You are approaching it like you have to discover a handicap so that you can fix it, as if there is something terribly wrong with you. What if you can't solve the problem because in actuality you don't want more prosperity? What if you are getting precisely what you are wanting?

Sibel thinks about it for a minute.

— But I do want prosperity!

I take a sip of coffee, wondering whether to get into it or not.

— Close your eyes. Imagine you have reached the height of prosperity for yourself. You have a driver, really nice clothes, a large home that looks over the Bosphorus Bridge, and you have investments on top of that. You collect rent from a couple of different investment properties, and you never have to work in your life again but you do so anyway because your work is your passion. Imagine that scenario in great detail just for a couple of minutes.

She cringes . . .

— What is that cringe about?
— I felt guilty in that vision. Super guilty. Like, it's shameful. It is so hot all of a sudden, I broke into a sweat. I can't believe this.

She takes off her jacket.

— Open it up. What is the guilt about?
— Like, I don't deserve such a life . . .
— Why don't you deserve it, if you've earned it? No one said go and steal. You worked, you earned, you invested, and because of that you are living in prosperity. What is the shame about?
— It's not okay for me to have when others don't have! Oh my god! I did not see that coming!
— Then what would you say your GAIN is from not creating any more than just enough to get by?
— To avoid being shamed, to avoid feeling guilty. By keeping myself financially limited, I'm thinking I'm being fair to the rest of the world.
— Is anybody else responsible for what you are choosing to believe about prosperity?
— No!
— Why are you making yourself responsible for other people's choices?

How could she really help others with financial abundance, which was important for her? By keeping herself small and limited or by demonstrating prosperity and abundance is available and accessible to all?

The bottom line is that many problems about prosperity arise from believing resources are limited. When the lack game is on, then you either have characters like Sibel, who feel that having more causes others to receive less, or you have characters who become greedy and want to grab it all for themselves. The underlying belief for both is the same:

There isn't enough to go around.

Just for the sake of getting outside of your own box, how would your relationship with prosperity be if you knew for sure that all people on the planet had an ATM machine personally allocated to them, and they could go to it whenever they chose and withdraw as much money as they wanted?

Would your relationship to prosperity be different?

The core belief to examine here is what you believe about resources and abundance.

Do you believe resources are limited or unlimited?

The source of all resources is the creative force of the Universe, and therefore resources and possibilities are unlimited except by our own perceptions and capacity to limit ourselves.

For example, what did we get out of our fear of running low on energy sources?

It brought out new ideas for creating energy sources from new resources, such as the sun, wind, and ocean. I don't think those will be running out anytime soon.

So, do we just sit there and worry:

— Well, if my house has too many solar panels compared to my neighbor's home, I'll deplete the sun. I won't heat up my home too often then.

There are different GAINS for different people who restrict the flow of prosperity.

Some people cringe because they believe that in becoming prosperous, they will end up alone, as the ones that don't have enough will end up hating them for it. The GAIN is to be loved. Others cringe because they believe they will attract a lot of jealousy and people will try to bring them down for it. Therefore, the GAIN is to be safe.

Women sometimes believe that if they make more than a man, the man will feel lesser and therefore end up leaving. The GAIN is to be acceptable. Yet others believe that resources are limited, that money is the root of all evil. The GAIN is to remain in the "good people's club."

Some believe prosperity comes with dishonesty. The GAIN is to protect integrity and honesty. Others believe prosperity takes away their freedom. The GAIN is to protect their freedom.

Some believe money corrupts and that one can't be rich and spiritual, as if the two have to be mutually exclusive. The GAIN is to remain pure.

And the list can go on and on.

Let's look at one last client story. This one relates to health.

Sharon came to see me due to severe body aches. The doctors couldn't figure out the problem; however, the pain would get so severe at times it would cripple her. There were even times when she would be in bed for months, hardly able to move even an inch.

— What's your GAIN in experiencing the pain?

When we got down to it, we figured out that the problem was in her being a perfectionist. When she was a child her mother rewarded her only if she did something perfectly. She got love and approval only when she performed impeccably. Anything less was met with her mother's extreme disapproval.

A parent's love is essential for a child. Love is not just an idea but also a frequency, a state that is tangibly felt, especially by little ones. Children are extremely sensitive to being loved, and when that love is under threat by parents who mean well but withdraw it as a weapon to get their children to do what they want them to do, it can be very damaging.

As a little girl, Sharon had reached the conclusion:

**I am worthy and deserving of love as long as
I am performing perfectly.**

She hadn't been aware this was what she actually believed.

AHA!

When we wake up to a pattern, the *aha* comes with it. It is like trying to figure out the combination to a safe. When you get the right combination, all of a sudden something just goes *click,* and it opens up and you can clearly see what is sitting inside.

— Wow! This is what I believe!!!

Sharon had continued on as a perfectionist into adulthood and was applying the exact same level of perfectionism and expectation to her own daughter. This is how patterns get passed on from one generation to another until the code is cracked and the pattern is released.

She would run around and clean her house perfectly, make sure that her daughter's homework had been completed perfectly, that the food was made perfectly, that the table was set perfectly. God forbid a knife and fork weren't perfectly positioned next to a plate. After everything had been taken care of at this level of perfection, she would finish each day completely exhausted. Perfectionism was her obsession due to her limitations around how love is deserved.

How could she take a break from life?

— If performing perfectly were what allowed you to be worthy of people's love, what would not performing so perfectly be equal to?
— Loss of their love and respect!
— What can be an ideal way or scenario of not performing perfectly and having a great excuse? How can you be off the duty of perfection without anyone loving you less for it?
— Oh my god!! Getting sick is my way of taking a break without the risk and threat of love being withdrawn from me!!!! It's the only way I am giving myself permission to not be perfect.

(Hallelujah!)

— This is insane! I don't need to feel sick to get off the hook. I don't have to be perfect to deserve love. Heck! I don't even live with my mother anymore.

(Roaring laughter)

— Apparently, she still lives inside of you!

At that very moment, she let that belief totally go, and the aches in her body left with it.

It's been three years since that day. She has never experienced those pains again and her relationship with her daughter is much better now. Sharon no longer pushes her daughter to be perfect and is experiencing the sweetness of being a relaxed and truly loving mother.

Unconditional love of self is indeed the best medicine.

Exercise #1: Finding the GAIN

The great thing about finding your GAIN is that doing so also simultaneously pinpoints your belief. It's like hitting two targets with one arrow.

1. Close your eyes and relax.
2. Visualize your goal.

If your goal is to increase your prosperity, for example, see yourself as having already achieved it, but exaggerate the outcome and take it to the extreme as I did with Sibel. Put yourself in that picture totally and visualize it in detail.

a) What is it that you don't like here? What makes you possibly cringe? What is your resistance about? What do you possibly lose in solving the problem? Write down what comes up.

b) What is your GAIN in holding on to the problem?

c) What is your belief around the problem?

d) What is more important for you: to keep the GAIN or make the change? Why?

e) What new perspective do you have about the problem now, at the end of this exercise?

Alice: Would you tell me, please, which way I ought to go from here?

The Cat: That depends a good deal on where you want to get to.

Alice: I don't much care where.

The Cat: Then it doesn't matter which way you go.

— *Alice in Wonderland*, Lewis Carroll

ONCE UPON
A TIME

Everything can be defined as a relationship. The relationship of A to B regarding any subject:

- My relationship to Self
- My relationship to Others
- My relationship to Resources
- My relationship to Money
- My relationship to Success
- My relationship to Love
- My relationship to Marriage
- My relationship to the World
- My relationship to the Earth
- My relationship to the Universe

A = the person's belief
B = the subject

Think of a two-point relationship with an imaginary box surrounding the two points. The box contains all the experiences possible in both the present and the future as defined by the relationship between A and B on any particular subject.

For this box to change, or in other words for what the person experiences to be different, the relationship between the person and the subject would have to change too.

Self-definitions of various kinds end up creating our reality. If we don't like what we are experiencing, it is always possible to look at that relationship and the mental construct we have set up and change it to experience something different.

Another way to look at it is like a train ride. Let's say a person has come to believe:

I am not worthy.

Maybe our father smacked us on the head when we were a child and called us stupid because we had a hard time solving math problems.

Maybe our neighbors were better off and their children got to have lots of goodies and we didn't, so we concluded that we were inferior and undeserving of nice things.

No matter how we arrive at such limiting conclusions, the journey is going to be the same as long as the conclusion remains active about a specific subject. The train is going down the track of "I am not worthy"-ville. On this journey we will stop only at stations giving us experiences that match this sense of unworthiness, i.e., situations and people that help us feel unworthy.

On the other hand, as I mentioned earlier in the book, if we change the definition of how we see ourselves or a subject, it's like we're on the midnight express going full speed and all of a sudden it crisscrosses and jumps to another track. Now the stations will be entirely different—in terms of our current and future happenings, and also in terms of how we feel about our past. It's an entirely different reality we are living in now.

Let's use my client Sibel's relationship to prosperity from the last chapter as an example.

A = Sibel's belief
B = Her relationship to money because of the belief

What was it? Do you remember?

A = It's not okay to have more when others have less.
B = I am not allowed too much prosperity.

For her to be prosperous meant shame, guilt, and exile from the "good people's club."

What kind of reality did that belief create?

C = A reality in which she made enough to comfortably get by, but nothing more than that.

What was her desire?

D = Prosperity.

This meant that A (her belief) hence her relationship to B (prosperity) creating the C (her current reality) had to change.

Not only that, but to get out of her C (current box/reality) she would have to clearly define a very exciting D (new understanding of prosperity, a new reality) for herself.

If D still contained shame and guilt, she was not going to get there. If D contained a picture full of inspiration, a picture of prosperity that resonated deeply within her, then she was going to get there. And once she changed how she related to prosperity and defined a new picture of prosperity for herself, she would be inspired to belong to that picture and it would automatically clearly signal this direction to the Universe as well, just like a specific address given to a cabdriver.

Clarity is a super necessary ingredient for creating the reality we prefer.

We can't get in a cab and say:

— Take me somewhere!
— Where shall we go, ma'am?
— I don't know! Anywhere!

It's not going to work.

First of all, the cabdriver will assume we have lost our marbles, and second of all they won't be able to drive us anywhere without direction from us.

Say we want prosperity. But just as in Sibel's example, if prosperity is synonymous with guilt and shame, we then get in a cab and say:

— Whatever you do just don't take me to prosperity!

The cabdriver isn't going to judge us. They are just not going to drive us to the land of prosperity; on the contrary, the cabdriver will drive us in the opposite direction. We need to know where we are and where we want to go for the cabdriver to take us to our desired destination.

In Sibel's case, initially she did not have a conscious awareness that she had loaded up her understanding of prosperity with guilt and shame, and therefore she had not generated an exciting, wonderful picture of the kind of prosperous person she wanted to become.

How and why would the Universe help her get to prosperity in that case?

Finding out what our real belief about a subject is and therefore the GAIN from creating and remaining at point C (our current reality) is like an orientation exercise. Once we are clear on where we are, we are free to decide whether to keep staying there or not.

There is a vast difference between what we consciously think and assume we believe versus our real and actual beliefs about things. More importantly, when we discover our actual beliefs, we know the address we're driving to at that point and no longer have to guess about why something is or is not happening.

Remember Sharon with the body aches? She found her current address of creation, but that is not where she stopped; she also defined a clear new address for where she wanted to go.

I deserve to be loved whether I am perfect or not.

She no longer had to live a life in which she performed like a racehorse all the time to deserve love and respect. She could relax and enjoy her life and free herself from physical pain.

You've got to let the cabdriver know where you want to be picked up and where you want to be dropped off.

One way to define and clarify your new address is to write down or picture what your new destination is going to look like until you activate a great sense of excitement about it. The excitement and inspiration will be an indication you are going in the correct direction for you and that the vision deeply resonates within. Write it down or picture it like you are watching it as a movie and you're the star.

If yours is a journey of prosperity, what does being prosperous in a really beautiful, graceful, and exciting way look like for you?

Another exercise is to find twenty separate reasons why you want to be experiencing your preferred reality.

Darel, for example, would give this exercise to prospective clients, especially if they wanted to work on prosperity. If someone couldn't come up with twenty reasons why they wanted what they wanted, he wouldn't even bother taking them on as a client. Darel would say:

— I can't help someone who hasn't made a clear choice as to where they want to go!

Neither can the Universe, as it can't decide for you.

Prosperity was no walk in the park for me either. I think the worst of it was when Ike and I, having just met, went to a yoga camp in Española, New Mexico. Neither of us could afford the camp, so we both signed up to work in the kitchen or greeting area in exchange for the course. On the way there, we spent money only on gas and coffee, and were proud of ourselves for being so careful. But it turned out that I had no money left in the bank, so every time we bought a cup of coffee for $3 or gas for $20, I was charged a $25 overdraft fee by the bank.

When I returned to Los Angeles, to my utter disappointment the balance on my account was minus $550. I learned this in a letter from the bank saying my account had been closed indefinitely. This is what a perpetual relationship of ignoring one's financial situation and bank account can look like.

I was too afraid to deal with how bad it was. I had always hoped somehow my financial ordeal would figure itself out someday.

I paid the debt with help from my parents. However, in the meantime, my bank had reported me to some general blacklist that banks apparently had back then. Not only did they close my account and kick me out as a client, they also put me on this list. As a result, I was not allowed to open a bank account in any bank in the US for three years or so. I was treated like a criminal although I had paid off my debt. It was an awful experience.

Many people have a tendency to live this way, hoping and praying for the best, oblivious to the fact that their thoughts, feelings, and beliefs impact their realities and choices every single day.

For me, even though I had received a great education, from my early 20s all the way into my early 30s, I was either working for free on a film set in Los Angeles hoping that one day my resumé would be good enough to get hired for actual pay, or working in a shoe store or a carpet store for minimum wage just to pay rent. It was always a situation of doing something I loved to do for free together with doing something I hated to do just to earn money.

Does the above scenario give you any hints as to what my personal beliefs around money could have been?

Once in a while, however, I would put into practice something that came from my own intuition or a thing or two I had read in a self-help book that resonated with me and miracles would take place. Jumping up and down because of one miracle or another, I would assume all my troubles had ended and I had finally "arrived" at my destination— only to come crawling back to the same old familiar box soon after.

In the middle of all of this up and down, at a time when I was very stressed and overwhelmed and had started questioning whether it had been worth it to leave my home and ability to earn a better living in my own country and basically just questioning the meaning of life in general, I found something that saved my life: Kundalini Yoga. Disillusioned and depressed and not knowing where to turn, one night before bed I got on my knees and begged the Universe to help me find my way, as I felt totally lost and desperate, not to mention very alone.

The next day, while walking around the block crying, I saw a red brick building, and a voice inside told me to walk straight in. Who just walks inside a building for the hell of it? Well, I did.

I found myself in a yoga studio and was informed that the first class was free. As if hypnotized, I walked into the class of a woman who dressed and spoke like an angel, Gurmukh Kaur Khalsa.

I came out of my depression and drug abuse in a matter of months. I felt as if I had discovered gold. I fell so in love with Kundalini Yoga that I became a teacher myself. I wanted to earn my living by teaching something I loved and was truly passionate about, but since yoga hardly brought in any money, I still had to work somewhere else to sustain my newfound passion to teach.

Ike, on the other hand, had been even worse off before we met. There was a time briefly when he had to sleep in Central Park because he could not afford rent. By the time I met him, he was pursuing acting but making his living as a waiter. We both had some sort of income, but it was still an utter struggle to make ends meet.

Today, as I mentioned at the beginning of the book, we have our own business and work from our home in Hawaii. We have increased our income by exactly a hundred times over. I want you to think about that for a moment. Take out a pen and paper and write down your current income and multiply that by a hundred. All this happened in less than a decade. We work four hours a day, four days a week and take vacations whenever we want. Having to take a vacation from Hawaii is a sweet life.

Did my financial situation sort itself out like I had originally hoped? No!

I first had to sort myself out.

Are we the spider who weaves the web or are we the helpless prey who gets caught in it?

What is destiny?

Do we create it?

Or do we simply play out what has already been created?

When I got on the phone for the first time with Darel, many years ago, I had no idea it was the day of my first step toward financial freedom. Much later, thinking back on what had happened, I realized I had made a new BEING choice shortly before I met him. However, at the time of the call, I was not even aware of that.

At first, I complained about how broke I was and that no matter how much I tried, I could barely make ends meet. Darel slapped me with this question without wasting too much time on my whining:

— Esra, what do you think of rich people?

I was silent.

— What did that have to do with my situation?

It's not something that anyone had ever asked me straight up, and I had never consciously thought about it before. Throughout our session I discovered I disliked rich people. It was as if the rich were the root of all evil and responsible for all the poverty on earth.

— You can't have something you reject. That's why you are experiencing such financial problems.

True. There I was supposedly asking for more, but I didn't like what money stood for and didn't want to become one of "them." All of this was like a news flash for me. There was a total rejection going on, which I had never been aware of before. It really was breaking news.

He proceeded to ask me how much my rent was, how much my expenses were, and what I did for a living.

— I teach yoga.

He cut me off before I could tell him about my second job, needing both to make a living.

— Why don't you charge more per session? If what you do doesn't even cover your basic living expenses, what's the point of working?
— Oh! No! No! I can't charge too much for yoga! Yogis don't make money, and besides I do what I do because I love it, not because I care about money.
— If what you do hardly pays your rent, it is not a business but a hobby.

In the meantime, the yoga center I was attending was probably a more than million-dollar business, which my perception deleted at the time, although it was a fact they were not operating via donations.

Even as I was answering, I began to see that doing something I loved and deemed valuable went hand in hand with me rejecting money. This was a new awareness for me.

But why?

He asked me to connect to my earliest memories about money.

I was immediately transported in my mind's eye into my grandmother's living room, where there was a crowded group of guests she had invited for afternoon tea. I was in the background supposedly minding my own business as a 7- or 8-year-old. It looked like I was watching TV, but I had my ears perked up like a little rabbit, tracking the conversation of the grown-ups very carefully.

One super loud, know-it-all woman was talking about a young girl who had been married off to some prominent old doctor. I think he was three times her age or something close to that. This woman was praising the young girl for making a materialistic choice:

— A woman is stupid if she marries for love. Even experts claim love is just a chemical phenomenon, naturally over in just four years. She was smart and bowed down to this arranged marriage. This is how a woman should be, obedient and smart.

- What? Love was stupidity?
- What planet were these grown-ups on?
- What were they drinking?

Hitting alarming levels of existentialist panic, I peeked from behind the wall to examine how all the other women were responding to this proposition of utter insanity. They were all nodding their heads in agreement as if they were the chorus in a Greek tragedy, though I couldn't tell for sure if it was real agreement or masked boredom.

I was livid, and more than that I was afraid and felt alone, especially because I was not allowed to voice my own opinions as a child. They would have ridiculed me for being too innocent and chided me for meddling in grown-up affairs.

— Are these the grown-ups I am meant to be guided by?

I didn't think so, therefore I went to the bathroom, locked myself in, looked at the mirror, and declared with passion the complete opposite:

— I will always say YES to love.
— I will say NO to money.

No wonder I couldn't make a living as a yoga teacher. Yoga was something that I loved. Therefore, money couldn't be in that picture according to my setup.

Money and love had been rendered mutually exclusive for me; they could not co-exist. I was only a child when I came up with this myth. That day, standing in front of the bathroom mirror, I had willfully chosen to reject money for the sake of siding and aligning myself with love.

When I came back to my conversation with Darel, I was shaken to my core by my discovery that indeed I had been the precise architect of my own reality all this time. I couldn't believe how clearly I was seeing that it had been a choice all along. The perspective of a little girl had been in charge of my entire financial life for thirty-one years.

It was so empowering and also kind of weird too, as the setup started to crumble all around me. My reality was experiencing an earthquake. I remember lying down on the couch after I got off the phone with Darel, with one hand on my head and another on my stomach, and it felt like the room was spinning. It was as if my entire life experience was comically dancing before me, the illusion unraveling like an old sweater when a loose thread is pulled.

No wonder rich people had been so annoying to me. No wonder I turned down any guy who was rich as a date, whether they were a show-off or not.

I laughed out loud at how great it was that Ike happened to have been a waiter—otherwise I probably would have rejected him too without ever getting to know him at all. He also had a vision of first finding love and then making it—wanting to make sure he was loved for who he was. Obviously we had found each other at the perfect juncture in our lives, just before things turned around.

As I was reviewing all this, still lying on the couch, another layer of belief dropped by to show itself before it flew away.

Money turns people bad.

This one I owed to the Turkish movies. The good were always poor; the bad were always rich. Most of the artists and moviemakers in those days were inclined toward heavy socialism, so their views on money were not surprising.

Goodness! All these layers of conditionings!

It felt like we were all living in the theater of the absurd.

Lying on the couch, I knew nothing would be the same again, and that ended up being exactly true. The golden nugget of the session and the real wealth, without a shadow of doubt, was this realization:

— The Universe reflects exactly who we choose to BE.

I was now free to experience both love and prosperity together, as the illusion of my own myth about money had been broken.

Now, you might assume that my prosperity changed because of my mentor or because I took coaching sessions or because I did the exercises. However, all of the above came to my experience because of something else I have hinted at already, the BEING choice. Without it, none of this would have or could have even begun. That is the subject of the next chapter.

Understand and discover the reasons and the personal power with which you create point C (your current reality), then choose and define your point D (your preferred reality). What would that next expanded version of you look like? What would the picture of your preferred reality or abundance definition include? How would you personally wear and carry abundance?

- Does it excite you?
- Does it inspire you?
- Does it give you joy?

If the Universe is your cabdriver, clarity about where you are and where you want to go will give you the two addresses you need. The emotions of excitement, inspiration, and joy are not only the fuel but also the GPS, to ensure that you will persevere and are on track in the preferred direction of your journey.

This is why we don't have to know the "how."

As long as you know the above, the cabdriver will take care of the rest.

Exercise #1: Activation

Write down twenty clear reasons why you want your destination. If your goal is prosperity, write down twenty reasons why you want to be more prosperous. However, all the material stuff can only be one reason—a car, house, clothes, etc., count as one single item, so you have nineteen more reasons to come up with.

If you can't come up with nineteen more, re-examine why that's the case. Examine whether prosperity is really something you want and examine your beliefs about it.

See how you feel after the exercise. What is different? If desire, inspiration, excitement, and joy have been activated, then you are on the right track.

Exercise #2: Clarification

Make a list of your priorities. As simplistic as this sounds, it's amazing how much clarity of action, organization, and time management this basic list can bring. So often, without realizing it, we give our attention and energy to too many things at once, depleting our energy unnecessarily and losing our clarity in the process.

Exercise #3: Busting the "I Don't Really Know What I Want" Syndrome

This is a big lie we tell ourselves. If you want to put this to a test, make a long list of everything you don't want to be experiencing, whether at work, in a relationship, or in life in general. Now that you know what you don't want, write next to each sentence the total opposite of what you just wrote.

See how clear you are? Do you have the guts to choose it?

To Be
or
not to Be,
that is the question.

— *Hamlet*, William Shakespeare

THE
BEING CHOICE

The BEING choice, a term coined by Darel Rutherford, is one of the most powerful, magical understandings for using the creative power that lies within each and every one of us, over and over again. It is so easy to utilize and yet, ironically, one of the most difficult concepts to get across.

We are the force of the Universe, individualized in the here and now, carrying the seed of unlimited creation and creativity inside us. The creative power is nothing we need to learn but rather just realize and remember. Everybody has it but most do not consciously utilize it.

I have witnessed so many times in my own life and our clients' lives what most people would consider to be a miracle. A "miracle" can happen in any area of life once this inherent power is understood, re-awakened, and put back to conscious use.

The Universe is full of possibilities. There are as many possibilities in the Universe as there are stars to count in the night sky, but of these infinite possibilities available to us, we get to experience only one choice at a time.

As mentioned earlier, we cannot be . . .

Fat and fit
Rich and poor
Pregnant and not pregnant

. . . all at the same time. Therefore, we make every choice at the expense of another possible choice. When we make a new BEING choice from the myriad infinite possibilities swirling in the Universe, just that one collapses into our own experience and we call it reality.

It's like changing the channels on your TV. You make a choice to stop at one station after browsing for a while, and that is the movie or show you start to watch. If you don't like it, you can always pick up the remote control and switch the channel once again.

A BEING choice is a decision point that defines which specific possibility you are bound to dance with for a given period of time.

When you make a new BEING choice, it is a total reality shift, just as if you're switching the TV channel from *Jaws* to a documentary about food and travel in Bermuda. Everything changes with a new BEING choice.

Although I'm afraid to introduce the word "quantum" here for many reasons, I will. My hesitation is due to every other thing being called a quantum this and a quantum that these days. Just to be clear about what I mean, I will define quantum in my own terms so that we are on the same page.

For me, the quantum field means a swirling sea of unlimited potentials and possibilities. In this field everything that "was" and "will be" already exists and is potentially available in the now. All time frames and spaces exist simultaneously.

It is the space of Oneness that we all belong to and are extensions of.

Looked at from this perspective, as far as creating our realities is concerned, even what we call "time" is just the speed at which we give ourselves permission to have access to something or not. Once again, we are limited only by our own beliefs.

Out of that swirling sea, what becomes our specific experience is based on our beliefs, conditioning, feelings, and therefore expectations.

For example, if you try to punch a brick wall, you will end up with a broken hand. But a master who has been training to use energy can effortlessly break many layers of bricks with his hand, no problem. What is impossible and detrimental for one person is very possible for another, as the two people relate to the bricks differently. That difference in relationship yields two very different outcomes. Both are people, both are working with bricks, and the only X factor is the difference in their consciousness.

Whether with money, health, weight, or relationships, we need to relate to a concept differently before anything can change. A BEING choice is always outside of our current box, without exception. It is beyond our current paradigms. Therefore there first has to be a desire, a dream to reach beyond the box. This is followed by a choice to belong to what we are asking for before the quantum field can move to match it.

This is easy to realize when we look at innovations and inventions. At first the concept of an airplane did not exist; someone had to dream it up before it became the reality that we all take for granted now. At first it wasn't possible to be thousands of miles away from each other and hold a device through which we could talk and see one another in real time. Someone had to dream it up before it could be experienced as a reality. Imagine going back only a hundred years ago and trying to explain to someone the current capabilities of a cell phone. They would think you were crazy! Innovations and inventions are based on being able to go beyond the box of the regular, accepted beliefs of a certain time, be okay with perhaps being called crazy, and then pulling out from the ether an idea that when focused on long enough finally becomes a reality.

A new BEING choice is made when:

We are able to step out of the box holding our habitual, regular perceptions in place.

This is when what was considered impossible just a second ago becomes possible this second. In moments of shock, this experience is rather common. There are many examples of people stepping outside of their perceived boxes for just a bit and then returning to them once their situation is over. It doesn't stick for them because it is not a conscious new BEING choice. Nevertheless, it happens.

One example, out of many such stories, is Charlotte Heffelmire.[3] She lifted an entire pickup truck, weighing tons, to save her father who was pinned underneath it. She was awarded the Citizen Lifesaving Award for her heroism. I like the way she describes that moment:

— I didn't feel like I lifted anything. I really felt like I was lifting a piece of paper.

Her father calls it adrenaline; others call it the grace of God. I like to call it accessing another possibility when we get out of our perceptual limitations, even if just for a few seconds.

I remember one day when I was a teenager. I came home and found my grandmother collapsed on the floor. I thought she was dying and somehow was able to scoop her up and carry her to the couch, even though usually I would not have had the strength to do something like that. Next I went to her medicine cabinet and somehow knew out of maybe ten bottles of medicine which specific one she needed, even though I had no prior knowledge about her medications whatsoever. I had no doubt about picking the correct bottle and making her take it, which brought her immediately back to normal. Getting out of my box for just a couple of moments allowed me to have access to information about her medicine that had not previously been available to me.

When it comes to quantum physics, people scratch their heads trying to understand what it is and how it works based on various interpretations. Regardless, even from a scientific perspective, it has begun to kill the more mechanistic and linear outlook of the world in general.

"It's not the physical act of measurement that seems to make the difference, but the 'act of noticing,' as physicist Carl von Weizsäcker (who worked closely with quantum pioneer Werner Heisenberg) put it in 1941. Ananthaswamy explains that this is what is so strange about quantum mechanics; it can seem impossible to eliminate a decisive role for our conscious intervention in the outcome of experiments. That fact drove physicist Eugene Wigner to suppose at one point that the mind itself causes the 'collapse' that turns a wave into a particle." [4]

If the mind of the experimenter or scientist is thought to impact the outcome of an experiment through the "act of noticing," why would it be far-fetched to understand that the exact same thing happens as we relate to our own reality?

When we look at all this and tie it to prosperity, how we choose to relate to prosperity and what we choose to "notice" about it defines how it shows up for us in our individual experience.

— Making money is so hard!

Is it really?

OR

Does that become our experience because of our beliefs? Who would I be BEING if I were already prosperous?

The value of the question and where it can take you, if it can be asked and answered with sincerity, can't be emphasized enough. It's a question that has the capacity to kick any one of us out of our box of habitual perceptions about the subject.

Who would I be if I were BEING the solution?

Again, the question can kick any one of us out of dwelling within the paradigm of the problem, which is precisely what keeps us re-experiencing the problem anyway.

Who would I be BEING if I were already prosperous?

When I asked the first question above to myself during the times of financial limitation in my journey, the answer was so simple:

— I wouldn't feel lack.

Who would I be if I were BEING the solution?

— I would generate feelings of abundance inside myself instead of waiting around for my circumstances to change so I could feel prosperous.

Therefore, I created a specific gratefulness ritual, which you can find as an exercise on page 357, and practiced it with Ike every day for 365 days.

If you had asked me how abundant I felt back then on a scale of zero to ten, I would have answered a three or four. In time and with practice, the feelings of abundance and prosperity started spinning around an eight, nine, or ten. I walked around feeling like a millionaire. In December of that year, my income had already increased fifteen times over. Ike's as well. It was that easy, that fast.

We don't have to find a solution. The solution is already in the field. All we have to do is make sure we belong to the outcome, and when we do, the solutions begin to fall in our laps.

Ask me if I made any particular effort to make more money:

— Nope!

Clients increased, new offers started pouring in, new ideas and opportunities started appearing, and all I had to do was sit back and say:

— Yes.

The more abundant I felt, the more came in.

When we make a new BEING choice, the quantum field has to provide everything that belongs to it. Abraham-Hicks calls this phenomenon the Law of Attraction.[5] I like to call it the Law of Belonging.

If the way we are looking at something is not serving us, changing our perception opens up new possibilities. The Universe, or the quantum field, doesn't lack anything. It is already pregnant with ALL and ready to provide the baby once you have made a BEING choice to belong to what you are asking for.

Let me give another quick funny example to underline how practical our daily lives can get with this understanding.

One day my parents came home from a vacation. However, both had forgotten the combination to the lock on their baggage and neither had written the number down. There they were wondering how to break the luggage open, scratching their heads trying to recall the number. I was sitting on the couch watching the whole episode like a funny TV series, extremely detached from the result, knowing there was nothing I could personally do to help. After all, they'd never told me the combination. Out of the blue, silently, I asked myself:

— What would it BE like if I already knew the combination?

I was just playing around. A very specific number showed up in my mind's eye. It just dropped in front of my eyes out of nowhere. I was surprised and wondered where this number had come from.

I blurted the number out and asked them to try it. My father gave me a look as if to say:

— Are you nuts? That's so not the number.

However, my father tried it and the baggage unlocked.

We were all surprised. There was a momentary silence and then we all carried on as if nothing out of the ordinary had happened. My dad categorized it as luck and my mother proceeded to ask what she should cook for lunch.

The EGO immediately brings us back to our habitual limitations, successfully erasing any happenings outside of its regular box.

A BEING choice is a moment in time in which we step out of our habituated perceptual limitations about who we are and what is possible and get to stay out. It is a clear and committed decision to belong to something new in a manner that is stronger than the will of the EGO to keep us in the same box.

All of the examples I have given in this chapter have been a little extreme, just to drive home the point that all of a sudden, we can have access to a whole range of different possibilities once we get out of the box. However, not everything has to be an emergency or a shock for us to be able to get there, and not everything can be such a quantum leap.

As a matter of fact, big leaps are really difficult and not such a good idea. It's like eating so much food that your digestive system can't handle it and you puke it right back up. Little baby steps are a much better and more grounded way of expanding.

In a minute, I will share more down-to-earth and practical examples of a new BEING choice, and an exercise at the end of the chapter will help you remember and understand that you have been using this power all your life and just didn't know it.

But first, let me ask you:

— Who would you be BEING if you were already prosperous?

Think about it! Better yet, close your eyes and then ask the question, then feel it. Write down whatever answer comes up.

What is your answer to that question?

Let's look at some other examples:

During a course Ike and I were teaching, I was searching for the definition of unconditional love and its possible relationship to prosperity. I said:

— We can feel abundant before the money ever shows up, or feel like we are in love before the partner comes, or accomplished before we receive our version of an Oscar. Feelings are free to feel and available for us to activate whenever we want to. Nobody else has control over how we choose to feel. Unconditional love is the permission we give ourselves to feel what we want to feel, without needing conditions or other people to be different first.

Reyhan, a client who really understood this, later shared:

— When you said that, I realized even the right to love myself was tied to a million different conditions to be fulfilled. How far was I from self-love? Very far! I changed my mind about who I was BEING, and decided to BE someone who allows herself to feel whatever I am inspired to feel without expecting anything to change first. A car, a house, a vacation didn't have the capacity to make me feel what I wanted to feel. I had that power. My smile was prosperity . . . My breath was prosperity . . . The joy I felt was prosperity. I started to feel rich in every way. This is the way I started to live my life. Soon after, my finances doubled. The more I gave myself the right to feel prosperous, the more income started flowing to me. I was living with my parents; now I have my own home.

Prosperity consciousness is so much more vast an understanding than just making money. When we truly understand and dwell in this consciousness, money automatically comes with it. Ironically, the more you are in prosperity consciousness, the less you need things; and the less you need things, the more comes to you.

Who needs less? . . . Those who already feel full.
Who constantly needs to buy things? . . . Those who feel hungry.

It is important to find out what that inner emotional hunger is about because buying stuff is just a temporary release until the credit card statements arrive at the end of the month.

Are we spending a lot of money because we are trying to feel prosperous, worthy, loved, entertained, or important? That is not real fulfillment but rather an insatiable hunger that is satisfied temporarily only by buying more. An unhealed wound will resume bleeding when the bandage is pulled off.

Or are we already feeling so much gratitude and fulfillment deep inside that we are naturally a match and a magnet for a life of so much more?

The second state of BEING automatically belongs to prosperity by activating the state of wealth within. And since like attracts like, one becomes a natural magnet for prosperity. Just like fish belong to water and birds to air, abundance belongs to the one managing to feel prosperous.

> The one in prosperity consciousness needs less;
> the one in poverty consciousness always wants more.[6]
> —Darel Rutherford

When we are in the first state described, it pushes us to be under the influence of the Spender's Law. We are under the thumb of the Spender's Law if our expenses are more than or equal to our income. Meaning, there is no positive cash flow. We cannot be in the Spender's Law and in prosperity consciousness at the same time, but more about this later.

When we are charged up with more self-worth, self-nurturance, self-love, and self-fulfillment from the inside out, and provided we also don't have a GAIN in rejecting prosperity because of a belief system, then abundance arrives beautifully, gracefully, and easily.

Now I can almost hear someone say:

— Well, I'm grateful all the time but prosperity doesn't necessarily come to me!!! How come?

I have found through my own experience and through working with clients that people think they are grateful and self-fulfilled when in truth they aren't.

When fulfillment is not a real thought pattern, it doesn't count.

There is a difference between thinking one is grateful and actually BEING grateful as a natural, everyday habit. One is just a concept, the other an actual state of BEING.

For example, Aynur claimed she was doing her gratefulness exercises and that she was also creating and minding her budget in detail, both of which are mandatory practices in our certification program.

— Nothing is changing in my life! What am I doing wrong?

She was not doing anything wrong, but she was trying to make it happen from a DOING attitude. I had to find a question that would wake her up to the fact that she hadn't really made a new BEING choice to be prosperous yet:

— I am going to ask you a question but I want you to answer quickly without thinking about it. What is the first thing that comes to your mind when I say the word "refrigerator"?

Empty! Always empty.

— Do you see? Images of lack are floating in the foreground of your mind. How is what you are doing going to work if your focus and therefore state of BEING are in constant lack?

AHA! Bingo. She got it!

A week later she got a sum of money from a vacation she had paid for the year before that ended up getting cancelled. Three weeks after that she got an apartment due to an inheritance.

You can call it all a coincidence if you wish.

All of her family members were fighting over which apartment each of them wanted in the building. She was laid back, relaxed, and did not get involved in the fight. Aynur decided she would get the last apartment left over, as she was too busy celebrating how abundance had already started to flow her way. After everyone had chosen the apartments they preferred, she ended up with the one no one else had claimed. It had the best view and therefore the highest value.

How on earth did that happen?

The Universe always reflects back exactly who we are allowing ourselves to BE. It never needs to take away from others in order to do that. Since the Law of Belonging governs us, nobody is left out in the cold, but also nobody is helped any further than what they are allowing through who they are choosing to BE. It is an exact reflection.

I asked Aynur:

— What changed for you?
— I started thinking of my fridge as being full all the time even when it wasn't, and frankly I started the practice of observing prosperity everywhere I went in a very conscious manner.

Choosing out of: "I don't have,"

Her focus became: "I have, I have."

> For those who think they have,
> even more shall be added unto them,
> those who think they have not, even that which they have,
> shall be taken away.
>
> — Matthew 13:12

We can think of prosperity like the ocean. It's vast and unlimited and anyone can get in; it's free. However, how are we, and why are we, limiting ourselves from entering? How are we putting on the brakes? The answers to these questions are different for each person.

Let's look at another example of a client, Inci:

— The first session I had in the course was one of the hardest things I ever experienced in my life. You guys confronted me with being a control freak. I fiercely denied it and was so upset, but soon after I accepted it, as I knew deep inside it was true. That was the first step toward prosperity for me. I realized in my need to control people, I was limiting my own energy and therefore my self-worth. It's like I was not allowed to have until others had. I was trying to course-correct other people's lives at all times. When I realized everybody is as free as a bird to create their lives in the way they choose, whether that is moving toward limitation or away from it, I stopped feeling responsible for others. I stopped the constant energy leakage. I lifted my foot off the brake and boy did I fly. Taking care of myself, caring about the way I feel, gave me more self-worth. I'm allowed to have if I choose, and other people's choices don't have to limit what I am creating. Now I am helping hundreds of people do the same.

Inci's income increased and yielded quantum results. It started with baby steps, but as the momentum sped up, she reached more than twenty times her income per month in a very short time, and it just kept accelerating from there.

She stopped trying to BE a savior and started focusing her energy on herself, and later on those who truly wanted to be helped by going to her classes and paying for those classes. The giving and the receiving were in balance and she no longer had an energy leak.

Her old choice was:

**Everybody else has to be fine before
I am allowed to have.**

Her new BEING choice was:

I am allowed to have even if others choose not to.

A new BEING choice is the seed planted for a new reality to flourish; it's no different from getting pregnant.

Just as you would not ask:

— How do I grow a baby for nine months?

Because the answer to that is simply:

— You don't. It grows itself.

Your part goes only as far as deciding whether you choose to BE a mother or not. In the same manner, your part goes only as far as deciding whether you choose to BELONG to prosperity.

— Do you really choose to BE prosperous, or not?

Notice I did not ask, "Do you want to be?" That is different.

Wanting is only a state of lack. It is only in the choosing that we get to actually belong to what we prefer.

I WANT to clean my car, or I WANT to be prosperous.
Where is the choice point? In the future sometime.
Result? Not happening yet.

I AM cleaning my car, or I AM prosperous.
Where is the choice point? In the now.
Result? It is already happening.

Which side are you claiming?

Looking back at my own journey from financial restriction to
financial freedom, I know the exact moment I made a BEING
choice to be prosperous.

Our mentor Darel Rutherford, all the coaching sessions, all the
endless practice in the living room with my husband, all the
opportunities that kept showing up, and all the financial freedom
that followed came after I made a new BEING choice to belong to
prosperity.

From my time as a student up until that BEING choice, nothing
really changed much financially. I did whatever it took to survive
but ended up remaining financially limited. If I wanted to start a
business, I didn't have the money to start one. If I wanted a baby, I
didn't have money to take care of one.

I was in my early 30s and still living the life of a student. I had
roommates in and out of the house as I was unable to afford my
own place.

In my mid-20s, I made the choice to be self-reliant; it's why I
left home early and why I tried to make it on my own. This was
wonderful and empowering and one of the best decisions of my
life, but on the other hand I wondered why I always had to be

in such a struggle and a feeling of limitation. I didn't know the answers to these questions back then.

On a day when I was reflecting on all these things, a flash of anger rose in my body. I was fed up with the way my life had been, and I had reached an explosion point. Like the volcano Pele, I was ready to burn to cinders the way that things had been.

Most of the time—although it doesn't have to be this way—we don't make a new BEING choice until we hit rock bottom. We wait and wait until we are truly fed up and then we decide. The benefit of knowing and remembering the magic of a new BEING choice is in realizing that we don't have to wait so long or wait until we hit rock bottom to make our choices.

Getting up from the couch, I found myself walking to the center of the living room, which by the way was only two feet away, and with one fist raised high in the air and the other fist waving fiercely next to it, as if speaking to some invisible audience, I declared:

— I will never be miserable due to money limitations again!

It was a dramatic moment. If anybody had been watching, it would have reminded them of a scene out of the movie *Gone With the Wind*. The point is that a new BEING choice is not just a casual, intellectual decision made as you chat away with friends over coffee. It is nothing less than deciding to let an old way of BEING die so that a new way of BEING can be birthed. You can be sure it is a BEING choice when you can feel the choice on a cellular level. One feels very different right after a true BEING choice has honestly been made.

When the student is ready, the teacher shows up.

A week later I was on the phone with my amazing, wise, humble, truthful, and out-of-this-world mentor, Darel Rutherford.

Was there any money around to pay for a life coach? Noooo!

A thirty-minute session with Darel cost $500.

A friend who was one of Darel's paying clients had invited Ike to Darel's sessions. When the friend dropped out, Darel offered to let Ike continue on for free, and Ike in turn invited me, as the third person, into our little power pact.

Although Darel had always been dead set against doing sessions for free, both Ike and I traveled on this journey with him for almost twenty years. We didn't ask, we didn't beg, we didn't hope. It just happened.

This is just an example of how everything gets taken care of once we are aligned to what we are asking for through the power of a new BEING choice. If we belong, it shows up.

Another client, Evrim, who attended our yearlong course, decided to get married and have a baby. Previously, she had visited Turkey's top three medical doctors, each one heading one of the three most prominent hospitals in Istanbul. They had all told her the same thing: It was impossible for her to have a baby.

The very last doctor she visited even said:

— With these poor values as evidenced by all the tests we have run, you can't get pregnant even with the test tube approach. It just won't work for you. I am really sorry but pregnancy is not possible in your case.

The doctors believed she was beyond the age for a pregnancy, and the test results clearly supported that picture. But she still chose to do a couple of things simultaneously. First, she made sure she was not attached to the result of getting pregnant.

How did she do that?

By making sure she was in a good feeling state and in a good relationship with the worst-case scenario of not being able to get pregnant.

In Evrim's own words:

— I had learned about manifestation in the certification program. I knew about the power of choice and if we wanted to create something, we also needed to be detached from the results by finding a solution to our worst-case scenario and making peace with it. Ours became the choice to adopt. We decided this choice would be full of gifts of a different kind and got excited about this possibility just as much. Most importantly I had learned to trust my own body, to trust the power of my thoughts and decisions. There was an unlimited trust in existence to mirror that.

Evrim had really started to understand the power of her own thoughts to impact her reality.

— I remember during the program I finally said to myself, if my thoughts can't create my body as I choose, damn me! That means I am wasting my time by not applying what I am learning here.

That is a BEING choice! Right there. Can you feel the strong, no-bullshit decision and commitment level of her choice in her wording?

She got pregnant on her honeymoon before they even got back home. It was that fast. She went back to the last doctor for a check-up upon her return. The doctor was completely shocked:

— What on earth did you guys do? It's as if the previous tests belong to the body of an entirely different person. This is nothing less than a miracle!

She had an extremely easy pregnancy, and her son, whose name means ocean in Turkish, is now one year old, and his eyes remind me of the infinity of the stars in the night sky.

Are you ready?

To BE, or not to BE; that is the question.

Indeed, it is the only question that matters.

Before going on, please complete the exercises to remind yourself that you have always had this power but have simply forgotten it.

A real committed BEING choice to belong to what we prefer, minus the attachment, is the formula to create the reality we choose. One cannot BELONG and BE needy at the same time.

Exercise #1: Reactivate the Remembrance of the BEING CHOICE

Take out a piece of paper and divide it into three columns. In the left-hand column, write down a major problem you experienced in the past.

In the middle column, write down what it looked like when the problem was finally resolved.

Finally, in the right-hand column, write down your memories of the moment you made a new BEING choice around this problem. Where were you? What were you wearing? What was the exact sentence of your new decision? Try to remember this moment in time, to track how your decision manifested in the solution.

(Try to write down at least five different examples.)

1. _____

   _____

2. _____

   _____

3. _____

   _____

4. _____

   _____

5. _____

   _____

EXAMPLE:

THE PROBLEM	THE RESOLUTION	THE MOMENT OF DECISION
I was broke	Met my mentor and became prosperous	In my living room when I decided money problems would never limit my life again
THE PROBLEM	THE RESOLUTION	THE MOMENT OF DECISION

Exercise #2: Stepping Outside of Your Box

Close your eyes and ask yourself the question below. FEEL the answer. Record it on your phone as you are feeling it.

— Who would I be BEING if I were already prosperous?

Exercise #3:

Same as Exercise #2 but related to another problem.

— Who would I be BEING if I were already _____?

NOTES _____

_____

_____

_____

_____

_____

_____

_____

_____

_____

_____

_____

_____

_____

_____

_____

There is nothing
either good or bad,
but thinking makes it so.

— *Hamlet*, William Shakespeare

YOU GIVE EGO
A BAD NAME

You might be thinking at this point:

— If it's so easy, then how come the majority of people don't exactly seem to be living a life they prefer?

It may seem that making changes in your life is being presented to you as if it is so easy. Maybe you even think that this is some sort of pipe dream.

When I experienced various limitations, I would get really annoyed if anyone tried to tell me it was so easy to change my life. In fact, I could have clubbed a yoga teacher of mine on the head when he said to me:

— Just do your meditations, follow what you love, and all will be fine in the end. You'll see!

Change or total transformation can be hard due to a function we all have, and it's called the EGO. Its main job is to protect the status quo, and it will do anything, anything at all, to keep us in the same old box.

The EGO is not evil. It is not there to sabotage us, nor is it an inflated sense of self. It is, however, the holder, the keeper, the protector of our belief systems, whether negative or positive, limited or expansive. Its job is not to figure out what is to our benefit or not, but rather to be the protector of our beliefs.

Beliefs have a life of their own, and the EGO holds them in place so that those beliefs can survive.

Why does it hold and protect so powerfully what we have come to believe?

The EGO encapsulates a belief to hold it in place so we can experience the belief as a reality. In a way, it is like a bookmarker so that we can return to the same page. If the EGO did not hold our beliefs in place for us, we couldn't experience a single thing.

It works the same whether we have decided we like coffee more than tea or whether, as in my example, we have decided money and love can't co-exist and therefore all rich people must be heartless.

In either case, the EGO will say:

— Your wish is my command!

The EGO is like the genie in Aladdin's lamp, who doesn't judge the wish but accepts it as a command. Unlike the genie, however, the EGO can't create on our behalf. But it does, through holding a belief in place, help us experience that reality and repeat it as an ongoing experience until we choose to step outside of that specific belief's limitation.

It was no coincidence that I never made money from a job I loved, no matter how good I was at it, and that I always turned down rich dates. My EGO held my unconscious belief in place so that I could experience that exact reality—love and money don't go together—until one day I chose to get out of that box.

Unfortunately, the EGO has gotten a bad name. Especially in New Age spiritual circles where anything perceived as bad or negative is dumped onto the poor EGO. That's taking us back to the Middle

Ages, when whatever people didn't approve of was believed to be the work of the devil. If you didn't like a healer, you called her a witch. If you didn't like a scientist, you called him the devil.

Perceiving the EGO as a bad thing is like saying a knife is bad. It isn't on its own. It can be used in the kitchen to cut food so that we can make and eat meals, or it can be used to kill somebody.

In either case, the knife isn't good or bad. It just has a function.

If we believe a negative story around money, such as the examples we have already seen, the EGO is going to literally protect us from money. It has so many tricks up its sleeve to do that, but not because it is a saboteur. On the contrary, it is a protector. If we hadn't given money a bad name, the EGO would not be there trying everything in its power to keep us apart from it.

Money is filthy.

OR

Money is the source of all pain and loss.

The EGO is going to be damn sure it protects us from having any. According to its point of view, you need to be protected from becoming a filthy person or a person who can experience pain and loss because of money.

What happened when we first put our finger into a burning fire?

— Ouch!

At that moment, we told the EGO without actually saying it:

— I don't like this pain. Keep me away from it!

The EGO says:

— Your wish is my command.

That is the reason we don't go plunging ourselves into fire. The EGO has learned to protect us from getting burned.

But if we want to learn how to walk on fire, that protection is going to be a big problem. We would need to retrain the EGO to understand that fire walking can be safe. That doesn't usually happen overnight. When in states of emergency, we can all of a sudden pop out of our usual beliefs and setups and get out of the box to experience things that are not a part of our habitual reality. But other than those times, it is important to train our EGO to hold the new reality or BEING choice in place.

Let us take the example of the woman who lifted a pickup truck and experienced it like a piece of paper. She won't be able to repeat it, as her EGO is not used to such a reality, especially when there isn't an emergency pushing her out of the box of her usual perceptions.There is also no motivation to stay out of the box since she will not be lifting pickup trucks for a living.

On the other hand, someone training for a heavy lifting competition at the Olympics can pick up really heavy things and break world records, as the EGO has digested the reality of picking up heavy things. Still, every new level of more weight is a challenge until the EGO accepts the new weight and can perform at levels considered impossible before.

It is important to understand this function, because if we are trying to change anything, anything at all, we will naturally and inevitably bump into the strong resistance of the EGO, which is dead set against anything changing.

You've heard before:

Mary is so full of herself
She has such a big EGO
You know, I hate Jim. His EGO is huge
These rich people! They are so EGOTISTICAL
Jane is not spiritual; she has too much of an EGO

Now write down some ideas you might have about EGO.

For example:

• I'm trying to get rid of my EGO
• I hate my EGO; it always gets me in trouble
• I'm not coming from EGO
• EGO is bad
• EGO is limiting
• EGO should be beaten into submission

With your specific list of sentences about the EGO, let's go ahead with a simple exercise.

Repeat each sentence but cross out the word "EGO" and replace it with the word "I." Using the sentences in the above example, the list will look like this:

• I'm trying to get rid of I
• I hate myself; I always get myself into trouble
• I'm not coming from myself
• I am bad
• I am limiting
• I should be beaten into submission

How does that feel? Not very good, right?

When we . . .

Dislike the EGO
Hate the EGO
Try to get rid of the EGO
Call everything we don't like the EGO
Belittle the EGO
Deny our own EGO

. . . we find ourselves automatically in conflict with the self. These approaches to EGO cause a relationship of disintegration from self as opposed to integration.

All that "EGO" means in Latin is: I (me, myself).

When we get into Universal Consciousness, the EGO does not dissolve; it actually expands to include more of the ALL that already is. Like the lens on a camera, widening and pulling back to see a more complete picture, the "I" identifies itself more and more widely and inclusively with the rest of creation.

At first:

I is just - "I" (baby)
I becomes - "we" (socialization)
I becomes - "we" (marriage or family)
I becomes - "the world" (leadership, care for the planet, seeing all the people of the planet as one family)
I becomes - "the Universe" (spirituality)

Therefore, what if the EGO can be seen as a neutral mechanism? A simple function that is there to serve a purpose? Otherwise, why would we even have it? Were we created defectively?

Based on the above, the EGO has two distinct functions:

1. To hold
2. To protect

Imagine we had to hold every decision we ever made always and forever freshly in our conscious mind. We couldn't. Once we learn something, it becomes automatic, and we don't need to consciously think about it anymore. The EGO is what puts those decisions on autopilot.

If the EGO were eradicated, you would wake up in the morning and look at your husband or wife in bed:

— Who are YOU???? And what are you doing in my bed? Get out!!

If the EGO were to disappear, you couldn't hold a single decision in place, and therefore would not be able to experience anything:

— Would you like coffee?
— Uh, I don't know.
— Would you prefer tea?
— Uh, I don't know.

Perhaps we can look at it like the relationship between a programmer, a computer, and a hard disk.

We, as the programmer
The computer screen, as life
The EGO, as the hard disk

Another way to look at it, especially if you are a travel lover, could be to liken the EGO to a passport.

It's far from having any capacity to appropriately define who we truly are, as we are way vaster beings than just our passport. I can't look at someone's passport and decide anything about the person.

It's just a number, a photo, and a nationality. However, the passport does decide which countries we have access to and which countries we are banned from entering.

Beliefs are like the different visas we have or don't have. The EGO is like the passport that carries these visas and decides which countries or realities we can or cannot enter (although it doesn't have the capacity to describe who we really are).

You could be the kindest and most giving person on the planet, but if you believe deep inside that you are not worthy and deserving of prosperity, you won't have access to the reality of prosperity. Your passport won't let you go there, even if someone comes and just hands you a million dollars.

I heard a story about a woman who was playing the slot machines in Las Vegas when all of a sudden she hit the jackpot. It was a crazy amount of money! All the bells started going off, the lights started flashing. She got so freaked out thinking she had done something wrong that she just fled the casino in a panic and never received her winnings. The money was hers to have, but she did not have the visa to access what came along.

Some celebrities end up broke even though they make twenty million dollars per movie.

— How could anyone make so much money and go broke?

It's so easy and so common. If there are beliefs that reject prosperity, the EGO will not allow prosperity to be an ongoing experience. One of the ways in which the EGO accomplishes a lack of prosperity is by keeping the person in the Spender's Law, which we already touched upon and I will go into much more detail about later. Or else seemingly random stuff happens and the money is lost.

For a long time, my feeling about money was:

No matter what I do, it is never enough.

Obviously if there is a belief system rejecting money in the first place, making a lot of it is not going to be a reality. Back then, I was so unaware of what I really believed about money. As far as I was concerned, I was trying very hard and it just wasn't working out. However, one day, since I had had enough, I made a new BEING choice outside of my box, and almost immediately that new choice was reflected in my life.

Sick and tired of working in a shoe store for $800 a month, I remember asking myself:

— What amount of income would really ring my bells, so much so that I would skip to work every morning instead of dragging myself there?
— What amount would help me dedicate my best potential to a job?
— What amount would excite me to really give all that I have to a job?

The answer came fast.

— $3,600 a month!

I had come to notice that it felt terrible to work in a job where I didn't care at all about what I was doing. I decided I wanted a job in which I could give and serve with my soul, and in return $3,600 a month was what I felt was the fair exchange at the time. I stepped out of the shoe store at sunset and stood on Melrose watching people go by. I remember feeling so good to be able to decide and really feel that what I had to offer was worth so much more.

— Where was I going to find such a job? What was it going to be? How was I going to find it?

A week later, my friend Sole got me an interview for a temporary TV project. The entry-level wage for the position was $1,800 a month. In the interview, I blurted out:

— I will not work for anything less than $3,600!

I remember that the person interviewing me almost fell off his chair. I too was taken aback by my audacity.

— Where was this kind of courage coming from?

Daring to feel more worthy, seeing myself as more worthy, claiming my greater self-worth was not my usual state of BEING whatsoever at the time. However, I had stepped outside of the box. I had made a new BEING choice without realizing it. This meant the mirror of my life had to reflect my new state.

Not knowing these concepts at the time, I had no idea about the possible outcomes. Neither did I make these connections until much later. But regardless, the principles work the same, whether we know about them or not. We all get rained on whether or not we understand how rain works.

Of course, my EGO was not silent about what was going on. Watching the whole interview and how it was proceeding, it spoke to me loudly in utter panic:

— Are you crazy?
— Have you gone mad??
— Who the hell do you think you are?
— Just take whatever they are willing to give you!
— You are being illogical!

Now that I was daring to claim a higher level of self-worth, my EGO was fighting me tooth and nail to protect the old core belief that I was worth less. It was simply doing its work like a loyal soldier.

This was a better job than those in my dreams. Though it was already in the process of becoming actualized, something inside me was still trying to stop me from believing I even had a chance.

The job was to get people from more than thirty different countries to come together as one big family for a special event, to celebrate the millennium and share their country's cultures. Everything would be broadcast live on TV, sweeping across the various time zones on a platform called Millennium Live. I was in love with the concept and could not imagine a more beautiful message to celebrate as we entered this new age.

I was potentially going to contribute to a message that said, "We are one big family on this planet." That was utter ecstasy for me.

The conversation continued inside my head:

— Don't push! Don't push! Don't lose this opportunity! You don't deserve it anyway.

I told my EGO almost out loud:

— Shut up! Shhh!

I had nothing to really show for or support my insane request for double the amount they were prepared to pay; I didn't even have any prior experience relevant to the position. Since the only alternative was going back to the shoe store, which was my nightmare scenario, it would have been so easy to cave in to the fear and accept whatever was being offered. However, because

I had truly claimed a higher level of self-worth and made a true BEING choice, it was easy to decide not to listen to the voice inside me demanding I keep myself small and okay with less.

The man interviewing me, having had time to collect himself after the initial shock of my demand, quizzed me:

— Based on what are you asking for such an amount?
— Based on who I am!

His eyes opened even wider. At this point I couldn't tell whether he admired me or thought I might be from another planet.

— I know I'll do a most excellent job, one that goes way above and beyond this position, but it's okay if you don't believe me. I have no proof, and I will understand if you choose to hire someone else.

— You just blew it! chimed in my EGO.

That is exactly what a new BEING choice looks and feels like. There is a clarity and commitment to the new position no matter what our EGO harps on about in the background. The EGO talks, defending the old identity through its nonstop mind-chatter, but rather than agreeing with its script, we can move forward regardless. It's not so much about courage as it is about having unwavering clarity about what it is we are choosing to belong to.

When we make a real and committed BEING choice, we are no longer attached to the result. This happens automatically as the BEING state itself is the fulfillment, therefore the results we hope to achieve stop mattering so much. That is the moment in time we start to actually BELONG to what we are asking for.

In reverse order, if we want to make a new BEING choice, we have to first find out what attachment of ours we need to let go of before we can step outside of the box and become more. In my example, choosing a higher level of self-worth required my willingness to detach from getting the job I wanted due to the high pay I was asking for.

By detachment, I mean we are still crystal clear about what we are choosing but there is a sense of being totally fine with not getting the desired result because the BEING choice itself has already become the fulfillment.

There was not much else left to say, so we politely shook hands and I left.

When I got back to my friend Norman, who had been nice enough to drive me to the interview, he asked me enthusiastically:

— How'd it go?

When I explained step by step what happened:

— You did whaaaaat? Are you crazy?

I shrugged my shoulders, as I felt so incredibly empowered by not having budged an inch from the new reality I had chosen:

— It is what it is!

Three days later I got the job, and they agreed to pay me what I wanted. It was the most amazing experience for a year, and a total miracle from beginning to end. It was as if an entirely new chapter in my life had opened up.

Although my job description was just coordinator, I found a sponsor willing to donate a million dollars to the project once we got closer to the air date. And I interviewed a prince in Saudi

Arabia who had gone up in space with American astronauts. He gave a stellar interview that highlighted the message the show had intended:

— We are one big family!

He talked of how that concept was really driven home and deeply seated in his consciousness and heart due to the experience he had in space:

— At first, we were all pointing at our countries . . . Then our respective continents . . . Then we realized in silence . . . there are no real countries and borders but just one beautiful planet, with one single family on it.

— Wow!

How had I found him?

My boss knew of him. He had mentioned him to me in passing, and I had set an intention to find him, without having a clue as to how. When I went to visit my parents in Saudi Arabia, as my father happened to be posted there as an ambassador for Turkey at the time, I met a producer. He responded to my passion as we talked about the Millennium Live project.

— What kind of a person would you like to interview?
— You know, someone who has had an interesting experience, who has a different perspective, who can see things outside of the box. Perhaps like the astronaut prince?

The next day I got the interview. I couldn't believe it. When talking to this producer, I hadn't known he had a direct connection. It was as if it manifested out of thin air.

But of course, nothing manifests out of thin air. All the way back in Los Angeles, I had set an intention to provide the project with an excellent interview with someone very special. When I heard about the astronaut prince, I was inspired. I knew a perspective from someone who had been to space would be an incredible contribution to the core message of the show. I set up a very strong intention to meet him without the slightest clue as to the *how*. I lived in Los Angeles, and he was in Saudi Arabia, and I had no connections to him. I visualized it happening. I was naturally unattached, since it was so incredibly far-fetched, but in about three months we were sitting opposite from each other having that interview.

You must understand what an unlikely candidate I was for such an event. I had no credentials, and I was not a journalist.

This whole incident happened the morning after I met the producer, who my mother had introduced me to the day prior. As I was having breakfast that morning, a phone call informed me that a car would be ready to pick me up within an hour for an interview with the prince. That was the first time I realized the producer had known the prince all along.

When we set a powerful intention from the heart without any attachment to the result and/or worry about the "how," the Universe has uncany ways and abilities of orchestrating events and synchronicities that would be impossible to calculate or figure out individually through the operation of our own mind.

Four things are needed for this to occur.

Intention from the heart. (Literally drop down to your heart space before you intend.)

Non-attachment to the results. (Find a way to let go of needing it to happen.)

Letting go of trying to figure out the how. (Don't think about it, just go with the flow.)

Belonging to what we are asking for. (Being choice.)

I had barely enough time to digest my breakfast, let alone process what was happening. I had to quickly take a shower, do my hair, and think of questions. The producer informed me over the phone on the way to the interview that the prince, rightly so, was very particular, and he had refused an interview with someone from a big-shot TV station only just recently, so I needed to be very careful.

I was already so nervous and the call did not help. I forgot my head covering, mandatory by law for women in Saudi Arabia, in the car. Showing up with my mermaid-like hair dancing on my shoulders to be greeted by a group of men who eyed me suspiciously as they took me to the interview spot was simply not the best start. I hid in the bathroom, preparing my questions, biting my nails, and praying that all went well.

It turned out to be a very successful interview. The prince was extremely gracious and put me at instant ease; he was very generous with his time too. The supposed fifteen-minute interview lasted a couple of hours.

My boss was floored and grateful. I was over the moon. The world was going to hear a wonderful message, and I kept my promise to be well worth the pay I had demanded.

From a shoe store, to a prince, to finding a million-dollar

sponsorship for the project, all of the above happened in nine months or less.

The reason I am explaining this story in so much detail is to underline and bring awareness to the absolute contrast of my life before and after that one day I stepped out of the shoe store and made a new BEING choice.

1. I had intended to find the prince from my heart because I honestly cared a lot about the project and the message it would broadcast to the entire world.
2. I was naturally not attached to the interview as nobody was pressuring me to find the prince nor did I really find such an occurrence to be very likely.
3. The "how" was naturally out of my league. How the hell did I know how to find some astronaut prince living on the other side of the planet?
4. I had made a BEING choice. First to provide amazing value for the project. Second, to do anything in my power to make sure the message of "oneness" got out into the world in the year 2000 as we entered a new era of humanity.

The rest was just about going with the flow and all of it manifested effortlessly.

You might ask if any of this stuck.

No!

But why not?

Millennium Live crashed two months before it was to air. The insurance companies pulled out for some reason. The baby we had all worked so hard to birth was lost before it could be born. It was very disappointing and heartbreaking for everybody at the company.

After that, I found myself selling carpets in a carpet store.

My EGO successfully took me back into my box.

— Who did you think you were, anyway?
— It was all just a random chance, a fluke.
— You just got lucky.

My reality went back to retail stores because I gave up the power of my original BEING choice and transferred it, once again, to outside sources and circumstances.

- I had been successful because someone gave me a job.
- I had been able to open doors because there was a company behind me.
- This was perhaps a once-in-a-lifetime chance that didn't pan out.

Do you see the difference in the thinking and attitude?

I didn't know about the EGO. I didn't understand its tactics, let alone have any idea about how to manage it. I didn't understand how powerful a new BEING choice could be or that it was essentially what I had used. I wasn't willing to believe how powerful our BEINGs can be and my old conditioning was able to get the upper hand once again.

Therefore, I went back to my old life and identity.

I just want to pause here for a second.

I've had these kinds of experiences of jumping from one extreme reality to another so many times, over and over again, ever since I was very young. It always frustrated me when I could not hold on to the good ones. In retrospect, I can so clearly see that all the ups and downs were a hardcore training in understanding how beliefs work and impact our realities so precisely. It was my theme of exploration in this life, and everything that happened or didn't happen was a part of this very specific learning.

In this sense, nothing we experience is a coincidence and none of it is wrong or without purpose, no matter how horrible or frustrating it might seem at the time.

If I had a chance to go back and change anything or speed things up, I wouldn't. It's been perfect as is. It is deep wisdom to know that all is well as we walk our paths in the now, rather than to figure it out much later when we get to see the bigger picture, or worse yet to never know it at all.

Trust that existence knows what it is doing even if it might seem illogical or you feel completely lost at times. The Universe always gives you what you need at the time for a larger purpose. See the gift in all things that come your way. Easier said than done but it's a good intention to have as you captain your ship across the ocean of life, through the good days and the storms.

Now let's take a look at what happened in the financial department of this same journey.

I had not yet discovered that I believed money was bad or believed that money and love didn't go hand in hand. In short, I was not aware whatsoever that I actually had a negative relationship with money. Logic would have it that since my income had more than quadrupled all of my financial problems would be left behind.

But it doesn't work that way.

It is not the amount of income we have that brings prosperity, but our chosen relationship to prosperity that decides whether we are truly abundant or not. Since there had been no conscious change in my relationship to money, although I was making more in terms of numbers, I still had problems paying rent. I had made a BEING choice to earn more income but I had not made a real BEING choice to be prosperous yet. The two are entirely different choices.

When we have an unconsciously bad relationship to money, we usually get caught in the Spender's Law without being aware we are under its influence. Which meant my EGO had to get rid of the incoming money.

I made more through the new job, but I also spent much more without realizing it. Working super long hours, I ate out three times a day, having convinced myself that I had no time to cook or even to make a simple sandwich. I bought a new wardrobe; I took a cab to work every day. My income had increased—the conditions had changed—but my story, and therefore my reality, hadn't. Once again, I threw my hands up in the air and fretted.

— No matter what I do, it's never enough.

If the beliefs and therefore the myths we tell ourselves don't change, neither does our reality. Either we go back into the old box entirely, without even realizing what is going on, as in my example around self-worth, or even though the conditions change, within the new conditions we end up creating the exact same reality, just as in my second example about money.

I made more, but I spent more. Therefore nothing changed financially.

The EGO will never let you see you are in the Spender's Law, but the test is simple. If you don't have savings and/or investments, you are in the Spender's Law.

Many years later, once I made a new BEING choice in relationship to prosperity and once my old reality died and a new one was born, the results completely reversed. This time, the EGO started protecting my new concept and reality of prosperity with as much strength and vigor as it had my previous lack of prosperity. I had come to know my EGO and trained it to hold a new story.

In 2008, when the recession hit, both my husband and I decided, and therefore knew, that the economic crash was not going to affect us. Although we were both involved in businesses that were considered luxury items, and usually those take the first hit when the economy goes down, our incomes increased. I had already started coaching, and my clients quadrupled that year. I made no price cuts. My husband was doing voice-overs for commercials and TV, and while everybody around him complained about not getting enough gigs, the number of projects he booked increased and his income tripled that year.

When we make a new BEING choice, one of three things has to happen:

1. We start getting winks from the Universe.
New people, new opportunities, new possibilities, new offers, new ideas, and new ways of feeling about ourselves begin to show up. We send out a different signal, and therefore what we receive begins to change. At this point it doesn't matter whether something is actually manifesting or not. The important thing is that something is different or we are feeling and reacting differently to what used to be. Time to acknowledge and celebrate.

OR

2. A powerful EGO resistance begins.
Whispering to us fear, doubt, and a sense of impossibility.
Defending the logic of the old box. A lot of mind-chatter. Your
EGO would not be acting out if a serious change were not really
happening. Time to acknowledge and celebrate.

OR

3. Both of the above happen at the same time.
An example would be when I manifested the TV job and my EGO
started screaming in the background.

If there is no new BEING choice, nothing is different.

The EGO's natural resistance is not to be condemned but
celebrated. It's an indication that a new BEING choice has been
made. Otherwise, the EGO would be asleep in a hammock with
a drink in its hand, listening to the sound of the waves, having a
vacation of its own. It wouldn't be on duty.

When we have a new idea, a new excitement, a new path or a new
decision and fear and doubt and what feels like self-sabotage begin
to kick in, that is fantastic news! No need to get disheartened; it's
really time to celebrate.

No need to resist the resistance. Just look at it, smile at it, and
know everything is on track. We will get to the section about how
to manage the natural resistance of the EGO in a bit.

Do you ever ask yourself, "How do I breathe?"

No, you don't.

You just breathe, because you know the oxygen is already there and
will continue to be available.

What if your relationship to prosperity could be like your relationship to oxygen?

A chance at prosperity can be as simple as a new perception about it—a new perception and a new relationship to it, provided you know how to deal with the EGO's resistance that is surely going to arrive with it to shut down the new movie.

Look at what a simple but real perception change can do for you in just a short time. We have the freedom to look at anything in front of us from whatever angle we choose. The question in regard to prosperity is:

— Is the way I choose to look at my financial situation empowering or disempowering me?

Here is how a client, Sinem, began to see it:

— I finally understood prosperity is a constant state of celebration. I decided to look at my finances not as an amount, but as a percentage. If my savings account went from $4 to $8, it was a hundred percent increase in prosperity and nothing less than that. Wow! It was amazing to look at the situation like that and it definitely paid off.

— Bravo!

She really had only $4 in her savings account when she first started sessions with us. Now she has $40,000 in savings and lives in a beautiful new home she bought for herself.

It is not hard. But it can be hard to figure out how easy it actually can be.

When the EGO is convinced to come and hold the new reality, you get a pattern of growth and ongoing expansion like Sinem's.

When the EGO is still busy holding the old reality in place and you aren't aware this is going on, your reality of financial struggle stays the same, just as in my previous example.

If we are a ship on the ocean, we need an anchor to hold us in place to experience a harbor. Otherwise we would drift forever. But when the time comes to move on from that harbor, we don't just cut the anchor loose, because we know full well it will be needed once again to hold the ship in the next harbor.

That is what the EGO does. It anchors a belief, so that we can experience it as a reality until it is time to move on. It serves a valuable function that we cannot discard even if we wanted to and for good reason too.

The thing to do is:

- Love your EGO
- Embrace it
- Understand it
- Converse with it

When we don't pay attention to what the EGO is, how it speaks to us, and how we can speak back to it—or at the very least learn to smile at it as it plays an old record of earlier conditionings, such as unworthiness or there is never enough—it's like we are ready to set sail to new frontiers but have forgotten to lift the anchor. We cannot figure out why the ship is not moving along, as we think we are doing all we can to set sail. That is when change and transformation becomes hard or looks like it's impossible to achieve. If you have a bad relationship with prosperity and abundance, money being just one single aspect of it, you can begin to talk to your EGO now:

— Money is not good or bad, but thinking it makes it so.

THE MEDITATION EXERCISES

Some of the exercises will now start to include meditations as well. You can pick out one meditation you feel drawn to and practice it for 40, 90, or 120 days, or you can practice a couple at the same time or even one at a time back to back, going through all of them in a sequence you desire.

A 40-day practice helps to break a habit; a 90-day practice integrates the new effect; a 120-day practice serves to confirm the habit so strongly that it becomes an ongoing aspect of the psyche, according to information provided by the Kundalini Yoga technique.

I'm giving a variety of meditations for two reasons. The first reason is to provide the mental, emotional, and physical benefits of each meditation. Secondly, I give them because they are amazing practices to train the EGO. Even if you will never become a meditator or a yogi in your life, practice awhile for the sake of learning to hear, recognize, and train the EGO.

The EGO is there to protect us, but when the EGO becomes the boss, it is a big problem. The EGO is meant to serve and not to rule or decide. During these meditations, the EGO will get bored, will complain, and will try to stop you from doing them daily.

To sit down and be with ourselves in silence while the EGO fights us and brings up all kinds of mind-chatter, dialogues, thoughts, arguments, and complaints is a wonderful way to master the art of mind-discipline. Meditation provides the opportunity to learn to observe the EGO and differentiate it from our true selves, and consequently be able to train it.

Give it room to express itself, hear what it has to say, but ultimately you have to make the EGO understand that you are the boss and decision maker.

When we obey the EGO, we experience a lot of problems. When the EGO is trained to obey us, we experience a lot of solutions.

Practice the art of training the EGO; it will open so many doors.

Exercise #1: Meditation to Clear the Subconscious Mind

Sit in a comfortable position either cross-legged on the floor or in a chair, making sure your spine is straight. Interlace your hands and make sure your thumbs are crossing. Bring this hand position or mudra to the level of your heart, palms facing the body, and rest your hands on your heart. This neutralizes the heart center and is very calming.

Breath: Inhale deeply and try to hold the breath for 45-60 seconds maximum. Silently chant the word HAR as you hold your breath. Exhale. HAR means creative infinity. Repeat.
Eyes: Closed and gently focused in between the eyebrows.
Time: To be practiced for ONLY 5 breaths in one sitting. NO MORE.
Practice: 40 or 90 days straight; 120 days in a row is ideal.
To finish: Inhale for 2 seconds and exhale for 2 seconds for a total of six times and relax.
Effect: Clears the subconscious mind.

You might have to take a couple of normal breaths in between each round if you have a hard time holding your breath. Start with however much time you can hold it in and eventually you will reach 45-60 seconds per breath.[7]

Exercise #2: Talking to Your EGO

Note: The point of this exercise is to soothe, convince, relax, and excite the EGO to come into your new reality with you. Beyond that it has an even more important job. You see, when we are talking to the EGO, we cannot simultaneously BE it. (Basically this is a conversation about your beliefs that are no longer serving you, and it trains your capacity to see the EGO from a distance and to build a relationship knowing you are not your EGO.)

1. Listen to your EGO's fears and doubts.
2. Let it know you understand how it's feeling.
3. Give it counterarguments and evidence about the direction you want to go, as in what you want to BE or experience or feel.
4. Let the EGO know what it's going to get out of the next reality. Give it motivation.
5. Let it know you are moving along whether it comes with you or not. Remember, you are the boss. The EGO needs to understand that.
6. Show it unconditional love. Be okay even if what it's defending and the negative dialogue don't change. Learn to smile at the EGO as you would a child having a tantrum.

Remember that you are not your EGO, it is only a part of you, often just defending the status quo.

Exercise #3: Meditation to Clear Obsessive Negative Thoughts

Sit in a comfortable position either cross-legged on the floor or in a chair, making sure your spine is straight. Bring your hands together like a cup, as if you are about to drink water from a fountain, your palms face up. Your right hand is on top and your fingers are crossing each other. Your elbows are relaxed on the sides. Your hands are in front of the heart center but not touching.

Breath: Inhale through the nose as you think of a negative thought, and let the thought just go as you exhale through rounded lips from your mouth, feeling that exhale on your hands.
Eyes: One-tenth open as you stare at your palms.
Time: 11 or 31 minutes.
Practice: 40 or 90 days straight; 120 days in a row is ideal.
To finish: Exhale all of your breath out. Pull in your navel point (belly button) as you hold the breath out and focus on each vertebrae of the spine as if you are counting each one, and inhale again when done. Repeat this ending breath 3 or 5 times before you stop and relax.[8]

And the day came
when the risk to remain
tight in a bud
was more painful
than the risk it took
to blossom.

THE EGO
VS.
THE BEING CHOICE

Each time I think of the relationship between the EGO and the BEING choice, I am reminded of the "Allegory of the Cave" by the Greek philosopher Plato, from his famous work *The Republic,* Book VII.

The allegory is a dialogue between Socrates and a student of his, Glaucon. In explaining to his student the nature of reality, he gives the example of a group of prisoners chained together and forced to look at the same wall in a cave since childhood.

Behind them is a big fire they can't see, since they are forced to look ahead at the wall by the chains on their necks, arms, and legs. In between the prisoners and the fire, actors on a raised runway walk back and forth with puppets, casting various shadows on the wall of the cave, like a modern projector casting a movie onto a white screen.

In this example, since the prisoners cannot turn around and look to see the source of the shadows and how they are being created, they take the reflections of the shadows on the cave's wall at face value. They think what they are watching is real, when in fact it is just an illusion.

The illusion they are experiencing seems to be the everlasting reality. The prisoners don't know of anything existing beyond the cave, as there is no reference point for them and they have never stepped outside of the cave.

Socrates goes on to explain what would theoretically happen if one of the prisoners were to be freed. The prisoner would have to be dragged out of the cave kicking and screaming. It would be like a death of sorts from that prisoner's perspective. And once the prisoner was dragged out of the cave, the minute the sunlight hit the prisoner's eyes, it would be blinding, making the prisoner run back into the cave yearning for the comfortable and familiar especially because he was dragged outside by force.

But let's say instead the prisoner endured being outside. Again, there would be the blinding effect of the sunlight and initial discomfort, and some time needed for the eyes to adjust to the new reality outside. If the prisoner had enough time and patience to adapt, however, the birds, the bees, the people, and the vast open spaces would amaze the prisoner.

Socrates continues to reason that if this person went back to inform all the other prisoners still chained inside the cave, pitying their illusions and limitations, and tried to explain what a beautiful life there was outside of the cave, the prisoner would be considered insane. Imagine this person trying to tell the others that nothing they are living is real! The other prisoners, not having experienced that reality for themselves, would have to deem all that was being shared as craziness and rubbish.

Since the freed prisoner returning to the cave would be blinded once again after re-entering the darkness of the cave, the other prisoners would consider the person not only crazy but also blind.

— This crazy idiot is blind to the truth!

Our belief systems work in much the same manner. Once any one of them is locked and in the cave protected by the EGO, that is the reality we experience, thinking it is the only truth.

The EGO successfully gets rid of any evidence coming from outside of the cave. If we believe . . .

Money is filthy.
Rich people can't be happy.
Money is the root of all evil.

. . . the EGO will deny, contradict, or erase from memory any information or evidence that opposes the beliefs outside of its cave.

A new BEING choice is like the sunlight outside of the cave. It is comfortable only once the eyes have adjusted to the sun. The EGO, on the other hand, is like the prisoners still in the cave. The EGO is afraid to step outside of the box and is convinced that going outside is not a good thing to do. It is there to protect whatever shadows our beliefs are casting.

The EGO always has to play the right and wrong game. As far as the EGO is concerned, everything inside the cave is right and therefore everything outside of the cave has to be be made wrong.

Hence, new evidence about a subject can enter our awareness only after we have made a new BEING choice to step outside of the old box to begin with. Otherwise the EGO will get rid of any evidence that doesn't fit the specific belief in the box. It will distort the evidence, make you forget the evidence, or will make you blind to the evidence.

— I will believe it when I see it!

Nope.

You will see it once you believe it.

If your belief is: **Money is bad.**

Your EGO has to make: Rich people wrong.

If your belief is: **Love is agreement.**

You will get super mad at people who do not agree with you, as for you, not being agreed with will translate into not being loved by the other person. In reality, that is not at all what is going on if there is a disagreement.

It's a given that we are never, ever all going to agree. It is not only impossible for everybody to hold the exact same beliefs, it is also extremely unnatural since variety is everywhere we look in nature. Variety brings color, contrast, and expansion. It would be a terrible tragedy if we all agreed on everything. Expansion would cease.

Even our heartbeat goes up and down; when it flatlines, we are pronounced dead. Without variety there is no contrast and without contrast there is no life or new desires or decisions to be given birth to.

To bring this discussion back to prosperity, if your goal is prosperity, or anything else for that matter, it is important to shed your own judgments about prosperity if you ever want to get out of the cave in relation to this subject. The judgments we hold keep us tied down and send us running back to the cave as soon as we catch a glimmer of sunshine on the outside.

What are my judgments?

- About money?
- About people?
- About men/women?
- About success?
- About myself?

Think about your answers to these questions, but make sure you write them down now.

You know why "now"?

Because even if you have a realization, by the time you have read more pages here, the EGO will make you forget. This is how well and quickly it does its job. Once we understand the natural resistance of the EGO, transformation becomes easier. Transformation is built into our systems; we have it even on a physical level.

Change is a constant truth of our realities, whereas the EGO is there to hold up the illusion of continuity and consistency.

- The earth changes in cycles.
- Trees change according to the seasons.
- Animals change in response to their environment.

Our bodies move toward change every day.

- Our stomach lining is totally new every four days.
- The skeleton is completely replaced every ten years.
- The surface of our skin is different every four weeks.
- Cells in the liver are renewed every three to five hundred days.
- We have a complete set of new eyebrows every sixty-four days.

It is not understanding how to deal with the natural resistance of the EGO that makes change appear to be impossible at times.

- It's too late for me.
- I'm unlucky.
- I'm not good enough.
- I'm trying, but I can't.
- I'm not pretty enough.
- I'm not young enough.
- I'm not old enough.
- I'm not smart enough.
- I'm not rich enough.
- It's unfair.
- It's because of my boss.
- It's because of my husband/wife.
- It's because of my children.
- It's because of the economy.
- It's because of people.
- It's because of the world.

Whatever the story of the resistance may be about, if we are not able to go where we want, it's due to the EGO's efforts to keep us safely tucked inside our caves. The EGO protects its cave for various reasons:

1. It's the EGO's function.
2. There is some sort of a GAIN for us in it being protected.
3. The EGO does not want to die, and every transformation is a death for the EGO.
4. It has to maintain the illusion of continuity.

The truth about reality is that it is ever changing. We can't step into the same river twice, even if the river is in our own backyard. The water flowing between our feet is never, and never can be, the same.

Yet the EGO holds up the illusion that it is the same river.

It is not at all an exaggeration to say change is the total enemy of the EGO, whether that change is positive or negative. If, however, we are able to bypass the natural resistance of the EGO, we have no problem getting out of the cave.

This also means that dragging someone outside by force doesn't work. Imposition does not really bring any lasting change. Someone with a problem can't truly be helped unless they have already internally made a BEING choice to move beyond their limitations.

This applies not only on an individual level, but also on a societal level. An innovator or an inventor is able to think outside the box, meaning beyond the accepted paradigms of society at any given time, because he or she doesn't mind being grilled, rejected, or criticized, as is inevitable. Just as the EGO can stop us on an individual level, society also gets uncomfortable with new things. It takes time for things to change and be digested.

There was a time when "being a good leader" meant conquering and killing as many people as possible. "Being peaceful" was considered a weakness and a lack of kingship and true leadership. To have different opinions or religious inclinations from that of the king or even simply falling out of favor was punishable by death. This was normal.

Just a short while ago, doctors would bleed their patients out up to the point of death. The medical community believed if someone was ill, their blood was vile, and therefore letting them bleed out was the cure. We now know that bloodletting often actually weakened patients and gave them infections.

A time will come in the near future in which the way we are currently doing things, living in society and running our governments, schools, and hospitals, will be seen as barbaric. However, even the best changes will never be totally and wholeheartedly welcomed, at least not initially, just because they are new.

> If I had asked people what they wanted,
> they would have said faster horses.[9]
> — Henry Ford

Just as we would do anything to resist dying if we were at gunpoint, in the same manner the EGO tries to stay alive with what it knows to be familiar and the belief it has sworn to protect, no matter what. Since it is just a function, it does this equally for both negative and positive decisions, not really having the capacity to know the difference.

In this sense, the EGO is never meant to be our guide. It is there to anchor the old or the new, but not to guide us out of the cave. For that, it is necessary to turn on our intuition, for intuition is the messenger and the sunlight from outside of the cave.

In that case, what is to guide us, both individually and as a society? What do effective leaders and innovators have in common?

- Love
- Vision
- Enthusiasm
- Inspiration
- Intuition

Love for the heart.
Without love and inspiration or at the very least without real motivation for something or another, courage is difficult and one can easily remain in the cave.

A vision for sight.
If we can't even see where we are going, we are blind on the path.

Enthusiasm for energy.
The kind of enthusiasm children have, when being alive is enough of a reason to be happy. "Enthusiasm" in Greek means the God within. When we are enthusiastic, we listen to the wisdom of creation, the voice that whispers beyond the cave, rather than to the comfort and familiarity of the EGO.

Inspiration for connection to spirit.
If creation is like a rainbow, each of us carries a very specific color that nobody else in the world has. Just as our fingerprint or the iris of the eye is unique, so is the spirit inside of us. Only we can do something in a specific way that no one else can do in quite the same manner.

Are we listening to the song that our spirit is whispering?

The connection to spirit is so essential that without it we would die. In fact that connection and re-charge happens everytime we go to sleep. That is why if someone were to be kept awake for days and days, the person would go mad and eventually die. This is also why people who may have depression may need to sleep longer hours. It is a much-needed recharge.

Are we consciously connecting to our spirit within in our waking hours? When broken down, the word "inspiration" means being in the state of spirit.

In-spirit-ation.

Or another way to look at it could be in-spirit-action. Inspired action.

When spirit is in charge, we feel inspired. It is critical to follow this feeling no matter how many naysayers are around trying to stop us from following that internal guidance.

Intuition for direction.
The ability to feel and hear the information outside the cave. It is hard to get out of the cave when we don't have our intuition in place. Intuition is the capacity to see without seeing, to know without knowing, to prescreen what exists beyond the cave so it is not too scary for us. Intuition is also the capacity to download information from the Universe when we need it, just like we do from the internet.

There is nobody without an EGO because there is nobody devoid of believing something or the other. We all need the protection of the EGO to survive, to remember, to repeat, to anchor, and to hold things in place so as to have experiences.

— I don't have an EGO.

Is equivalent to saying:

— I don't have a perspective about anything.

Which is like saying:

— I am not having any experiences whatsoever.

If that were the case, you would be pronounced dead.

However, when the situations and circumstances call, when our next best version begins to knock at the door and our spirit calls to move us along in the journey, do we sit tight or do we blossom?

Can we successfully bypass the natural resistance of the EGO trying to hold us in what was?

If we do step outside of the cave and let the spirit within us flow and blossom, we are met with renewal, revitalization, and rebirth. Then we can bring the fresh breath of air, the new idea, the new perspective, the renewal, and the springtime back to our homes and our society.

> There is a garden beyond right and wrong.
> I will meet you there.[10]
>
> — Rumi

Exercise #1: Vision

— What vision do I have about the next step of my life?
— What vision do I have for society or the world? In what small or large way am I contributing to that every day?
— What about my vision excites me? Gives me energy?
— Am I wasting my time and energy on stuff I don't really care about?
— Is something I am doing, or someone I am with, giving me energy or taking it away from me? If so, why?
— What can I do to retain what gives me energy and drop or change what depletes my energy?
— If I had no perceived limitations, what would I be doing? Who would I be BEING?

Exercise #2: Love

— What do I love? What do I care about? Country, children, fashion, flowers, fitness, nature, health?
— How much time do I spend doing what I love?
— If I am not spending much time doing what I love, why? What is the excuse? What is the story?
— What would it look like if I spent more time doing what I love?
— What would it be like if I made a living by doing what I love?

_____

_____

_____

_____

_____

_____

_____

_____

_____

Exercise #3: Enthusiasm

— What am I enthusiastic about?
— When do I feel this feeling?
— Do I follow it or do I stop myself? Why? What could be more important than listening to the voice of the creator speaking inside of me?
— What would my life look like if I gave this feeling more space and expression?
— What if I followed this feeling more often and allowed it to take me places without needing anybody else's permission?
— What stops me from being enthusiastic? Is it worth it?

_____
_____
_____
_____
_____
_____
_____

Exercise #4: Inspiration

— What inspires me?
— How much time do I spend being inspired? If not much, why?
— Do I intend to find what inspires me?
— Do I believe in the potential and power of my spirit?
— What is it really telling me when I connect?
— Do I believe that only I have a specific gift that nobody else has?
— What is that gift? What comes to me naturally?
— Does inspiration frighten me? If so, why?
— Why would I choose a life that would not include my inspiration in it? Is it worth it?

_____
_____
_____
_____
_____
_____
_____
_____

Exercise #5: Pranayama Meditation

Deep, long left-nostril breathing (to calm the mind and increase intuition).

Sit in a comfortable position either cross-legged on the floor or in a chair, making sure your spine is straight. With your right hand, keeping your fingers straight, close off your right nostril with your right thumb.

Breath: Breathe in and out with deep, long breaths through your left nostril only. To make sure you are breathing deeply, with each inhale your stomach should expand out as if you are pregnant, and with each exhale your tummy should contract as if you are getting into some tight pants. This is to make sure you are using the diaphragm when you breathe.
Eyes: Closed and gently focused in between the eyebrows.
Time: 26 in-and-out breaths minimum per sitting or 11 minutes or 31 minutes a day. Can be practiced any time of the day but is especially useful before bed.
Practice: 40 or 90 days straight; 120 days in a row is ideal.

Effect: Calms the mind-chatter. Increases intuition (the mind needs to be calm to hear the voice of our intuition), helps with sleep disorders, helps with weight loss and anxiety by calming the nervous system and activating the parasympathetic system.[11]

Exercise #6: Intuition #2

— Before you say YES to something—let's say it is a partnership with someone in business—write down what you feel about the person.
— Write down your feelings both negative and positive . . . Does it feel a hundred percent YES???
— If not, ask yourself why you are proceeding. Are fear and logic guiding you? Or intuition?

When an idea or a person pops into your mind, ESPECIALLY if it is illogical and seemingly random, do you follow up with it? If not, follow it for 30 days and see what happens. See where it takes you.

For example, you haven't seen or spoken to someone for six years. All of a sudden when you are having tea, for no reason, they keep popping into your mind. You see their face or have a conversation out of the blue with them in your head. Instead of bypassing this, call the person and let them know you reached out because you randomly thought about them. See if they have any useful information for you or if they need you for some reason. Don't be surprised if they say something that validates your intuition.

— I was just thinking about you!

OR

— I was trying to find you. This is crazy!

It's not crazy at all. It is intuition. But, the only way to learn it is to follow the hints so you can begin to differentiate between what is intuition and what is not. Intuition and conditionings are very different, but only through practice will you begin to know the difference inside.

I gave this self-created exercise to a client who wanted to develop her intuition. She decided to commit to practicing it. One day while she was watching TV, an old boyfriend of hers popped into her mind, out of the blue. She hadn't been thinking about him, and they hadn't seen or talked to each other for ten years.

She decided to do the exercise and texted him, at first hesitant but then curious to know if he had popped into her mind intuitively.

— Thinking of you. I hope all is well and you are okay?

He texted back:

— Oh my god, I just walked into my apartment to find everything stolen. I was about to have a nervous breakdown but your message saved me. It reminded me all is going to be okay and that I am not alone. This message means more than you can imagine.

My client was shocked and began to discover, in a playful manner, the power of her intuition.

NOTES _____

_____

_____

_____

_____

_____

_____

_____

_____

_____

_____

_____

_____

_____

_____

_____

_____

_____

_____

_____

_____

_____

_____

_____

_____

_____

_____

_____

_____

When I let go
of what I am,
I become
what I might be.

— Lao Tzu

THE NATURAL RESISTANCE AND FUNCTION OF THE EGO

Let's go back to the EGO and understand its important function with more examples.

Let's just say we want to quit eating sugar. The EGO is going to do everything it can to remind us how wonderful an experience eating sugar is. Maybe the little cakes in our local bakery are going to start looking even more precious than before, as if they are smiling and waving at us as we walk by.

By the same token, if eating healthy has become a new BEING choice, the EGO will just as strongly protect this new place once it has adapted to the new reality. For instance, maybe we will look at someone stuffing their face with cheesecake and our stomach will churn. Here, the EGO is useful, as it will keep us from going back to eating sugar in our new reality.

Or, let's say you recently decided to get your financial life in order. You vowed to yourself you are going to get better at managing money. Your goal is to sit down and make a budget, but you just can't get there. You keep delaying the action.

Instead of judging yourself, ask:

— EGO, what is it that you are trying to protect me from?

Remember, it's there trying to do its job. If you understand what it is trying to do, you can manage the EGO better, just like a good boss manages an employee.

Let's say you have to pay rent. A friend owes you money and she promised a long time ago to pay you back but still hasn't. You know logically you have the right to ask for it back, but you just can't. Each time you think of asking for it, you feel embarrassed and shy away from the idea.

— EGO, what is it you are trying to protect me from?

Dealing with or caring about money makes me shallow.

Remember, the beliefs we are talking about are usually not immediately accessible by our regular awareness. It might need reflection to understand. If this is your program and you really don't want to be perceived as shallow, the EGO is going to stop you from asking for what you are owed simply because it is trying to protect you based on your belief system.

Money makes people bad and unscrupulous.

How is the EGO going to protect this idea and belief?

By making rich people wrong.

Happy people are stupid.

How is your EGO going to perceive someone having a good time and laughing with friends?

— Oh! She is so dumb!

As we underlined in the past chapter, one of the ways in which the EGO protects its current reality or box is by making wrong everything and everyone outside of its box.

Everything and everyone inside of its box is okay.
Everything and everyone outside of its box is not okay.

This does not mean we will necessarily perceive from the perspective of the EGO, but the EGO will judge to protect its box. We don't have to agree with the EGO or act accordingly. This is why it is so useful to know the difference between our true selves and the various acts of the EGO. When we do, we are able to make good, healthy, and beneficial judgments instead of being judgmental as a knee-jerk reaction.

There are many spiritualists, for example, who claim that they don't have an EGO. Yet these are the exact people who, just like everyone else, no different, make out those not seeing life from their point of view to be wrong. The only difference might be judging with clenched jaws with a fake smile plastered over it or maybe cloaked with the "I am holier than thou and you don't understand, little one" attitude. Needing to put oneself on a higher spiritual horse than other people is one such game.

Whenever we are playing the right and wrong game, we can be sure the EGO is in charge. I am not saying there is anything wrong with this, as everybody does it, but it is important to just be aware in those moments where we are coming from.

The EGO is never after a solution. A solution is not its function; its function is to defend and protect the perspective it has going. There are many places, situations, and moments when this is exactly what is needed.

For instance, if you are in the middle of a battle, you'd better not choose that time to have a philosophical debate with yourself about whether war is legalized mass murder. If you do, you'll get blown to pieces. You may want to contemplate the question after the war perhaps, but it is not a good idea on the battlefield. To stay alive, you'd better believe strongly in your EGO's box that says you are the "good guys" and they are the "bad guys." Otherwise you will not be able to do your job or protect the people relying on you.

On the other hand, if you are a politician and really care about a peace treaty being signed, you'd better not play the EGO's right and wrong game. That's not going to move anything to a resolution; it's not going to get either party out of any cave anytime soon.

Here, it is almost essential to let the past go to be able to create a win-win situation for both sides. Who is right and who is wrong cannot be a conversation if one wants to move toward peace and resolution. Focusing on the past, with the intent to punish, is not a vibration that matches peace or ever creates a win-win solution.

Another way in which the EGO upholds and protects its reality is by presenting the illusion of *no change*.

Do you think you could exist without a cell phone today?

Only fifteen to twenty years ago we existed just fine without them. But doesn't it now feel as though we were born with a cell phone attached to us like an umbilical cord?

Could you function just fine without a car? I could, but that is because I never learned how to drive. My EGO doesn't even know what it's missing since I never had the experience of personally owning a car. But for someone driving since they were 16, it will seem to their EGO like an impossibility, especially in a city like Los Angeles.

A friend of mine made a list of the ideal attributes of a home she would love to rent. Realistically she didn't have the budget to afford much on her list. But she made a strong intention and visualized a home with everything she wanted, maybe a couple of times at most. Then she forgot all about it.

Five months later she moved to a new rental. She was kind of happy, but it was no big deal for her. As she was unpacking she found the list she had made with the ten or so items she had requested. All of it, every single item, existed in this new rental.

What would have been a joy and total miracle for her only five months earlier was in her experience now, but her EGO had already adapted her to this new reality as if it were no big deal. As if no miracle had taken place.

This is how the EGO adapts us to a new reality, selling the illusion that it has always been a certain way.

To counter this, it is incredibly important to stay in a constant state of gratitude. Otherwise our dreams keep happening all around us but we still walk around complaining that our lives are just the same.

Since change is the enemy of the EGO, it never wants us to know:

* How easy change can be.
* How powerful we are.

Remember once again, the EGO is there to protect; it's not there to get you out of your cave.

The EGO will always suggest to you the possible dangers that wait outside the cave. But it's up to you to pick and choose what is sound and what is not.

If you are walking through a forest inhabited by wildlife and the EGO is being protective, you'd better pay attention to it if you don't want to be an afternoon appetizer for a hungry lion.

You are free to choose when the EGO's protection is useful and when it is a hindrance.

Another way in which the EGO protects us is by disguising certain limitations we carry around so we can't tell what is actually going on, as you will see in Vicky's example. These are our own self-constructed masks to hide and shield ourselves from a deep wound we may have not dealt with yet. A limiting belief waiting to be set free by us.

Vicky would not stand up for herself in arguments with other people. She would quickly end a discussion by telling the other party that they were right and she was wrong. Her EGO had her believing she behaved this way because she would rather keep the peace than be right about one subject or another. However, whenever she backed down, she wouldn't feel good about herself either. When she finally faced what was actually going on, she was so surprised to see the actual limitation. Vicky discovered she had a self-concept:

I am not smart enough.

Her EGO was trying to protect her from seeming dumb by immediately shutting the discussion down; it didn't have anything to do with protecting the peace. When this was revealed, she was appalled by the limitation she had placed on herself. It was the belief that was leading the communication or lack of it, not really her. With her new awareness she was able to speak up for herself and also felt empowered to remove the self-concept of being dumb from her identity.

This doesn't mean everyone not entering a discussion is doing it for the same reason. What is important is our own true reason behind the behavior. And when we can be coached to discover that piece of the puzzle for ourselves, the sky is the limit when it comes to the transformation that is possible.

Since the EGO's job is to be the keeper of our belief systems so that we can experience those beliefs as a reality, it sometimes cleverly packages patterns to look and seem different than what is actually going on. It is only awareness that brings it up to the surface for us to see what is really going on.

It's not the economy, circumstances, or other people that are the limiters of our experiences in life, but rather the self-imposed beliefs we carry around that we might not be consciously aware of. And the EGO, anchored at a certain reality, will do anything to protect its current box. Remember, its function is to help us experience any belief we hold as a reality.

But let's say you have chosen to believe something more in alignment with the truth of who you really are and you made a new BEING choice in that direction. The EGO will protect that just as strongly once it buys into it.

It's really hard to make a living.

Can easily become:

Prosperity flows to me because what I have to offer is of value.

It is well worth asking yourself:

Do I really believe what I believe?
Is this my truth or is it just my conditioning?

EGO's main job is to protect your choice, old or new, so that you can experience it as a reality.

The only reason I kept slipping back from more success and financial abundance in the stories that I have shared so far was because I kept falling for the natural resistance of the EGO, in its function to keep me in my old reality, instead of teaming up with it and commanding the EGO to keep the new reality in place.

Even when we move from our old apartment to a more beautiful home, we may have tears in our eyes as we say goodbye to the old. A part of us is not wanting to let go of what has been though we know full well we are going to a better dwelling. This is exactly what happens with our old identity too. The EGO dies with the old self-definitions and self-identifications to be reborn again in a new reality. It's natural for it to put up a fight as it dies.

That may even mean something as simple as resistance when going to a workout to be more fit and healthy. Just understand it, smile at it, and don't be conned by its act.

What does it look like and/or sound like when we are coming from our EGO's resistance?

- Mind-chatter
- Selling us a story to convince us to stay in the cave
- Defending the limitations
- Trying to prove something. (Possibly we are trying hard to prove something because in truth we actually believe in the opposite)
- Complaining
- Blaming
- Being the victim
- Paralyzing fear
- Paralyzing pain
- Playing the right and wrong game
- Playing the fair and unfair game
- Making us forget what really matters

When the EGO is protecting a belief that we align and resonate with, we simply don't have an issue in that department. That department flows just fine, until it doesn't because we have outgrown the belief due to an expansion in our consciousness.

Therefore every problem is a gift and a doorway for something new.

Other ways in which the EGO protects the cave we're in:

1. Removing from sight any evidence contrary to its belief.
2. Distorting the incoming information to fit with whatever belief is already being held in place

The EGO acts like the filter in a pool. What does a pool filter do?

It removes everything from the pool that does not belong in it.

In the same manner, the EGO removes all kinds of evidence and information that do not fit the sustained belief and reality.

Yasmin wanted to work on relationships, as she had gone through one bad experience after another in this department. She was always the one finding a reason to leave her relationships. As we dug in, it became apparent that she believed lasting relationships were possible only if one gave up on self-happiness and compromised. Yasmin believed she had to sacrifice self-happiness to make a relationship work long term. She knew of my relationship with Ike from his book *The Universe Is My Sugar Mama*.

— You have my example. I am very happy with Ike and I have never felt I had to sacrifice my own happiness or values to be with him. What do you feel about that?
— Oh, that! You see, I think you guys are just pretending in public for the sake of your careers.

I dropped the phone I was laughing so hard. This is exactly how the EGO functions. It re-interprets incoming information to match the current belief being held in place. It has to keep the belief alive, otherwise it has to change and get out of the cave, and it doesn't want to do that.

But you see, if Yasmin wants to eventually create a long-term relationship and be happy in it, she has to get out of her cave, which means she has to be willing to change her perception and make a new BEING choice.

We can think of the EGO as a dragon protecting its cave. If we want to get out of the cave protecting the belief we have constructed, it's not a good idea to get into a fight with the dragon. If we do, the dragon is probably going to burn us to a crisp. Instead, if we can befriend the dragon, convince it, consciously show it new evidence in the direction we want to go, then we can get on the dragon and fly out of the cave with it.

As long as she was on this train it was obvious she was going to keep re-experiencing the same patterns of choosing out of relationships before they had a chance to ever become long-term.

I asked Yasmin if she wanted to keep believing what she was believing.

— No!
— What would you rather choose to believe?
— Happy long-term relationships do exist, and I don't have to give up who I am to experience one.

After the session, I asked Yasmin to collect new information and evidence to show her EGO a new perspective, something she could only actually find, though, if she made a new BEING choice outside of her box. Otherwise the EGO would keep blocking any evidence, as it was already doing, that didn't match the idea:

**Relationships require one to give up
on themselves and sacrifice.**

— Okay. This week your homework is to look around and try to find real examples of people who are in long-term relationships and haven't given up on happiness.

Yasmin must have made a new BEING choice outside of her box, because the next week she was all excited:

— I found at least ten examples. They are all couples I know intimately enough to observe they are actually happy. I can't believe I never saw that before. The evidence was right in front of my face, in my own backyard, but I didn't see it.

This is just one example of how the EGO can successfully hide clear evidence of what actually exists so that we can keep re-experiencing the myths we have created.

Another example I can give from my own life is about someone who heavily rejected the love I gave. This hurt me deeply, because I felt as if I were being rejected and could not understand why. Once I understood how the EGO operates however, a lot changed for me because I stopped taking the action personally.

The person had the self-concept:

I am not lovable.

Hence, every time I gave my love in various ways, the person had to reject it, as my actions did not match the person's own self-concept. However that was not a rejection of me personally but of what I had to offer as it was not welcomed by the other party's self-concept.

We cannot believe "I am not lovable" as a self-concept and simultaneously be the welcoming recipient of love. If we have this belief about ourselves, we have to change our own self-concept and revisit this myth or we will automatically reject those who give us love by:

- Getting irritated.
- Barking at the person.
- Thinking they are being fake.

The EGO has to make wrong and toss out whatever it is that doesn't fit into its belief.

A lawyer, Ece, who attended our course, was sick and tired of being a lawyer, but at the same time she needed the money. She had recently been offered a huge salary for a big project as a lawyer but had rejected the job altogether. Instead, she started working as a coach but chose not to charge her clients any money.

In her session she kept on making the point:

— I don't really care about money.

She repeated this maybe five times in a five-minute period. That statement, right there, is an indication a person has a bad relationship with money in one way or another. If one is rejecting money, prosperity is not going to be theirs. Yet here she was attending a prosperity workshop—a simple example of the contradiction between what the EGO wants to protect versus what we want to actually experience.

The fact she had paid for the workshop and was actively participating in it was an indication she was ready to get out of her cave.

— I don't care about money!

What was the pattern holding her in her cave?

When we dug deeper it became apparent that in her childhood she had felt disregarded by her parents. Ece's parents had not been emotionally available to her, but to compensate for their inability to spend quality time with her, they bought her everything she wanted. She had all the new toys, the best clothes, and the newest gadgets, but was unhappy. As a little girl all she had really wanted and yearned for was their love, care, time, and attention. This is all that children want and need in essence.

When Ece would express how lonely she felt and how unhappy she was with the situation:

— But darling, we get you whatever you want!

Other people would chime in:

— You don't have a right to be unhappy. You have everything you want!

Ece felt dismissed, and in return rejected the money lavished on her. She felt it was given to her as a substitute for the love she so desperately wanted.

When children cannot experience the presence of their parents, due to stress or a busy life or whatever else is going on in the adult world, they tend more often than not to interpret this as not being valued and loved. Love is not just an idea or a concept; it is an energy that is expressed through presence. When there is no presence, it can't be felt, even when it is there.

— I don't care about money!

By rejecting money, she was trying to say that she had wanted their love and attention instead. She was stuck in that past, and the wounded little girl was ruling her financial life even as an adult. Her EGO was still busy trying to prove that:

Money doesn't matter.

This was a relatively recent session, and we will see how the story ends. But the journey that awaits her, if she chooses to leave that old cave, includes:

- Forgiving her parents for not knowing any better.
- Forgiving herself for still trying to punish her parents by rejecting money at the expense of limiting her own abundance.
- Realizing having money doesn't have to mean it's a substitute for love anymore.
- Realizing the past does not have to keep reoccurring in the now if she lets it go.

One of the ways we get stuck in the cave is by being too busy punishing others or ourselves for the past. In the example above, she may never choose to forgive her parents, and she doesn't have to. But the problem is that if we are busy punishing the past and keeping alive the fire of revenge, without meaning to we burn ourselves in the present too.

Ece's story also offers a great example of how prosperity is a matter of choice. If we claim we want prosperity but don't have it or make lots of money and then destroy it all, perhaps even faster than we made it, it's because a part of us is heavily rejecting it. It is well worth our time to investigate why that is the case. Once we find out, we may still not be interested in prosperity, which is fine, but at least it is not for any other reason than our authentic choice.

The goals that are seemingly materialistic are essentially not so. In this specific example, nothing less than letting the past go and healing a broken heart is the requirement for being able to move on to prosperity.

As Lao Tzu put it so succinctly:

> When I let go of what I am,
> I become what I might be.

Although some say this is not a quote by Lao Tzu and some claim it is, whoever said it said it well.

This becoming and transforming can sometimes be painful, and for good reason, too.

A while ago I was in the middle of a huge transformation and was feeling an incredible amount of sadness and pain. Today I can't recollect what it all was even about. Although I knew my new choice was a much healthier one, I was still having difficulty with the amount of pain that resulted.

— Darel, I can't understand why there is so much pain involved. I know with all my being I am making a much better choice for my life, but why all this pain?
— Your EGO is dying with your old self; of course there is going

to be pain. But instead of seeing it as an unwanted feeling, why don't you welcome it as a part of your healing?

At that moment, lightning struck my consciousness. I understood what so many of the masters talk about when they refer to death or dying while still on the journey of life.

Die,
before you die.[12]
–Rumi

When we leave the cave, the sunlight outside is going to initially blind us and make us uncomfortable, almost as if we are dying.

Avoiding pain is a big detriment to growth. One must almost be willing to walk through the fire and burn to rise back from the dead like the phoenix that resurrects out of its own ashes.

Pain is okay . . . Suffering is not.

First is the raw pain of getting out of the cave; it is temporary and transformational and brings us growth. This kind of pain deserves our presence, not our rejection, as the transformation takes place in the unconditional love given to it, just like a woman in childbirth. This is very different from the tears of ongoing suffering. In that case the person gets stuck in the pain exactly because they are avoiding rather than really looking at and accepting or learning from the pain, therefore it just keeps humming all the time underneath the surface. Suffering happens when there is a refusal and a rejection of the journey, an avoidance of the pain and a stubbornness to stay in the cave due to fear.

When the self-constructed identity dies, a fresh breath of spirit comes in, like the fragrance of early spring flowers heralding the birth of a new season. As this death of identity takes place, we attend the funeral of who we have been and the tears fall as we say goodbye, to become the fountainhead of the rebirthing.

Exercise #1: Meditation: Stress Relief and Clearing the Emotions of the Past

Sit in a comfortable position, either cross-legged on the floor or in a chair, making sure your spine is straight. With your hands in front of your chest, at heart level, bring them together like a tent, forming a triangle. All fingertips are touching, including the thumbs.

Breath: 4 times per minute. Inhale for 5 seconds, hold for 5 seconds, and exhale for 5 seconds.
Eyes: Slightly open and focused on the tip of the nose.
Time: 11 minutes.
Practice: 40 or 90 days straight; 120 days in a row is ideal.

Effects: Helps deal with stressful relationships and clears past family issues. Also helps with disturbing thoughts that chase us from the past, and fears and phobias.[13]

NOTES _____

We create our
own problems.
We find our
own solutions.
In between
we discover
who we really are.

— Darel Rutherford

THE JOURNEY OF CONSCIOUSNESS

Do you know those Russian wooden dolls? As you open each one, another smaller one pops out until you reach the smallest one of all. They are called matryoshkas. Just like these dolls, we have layers and layers of consciousness within us, with the ever-so-small self being cradled by the larger self, expanding out to the Universe. The larger self is the Universal mind or the quantum self.

Imagine casting a stone into the ocean. The ever-widening ripples grow from small to large, expanding out into infinity, gaining more and more access to what already is in that big ocean.

For this chapter, before we begin:

1. Close your eyes.
2. Imagine yourself by the seaside.
3. Find a pebble or a stone as you walk by the sea.
4. Let it represent your intention.
5. Pick it up and bring it to your heart. Make a wish and an intention from your heart.
6. Now in your mind's eye, throw it out into the sea and watch the ripples expand out.
7. Know that in having made an intention from your heart, you have been heard.

From ultimate loss to finding the ultimate treasure, from self-rejection to self-love, from weakness to heroism, from sickness to health, from poverty to prosperity, from limitation to expansion, from fear to courage, from the victim to the victor.

These are the very themes and fabrics of the great stories that inspire us. Cinema, art, and literature—anything or anyone with a good story—captivate us not necessarily just by sharing such rousing tales, but also by successfully capturing the journey of the unconscious mind in great symbolic expression. These mediums bring about a catharsis, a purging of repressed emotions and energy of renewal and healing for the individual experiencing them. This is what art was about in ancient Greece.

These stories can really awaken the hero's potential and cause an expansion in consciousness, enabling one to victoriously complete a certain path. This is the stuff that belongs to the realm of dreams, art, rituals, movies, and poetry that never dies; it is so encapsulating of the Universal journey and a dance that we are all intimately connected to. These stories remind us that whatever that next journey might be about, it is never-ending. Just like the ripples of the stone cast into the ocean, they cause ongoing expansion.

Such tales capture us again and again, no matter how many times they are retold. There is something about them that resonates deeply inside and we feel a truth; somewhere deep down there is a stirring, as if an ancient song is calling us out of our slumber in the cave.

The author of *The Hero with a Thousand Faces,* Joseph Campbell, maps out the journey of the individual for the sake of individuation and self-realization with incredible mastery. By drawing from myths, history, and the arts of the various cultures, he gives a sense of the Universal language that speaks through all of us, regardless of which culture, religion, race, background, or time we come from.

There is a specific formula or rather a specific understanding of how the cycles work and the different levels of what the individual consciousness needs to confront before a journey can reach its completion. This understanding is Universally so resonant that the Hollywood movies created from this space capture audiences worldwide, as an expression of a common language of the unconscious mind.

For this book, I will oversimplify some of Campbell's steps and put them on a map according to my own point of view and tie it to the subject matter we have so far explored. The purpose here is to show that for any lasting change and transformation to occur, a change in who we are BEING is not a luxury but a requirement.

This is simply why solutions alone, although helpful, are not a real answer to problems.

A widening of our perceptions so that we can have automatic access to certain new solutions and a deeper understanding of the self becomes the necessity here. The beautiful thing about problems is that without them there would be no journey forward. In this sense, problems are not nuisances but great blessings. We go to a movie to see how the hero will overcome the challenges presented, yet in real life the tendency can be to reject those challenges or see the problems as a negative, when in fact those problems are an opportunity for a new choice point.

— Mary was born; she was great, successful, and happy; and then she died.

No story here. Now think of your favorite movie reflecting the journey of the hero and follow the steps.

The first one that pops into my mind is *The Matrix*.[14] Neo is just a struggling guy who is called upon a journey. There are claims he might be the ONE to save the world, and if that is true, it's his destiny to do so.

Does he go skipping along on the journey? No!

At first there is a refusal, a hesitation, a denial. After the acceptance of the journey, there is a period of gathering information, a preparing. Only after that does the help arrive, in the form of an oracle, to give him some answers.

— Am I the ONE?

After the hoopla, once everybody is convinced and depending on Neo, he turns out not to be the savior after all. It is the anticlimax of the movie. This is the exact juncture where most people give up in real life, when a dream or a goal or a hope or an expectation doesn't reach the desired result.

What makes a hero a hero is their decision to continue and believe regardless of the upsets, the setbacks, the betrayals, or the obstructions bound to arise.

After much hesitation and setback, at one point in the movie Neo claims to BE the savior of the world, even though it might mean his death and despite being told it is not his destiny. He claims to be not who he was expected to be, but who he chooses to BE. A hero's journey is always self-made. Isn't it interesting how much this concept attracts people? These stories, if they hit the right notes, have a way of lasting long after we are gone.

Neo makes a new BEING choice and in the transformation that follows, he becomes much more powerful than before. He gains his powers in accordance with who he has chosen to BECOME.

He has to penetrate the fear of failing and not being good enough or strong enough, of not being the chosen ONE, not only to follow his journey but to actualize it at the end, as he is being beaten nearly to death by the enemy.

This is Neo's final test, or rather his final claim of himself.

— Are you really going to be able to demonstrate BEING the new you, or are you going to go back to the cave if scared or desperate enough?

The story of the phoenix rising from its own death. A bird in Greek folklore who could live up to five hundred years, only to combust and crash in flames, decompose, and rise back up from its own ashes.

No story starts without a problem or a limitation. The limitation itself is the catalyst, as the contrast is the birth of the desire to become more. If there were no limitations, there would be no new desires. This is the benefit of the contrast the limitations provide, serving as the springboard for the new expansion to be born.

Usually the hero is found sitting in a cave or some sort of limitation where it seems like the problem is impossible to surmount.

For example, a monster threatening a whole community, or Cinderella cleaning ashes in a fireplace day in and day out, or the ugly duckling who is so upset because of all the abuse he gets from others. This is the point of contrast, of being in a corner in the cave, feeling helpless to do anything about it but wishing things could be different.

What is the limiting belief that is holding you stuck in the problem?

For the hero having to deal with a monster attacking the whole community, perhaps the limiting belief is:

I am not powerful enough.

For Cinderella who wants to go to the ball but can't, perhaps the belief is:

I am not worthy enough.

For the ugly duckling, perhaps the belief is:

**There must be something wrong with me because
I am so different.**

The first thing that happens when one is being invited to leave the cave—the status quo, the box, the so-called normal way, the safety zone, the rules of society, the accepted ways of behavior, the habit, the problem—is an initial refusal or denial of the call. The refusal of the call is so textbook it's kind of funny. I can't think of a good movie without this part.

This initial refusal of the call is exactly like the natural resistance of the EGO to change. The EGO is not up for an adventure or for diving into the unknown, but only for protecting what has been.

This is the stage of immense avoidance: fear of seeing, looking at, or facing something about the self or the situation that needs to come to light. If it does, there is healing. If it is successfully repressed and swept under the carpet then eventually there is disintegration, darkness, depression.

This is the stage in which the hero refuses to accept any responsibility, feels like a victim, and/or blames others for the problem being experienced. As long as there is no responsibility taken for creating the problem and for being and remaining in the cave, there is no movement forward in the journey, period. If one is stuck at this stage—the resistance in facing the real problem and the initial pain of getting out of the cave—then ongoing suffering sets in as a result; it is unavoidable.

The hero always has a choice to either be a winner or a loser.

One way to get out of the box is to ask the self these questions:

— What pain am I trying to avoid?
— What is it that I am afraid to face in myself?
— What would my worst-case scenario be?
— What is it that I am so desperate to protect rather than leave behind that I am willing to stay in the cave forever?

For Cinderella: Perhaps ridicule.
For the Ugly Duckling: Perhaps being wronged and shunned.
For Neo, from the movie *The Matrix:* Perhaps being unable to live up to the expectations of others.

Does any of this sound familiar?

When there is an attachment to protecting something, the EGO is in charge and one remains in the cave, no matter how painful and dark the cave itself might be.

Maybe . . .

—You can't leave a dysfunctional marriage because there is too much fear about ending up alone, or feeling like a failure because it did not last.
— You don't create a relationship because there is the fear of eventually not being liked and therefore abandoned.
— You can't create more abundance because it requires you to grow up and no longer be a child, needing others to survive and be rescued by.

What is the pain I am avoiding?

What am I trying to prove or protect by remaining within the confines of the problem?

If there were nothing to prove or protect, a solution would have already come.

During WWII, Darel's job was as a glasscutter. The broken glass from all the bombed buildings had to be cut perfectly to be reusable. In his group were many great glasscutters from various countries, but Darel really sucked at this job. When it was his turn, he attempted his best but shattered the glass twice. Everybody made fun of him and it was really embarrassing for him. He had inherited from his father, who used to slap him on the back of his head and call him a dummy, the belief:

I am dumb.

Finally, he was done being embarrassed and laughed at himself for feeling like a dummy.

He decided:

I don't care what people think of me!

On his third try, he cut the glass perfectly and everybody was surprised and started clapping. Because he stopped giving his power away to what others thought of him, he got out of the cave and achieved not only the perfectly cut piece of glass but also a perfect new perspective about who he truly was.

— I am not dumb; that's just an old story playing over and over in my head because I chose to believe and take to heart what my father said.

When the hero shows courage and faces the shadow inside, when the hero decides to leave the cave, help always arrives in some form or other. This could be a new opportunity, the help of a friend, money showing up out of nowhere, or simply feeling different in the face of a familiar problem.

In the Cinderella story, once she decides to be a part of the ball even though she has no idea how to get there, help arrives immediately. If she had held on to the "I'm not worthy" story, nothing would have happened. The decision to be a part of the ball is an indication of the up-leveling of her sense of self-worth. The help arrives in the form of a fairy godmother. Cinderella magically gets everything she needs to go to the royal ball: a beautiful dress and a royal carriage with a driver, all from a pumpkin and a mouse.

This is so symbolic of the kind of true alchemy that happens with a new BEING choice.

What is the first thing the fairy godmother says to Cinderella?

— If you had lost all your faith, I couldn't be here, yet here I am!

The real battle, however, isn't won until there is a true stabilization of the new BEING choice that has been tested by the events and the situations to follow. Hence, even the fairy godmother isn't allowed to help entirely.

To play the game of life on a new level, an equal up-leveling of self-worth to match is a must. How many movies have we seen in which the hero is enlivened by making a new BEING choice and courageously embarks on a journey, getting incredible support and knowledge up to a certain point—only to experience an unexpected blow?

Just because someone has penetrated the fear, or has overcome the first illusion of the dragon and exited the cave, does not mean the light outside won't blind them.

The question is: Will the hero keep going or give up and go back inside?

This is the real point of a true decision.

Can you get up once you have failed?
Can you deal with the blinding sun once you have left the cave?
Can you detach from your status and/or your treasures to do what you believe is the right thing?

At this point, almost always, something needs to be given up to move forward. Some form of attachment.

What is that?
What attachments are you carrying on your back?
What is the cost to pass through the second threshold?

Is it the approval of others?
Is it the fear of being shamed?
Is it the fear of failure?
Is it the fear of not being loved?
Is it criticism?
Is it abandonment?
Is it admitting you have been wrong?

What is the avoidance? What is the shadow? What is the even bigger dragon that needs to be faced? What is the attachment that needs to go? If the real dragon inside is not faced and fear wins again, there is a descent back into the cave. The journey temporarily shines but ends before it has truly even begun.

In real life, this part corresponds to a one-time victory. A star that shines but is never again seen. The incredible but one-time move of success in a business. A great opportunity arises, only to disappear into thin air.

The above happens when we have made a new BEING choice but are not able to deal with the resistance of the EGO, and so we return back to our old way of BEING. If the hero successfully passes the first threshold the hero might think the problem has been conquered.

That "first victory" might go to the hero's head.

— I did it and I'm done and I'm it! I'm enlightened now!

But the true victory is yet to be claimed. The outer, obvious dragon might be conquered, but has the real dragon inside really been faced?

This second level is when most choose out of the real journey and go back to the cave, mistakenly thinking that the first level was the real victory, and wanting and needing to hoard the treasures achieved on this first level. This could be someone who has gained a position of political power or a celebrity who has gained popularity only to get caught up in the prison of attachment to their status or image. This is when what starts off as well-intentioned leadership can turn into utter corruption. The hero perhaps misses the courage to put everything on the line to reach for the truth of being, no matter how small or big the losses can seem.

In the Cinderella tale, this moment would have occurred if, after the royal ball and her dance with the prince, she went back to her old life and old self-image. That time with the prince would have been just a cute story to tell her grandchildren one day instead of becoming the fairy tale.

In the example of Neo, when he is being beaten to a pulp on the floor, it could have easily been his choice to never get up again.

This is the moment in a movie when we hold our breath wondering how the hero will spring back. How will the hero overcome this seemingly insurmountable situation? We root for the hero because we are wired to win. Not just to win any old outcome, but to win the awakening of the awareness necessary to victoriously complete the journey.

This is the darkest hour before the dawn—but the sun always comes up in the end.

This is the faith the fairy godmother is talking about when she appears before Cinderella at the beginning of her journey.

We deserve to the degree we believe.

What needs to be unloaded?

When the enemy defeats Neo, the physical pain is symbolic of his old identity dying; he is renewed because he lets his attachments go. His biggest fears have already happened and there is nothing left to be afraid of anymore. He has already accepted and even faced death.

He gets up and is a completely new man. As he lets go of: I am not.

And claims: I AM.

With that, a whole new range of powers is downloaded to him and the enemy is beaten effortlessly—the enemy being only the shadows of one's own mind. Once the shadow of not being good enough is penetrated, Neo is able to fight using just one hand, and the thousands of bullets fired at him stop in mid-air. Some that have reached him fall right in front of him. It takes no effort to win the battle in the outside world, as the real battle inside of him is already won.

When we BELONG the solution arrives at our feet and fits our situation perfectly, just the way Cinderella's slippers fit as her prince finds her without her having to do anything about it.

This is the point when the ugly duckling figures out he was a swan to begin with and can now travel with ease and grace, expressing the true potential he had all along.

This is the point when the prince and princess sail into the sunset happily ever after, until it's time for the next cycle to begin. However, for now the credits read:

THE END.

Exercise #1: Let's review the steps of consciousness

1. THE CALL happens when a person is being invited to an expansion of sorts, to a better version of the self, a new journey through the problem or limitation being experienced.

2. THE REFUSAL of the call
- Victim mode
- Denial
- Fear
- Resistance
- Delay
- Escape
- Defending the problem
- Holding on to the GAIN in the problem or limitation
- Not recognizing the limiting belief
- The refusal has to be released before the new journey can begin

3. THE ACCEPTANCE of the call and embarking on the journey.

- Courage, An increase in self-worth
- A BEING choice to belong to something better or more expansive

The above choices need to be made to pass THE FIRST GATEKEEPER.

4. THE HELP ARRIVES, as in the fairy godmother, a friend, a parent, a stranger, in the form of money, connections, valuable information, or whatever is needed. This is the part most people label as luck but it really is the changed vibration that is attracting new possibilities. Morpheus is the name of the Greek god of dreams. It is no coincidence that Neo's guide is given this name. When we make a new BEING choice, everything that belongs to the new choice must be provided by the Universe.

In the case of Neo, Morpheus shows up as his guide to help him become aware that he has already decided to embark on the journey.

5. THE FIRST GATEWAY is crossed and there is a victory of some kind.

Much information is collected at this stage: new perceptions, new possibilities, new awareness, new realizations. It's as if the person is in training for the more to come, and it is a period of general strengthening and growth not to be confused with the actual victory or mastery.

At this point Morpheus begins to train Neo both mentally and physically to a new potential. Neo begins to win small battles with the enemy, but it is always through the help of others, and at various times he almost doesn't make it. For Neo in this stage, there is a lot of learning but also still self-doubt.

The moment arrives to pass THE SECOND GATEWAY. The new BEING choice at the beginning of the journey will either be tested to see if it is sustained or the hero will need to make an entirely new BEING choice as the hero faces his/her shadow. This is when the hero finally faces the sunlight, can see the truth, and is almost blinded by the light. Will he or she jump to this new reality or return back to the cave? In Neo's case, he finds out he is not the savior he was being groomed to become.

Now he has to make a choice: **To BE or not to BE?**

- Making the worst-case scenario all right (even something to be excited about)
- Releasing the attachments to the old
- Releasing the attachments to the result
- Successfully overcoming the EGO's natural resistance
- Learning to smile at and embrace the shadows of the self
- Strengthening the original BEING choice or making a new one

Neo's new BEING choice is to save the world whether someone said it was his destiny or not. But he only morphs into his BEING choice after he goes through some of the above. We will look at some of the above more closely in the next chapters.

6. TOTAL TRANSFORMATION is achieved. The second gateway is successfully penetrated and the prisoner is out in the sunlight basking in the delight and awe of the new reality.

Neo beats the army single-handedly and without much effort. He has become the savior by breaking all his beliefs in limitation and by choosing to become the ONE.

7. REPEAT when the next cycle arrives.

Exercise #1: Meditation: Sat Kriya

Sit on your knees with the knees together, which is the ORIGINAL sitting position for this meditation. If it's too uncomfortable, sit cross-legged on the floor or sit in a chair normally, making sure your spine is straight. Clasp your hands together with the fingers interlacing. Only your index fingers are straight. Arms are hugging the face. Remain straight and still.

Men: Right thumb is on top of the left thumb. The left pinky is at the bottom.
Women: Left thumb is on top of the right thumb. The right pinky is at the bottom.

Breath: No direction. The breath will regulate itself with the rhythm.

Eyes: Closed and focused on the point between the brows.

Time: Start with 3 minutes. Can be practiced for 5, 11, or 31 minutes daily. It is best to start with just 3 minutes and work your way up, as it is a very powerful and detoxifying meditation. Start lightly; 11 minutes is a perfect goal to reach, but the lesser times have a powerful effect as well.

Mantra: Chant SAT as you pull back and lock your navel point in and NAAM as you release your belly button. You are activating your diaphragm and massaging the heart. You can focus on the 3rd eye as you chant NAAM.

Practice: 40 or 90 days straight; 120 days in a row is ideal.

To end the meditation:
1. Inhale deeply and hold the breath as you squeeze all your muscles. Focus mentally above your head.
2. Exhale all the breath out. Hold it out for 5–20 seconds as you squeeze all your muscles. At the same time, apply all three locks. This means you squeeze the anus and the sex organs, squeeze the navel point back and in, and also lock back the neck by pulling your chin in. You do this by keeping the chin parallel to the ground and pulling the chin slightly back as if there is a wall right behind and you are pushing against the wall with your head. Relax and ideally rest on your back for double the amount of time you practiced.

Effects: Helps to balance the sexual energy. Uses the sexual energy for healing of the body and increasing creativity by redirecting the energy. It works on balancing all the chakras, but since it works the 3rd chakra powerfully, it strengthens qualities such as courage, personal boundaries, and our personal power. It releases energy that heals.[15]

NOTES _____

If ye have faith as a grain of
mustard seed,
ye shall say unto this mountain,
remove hence to yonder place;
and it shall remove;
and nothing shall be impossible
unto you.

— Matthew 17:20, *King James Version*

THE BEING POWER
AND THE FOUR KEYS
TO SUCCESS

As we walk our paths, the ideas and concepts we have about ourselves influence, very directly, the outcomes of what we create and don't create in life. Having coached thousands of people, I've seen again and again that whatever the problems or limitations individuals experience, when it comes to self-concept, it all boils down to a sense of self-worth and self-love in the end.

All of us have negative repeating belief systems about ourselves, whether we are aware of them or not. Some of us have very misaligned self-concepts that are not even true, but we make them real by believing in them. They're simply conclusions we have arrived at about ourselves as little children experiencing our environments, and nothing more. A lot of self-destructive behaviors (so called self-sabotage), destructive behaviors toward others, or limitations on success or prosperity, or lives lived in "quiet desperation," as Henry David Thoreau put it, are based on one's layers of negative self-images or limiting beliefs.

The wonderful news is that these negative self-concepts can be changed, and the process isn't that hard to do.

Here, I want to talk a little about my own past growing up to make a point about the BEING choice, its relationship to the EGO, and together how they impact our reality. Especially about how the EGO can bring us back into the old box almost undetected and without us realizing it unless we are alert and paying attention.

Once we have an awareness, though, as to how it engages, and if we learn to develop the habit of smiling at it while it tries to use its tricks, then it becomes so much easier to successfully maintain the new BEING choice and remain outside of our box.

If you want to make a new BEING choice, to belong to prosperity for example, two things are essential:

1. Find and choose out of your negative belief systems around money.
2. Increase your sense of self-worth to belong to a new reality.

First, some history:

In my childhood we moved from country to country because of my father's career. I was in a totally different world every four years in terms of friends, houses, cultures, languages, schools, and expected rules of behavior. This moving around did not entail just a move from one country to another, but from one wholly different psychological system to another—from the East (Turkey) to different countries in the West (Europe), back and forth in cycles. What was considered a virtue in one part of the world, such as speaking your mind, having your own opinion, challenging your teachers, and becoming an individual, was seen in another part of the world as rebellion, disrespect, and disruptive behavior. Individuality was a virtue in the West but considered a vice in the East.

By the time I was done with my studies, my school career looked like this:

- Two different kindergartens (Belgium, Turkey)
- Two different primary schools (Turkey, Greece)
- Two different middle schools (Turkey, Spain)
- Three different universities (Austria, Turkey, United States)

My life had been dragged across six different countries spanning three different continents. It was most definitely a very educational experience but at the same time a real ordeal growing up.

When I think of education in Turkey, I seem to always remember a teacher in middle school at Ankara College who went insane on me because I refused to open up my palm and get hit with a ruler. She was hitting everyone, one by one, as we had made too much noise in the absence of our regular teacher. When it was finally my turn, and after I had just seen my best friend shed uncontrollable tears of pain and shame for no reason, I was determined to confront the teacher about what she was doing. It was wrong and I was not going to be a part of it.

— I am here to learn, not to get abused.

She was livid, and meant to hit me hard across my face. I remember seeing the big wide ruler rise up in the air and aim for my face, but my eyes remained fixedly looking into hers, unflinching in silent rebellion. She simply couldn't hit me and instead the ruler came down hard onto the desk with a whipping noise and broke into pieces.

— Go to the principal's office! You disobeying virus!
— Why was I a virus now?

Although I wasn't in physical pain, my heart hurt. Even back then I knew that what they were doing to the children in the name of education was nothing less than ruining a whole generation. They were stripping away self-worth and self-power from kids at such a young age, and everybody in the culture seemed to think this was normal and gave this abuse their blessing by doing nothing about it.

But after a couple of years, without meaning to, I started to become a part of the system too, and started getting subdued, step by step, even if only partially.

After a while it was time to go back to the West, to either an American or British school. There I was criticized for not speaking up, contributing in class, or being creative or spontaneous. I was in a pattern of hiding just to be safe and not get in trouble again. In time I would start building myself up again to become more of an individual, as it was safe to do this in the West, only to be torn back down when I went East once more.

But the Western world presented a different set of challenges to deal with. For example, there was prejudice. I was ostracized from any contact with any playmate at school for the first year we were in Greece based on the verdict of Sophia, the most popular Greek girl at school. Though attending a British school in Greece, I wasn't able to speak English yet. I had no clue what was going on at school. All I knew was that all the children hated me; they would wash their hands if they touched me by mistake.

— Was I a virus, again?

After a year, once I began to understand the language, it became clear as to why. Sophia's grandmother had told her that Turks are barbaric and they kidnap and kill children.

Once I was able to learn English and successfully convince her that this was not the case in my country, and that my parents weren't going to eat her for dinner if she came over, we started to play and became good friends.

Another time, a good friend stopped talking to me because her mother had said I was a devil, since I was born in what was known to be a Muslim country. Anyone born in a Muslim country, practicing or not, was a devil according to her mother's perspective.

At a young age, having to deal with emotionally tough situations, I began to realize the strong hold beliefs have on people and how incredibly relative all of it is.

My good friend and I loved each other until her mother's religious beliefs got in the way. Sophia and I became good friends after her grandmother's cultural beliefs were out of the way.

In fact, we ended up writing a letter demanding peace between Turkey and Greece to then Prime Minister Papandreou, showing our 8- and 9-year-old selves as examples of what was possible in life. I remember feeling so freed up by this act. I realized most people did not intentionally mean to harm anybody and were prejudiced just because they were taught to be; it was just all the conditioning they were brought up with. So, I decided as a little child never to take prejudice personally ever again. If the other party was prejudiced, it meant they were ignorant, and that did not have to have the power to define who I was going to be unless I gave it power. It's of course no coincidence that I never, ever experienced a problem in that department again after that day.

My grades were sometimes really good and sometimes average depending on how many different levels I was battling for survival in what seemed to be such a crazy world. At home, my parents would disapprove if I wasn't performing my best as I tried to figure out which wound to lick first from school that day.

Naturally there were conflicts at home as well between how I was growing up and what I was permitted to do and be versus the allowance range my foreign friends had. The two were in stark contrast to one another due to cultural differences. As soon as I gained any sort of victory, balance, adaptation, or popularity at school, it would be time to move again, only to start the entire nightmare all over again.

In middle school in Turkey, a teacher called me a whore because a boy caught me as I was falling backwards from the top of the stairs. In my American high school, I was labeled a lesbian because I did not have a boyfriend at age 16.

Needless to say, it seemed I couldn't get it right no matter where I went or what I did. These experiences and feedback led me to believe I was and therefore to label myself as:

Not good enough.

While I did not buy into the prejudice, I identified with the above as a truth growing up. Cycles of feeling down, alienated, and like I didn't belong anywhere started very early and carried all the way through to my late 20s. Sometimes I felt I didn't even belong on earth. Little did I know at that time that those hellish experiences would become the exact blessings and gifts of the future. Once I dared to open up Pandora's box as an adult, each wound and the consequent belief attached to it would transform into the freedom of a butterfly, one step at a time.

After the near-death experience I mentioned at the beginning of the book, I came back to the body knowing full well . . .

- From the Soul level, even death is a choice.
- The Soul is much more a real identity than the body.
- The body drops but the Soul continues on its journey.
- The Soul identity is all-powerful and lacking in nothing.
- Love is not just a concept but a tangible vibration permeating the real fabric of all beings . . . without which existence can't be.

. . . it is the truth of existence.

Not wanting to leave the earth after all this remembrance, I was slammed back into the body, and the waves that had taken me under initially now served to surf me back to shore.

Life was indeed a beautiful gift.

As I struggled beneath the water for air, I worried the most for my parents. I wondered how they would cope and who would inform them of my death while I still tried in desperation to kick to the surface of the sea. A voice out of nowhere, close to my right ear, spoke with authority and clarity:

— Life is the dream. You are about to wake up!

This is when fear left me. I surrendered to death as the truth, and the remembrance of the words spoken washed over me. After many revelations and understandings, which took place in what felt like a lifetime or even longer beneath the sea, I was excited all of a sudden to be back in the world.

— Now that I have remembered, how will everything be different?

However, I was mistaken about that assumption, as the beliefs about myself, the ones my EGO held up for me, had not yet been transformed. I was in pure ecstasy for a couple of days and after that right back to the regular me. Especially after a couple of friends labeled the experience as weird.

Now let's fast-forward this movie to my early 20s.

It was my dream to live in the US and study some sort of art form. I chose film studies. America, because of my experience of the schooling system in Europe, represented freedom to me. I always thought of the Statue of Liberty whenever I thought of the United States.

One day, standing in front of the coffee machine at the TV station where I worked in Istanbul, waiting for my latte to fill up, I just knew that for better or worse I had to go to America. Within a day or so of that decision, I found the film certification program at UCLA, which miraculously cost only $7,000 instead of the hundreds of thousands of dollars the top universities tend to charge in their regular programs. Again, this is a perfect example of how things shift when instead of BEING the person who wants, you start BEING the person who chooses. Before this decision I had searched for years for a way to study in the United States and had never come across the above information.

Next I found and secured a scholarship for the program. Again, once I made a real BEING choice to BELONG to what I chose, the help arrived soon. A family friend, someone I will be grateful to for the rest of my life, helped me secure a scholarship.

I declared:

— I am going to America!!!

I hadn't even been to the United States as a tourist yet. I had no real idea about the difference between New York and Los Angeles. However, choosing UCLA and the filmmaking department determined the city I would end up living in longer than any other place I had ever lived before.

At the end of my studies, I was able to secure an internship with Oliver Stone at X-LAN in Santa Monica. As film students, we had to do a mandatory internship for three months to get our certification from UCLA. I kept on visualizing Oliver Stone for about a week. I had no idea how to find him, as search engines weren't that popular yet and all the accessible information we take for granted now was not that readily available back then.

Soon after, while waiting in line for food at the school cafeteria, I started chatting with a student right in front of me. It turned out he had just finished an internship with Oliver Stone and informed me that they were looking for a replacement. He gave me all the contact information. I went for an interview and got the position.

Initially, because I was so thrilled about being there, I was the world's most nightmarish intern. I think I jammed the Xerox machine three times and people had to come to fix it. When Oliver Stone called and it was my turn to be at the reception desk, I connected him to all the wrong people before I got it right. It was like a sitcom, and I was the joke.

On my last day, Oliver Stone gave the whole office a book called *The Fountainhead* by Ayn Rand. He wanted everyone to read it and share their feedback. I took the book home just for fun, as I no longer had a responsibility to do anything more for the office.

However, I fell totally in love with the book, and the inspiration to create an imaginary project was born. Just for the fun of it, I wrote a long character analysis for each and every character, watched an old movie of the book, and wrote a synopsis of how I would turn it into a movie myself. I slept with the book, went to the bathroom with the book, ate with the book, and talked everybody's ears off about the book. My friends were sick of me.

This went on nonstop for about a month and a half, every day from morning till night. In my imaginary project and world, I was explaining to Oliver Stone how the movie should be made on a daily basis. I found myself talking about the female character

Dominique mostly. In my imaginary world, I was the hands-down authority. There were no limits to feeling, to expressing, to BEING and acting as though this project were real. I was just like a child playing house with a friend, and in my head, he was really just there to help me collect my own thoughts into some sort of coherent package.

There was passion, inspiration, and nonattachment, as I was following my bliss without any expectations. I lacked attachment as the project was not real. It was playtime. Since I looked at it as having nothing to lose, I was naturally in the Winner's Attitude. We will get to the Winner's Attitude later on, but very briefly it is about feeling and knowing there is nothing to lose.

Unconsciously and without realizing it, I had figured out the four basic keys to success:

1. Following one's bliss and inspiration.
2. Committing to doing one's best.
3. Practicing non-attachment.
4. Adopting the Winner's Attitude.

Since I kind of happened to fall into it, I didn't put the formula together back then. My EGO couldn't ground it at the time as clear steps to follow each and every time. I would understand all this much later, when all the different pieces came together after similar experiences where practicing even just one step would turn things around as if by magic.

If the four steps above are the key, you are the keyhole that makes them work, by virtue of who you choose to BE.

Soon after I completed this dream project, Oliver Stone's assistant Brennan randomly called me to go for a couple of drinks in

Hollywood. We met to chat about the book. Interestingly, he called me almost as soon as I finished the imaginary project. When he heard about my ideas, he insisted that I fax over the entire project to the office as my feedback. Genuinely surprised by how his eyes lit up in total excitement over what I shared, I thought:

— What's the big deal?

Early one morning a week later, I got a call from X-LAN.

— Mr. Oliver Stone is on the line for you.
— Mr. who?
— Mr. Stone.
— What?

The next thing I know I am in a four-hour meeting with Mr. Stone and Brennan. I am so passionate about the project that I am just laying down my vision about the book and completely unfazed by the fact that I am talking to one of the most famous film directors in the world. I argue heatedly about several of the points in the book as if I am the director.

— But, Mr. Stone! If that was the author's true intention, then how come she has the Dominique character say the following quote? And the Roark character's response is the following quote?

I knew the book like the back of my hand. Mr. Stone would turn to Brennan and ask him to find the exact quote from the book for reference, and Brennan would look over at me as if to say:

— How am I going to find these quotes one by one?

In the meantime, on a much more important level, I was trying to come to terms with how exactly the way in which I had imagined things in my made-up project was now playing out for real right in front my eyes. Even my body postures were the same as I had envisioned.

— Was this some kind of a joke?
— What the hell was going on?
— Was my imagination this powerful?
— Did visualization really work out this exactly?

This aspect of what was going on had my attention so much more than the fact of having a brainstorming meeting with Oliver Stone.

— Were thoughts that powerful?
— That couldn't be! Or could it be?

It couldn't get any better than this opportunity for a film student.

I wanted to be hired by the company, and I asked for exactly that just before I left the meeting. Although my situation was a little complicated, as I was still on a student visa and did not have a work permit, Mr. Stone was excited about the idea and promised to see what could be done.

I was over the moon about what had taken place. Like a little gazelle caught in the headlights not knowing exactly which direction to skip toward, I left the office and went to a coffee shop across the street. Drinking my latte, I contemplated:

— All this couldn't be a coincidence. It was too precise.

OR

— Could it be?

Soon after, a phone call came with the decision to hire me

for X-LAN. I was to work with Mr. Stone's producer, Danny Halstead, but had to wait six weeks until the company found a way to legally hire me. For that period of time, I worked from home as a script doctor for the scripts that had already been greenlighted by the studios. They asked me and I jumped at the opportunity to do what I loved to do, analyze story and work on movies, but it was back to working for no money like an intern.

Remember my beliefs around money?

Love and money can't go hand in hand.

I was a master at working successfully and managing not to get paid for it.

In that month and a half of waiting, everything within me started reverting to my old patterns again: doubt, anxiety, attachment, fear—you name it! They were like weeds I couldn't seem to stop from growing in the garden of my mind.

Now that things had gotten real and serious, I went back to the self-concept I mentioned earlier:

Not good enough.

While I waited for the job to start, I practiced the total opposite of what I had been practicing the month prior when I took on the book as my fun imaginary project.

— What if I wasn't good enough?
— Didn't they remember? I was the intern who broke the photocopy machine like three times.
— What happened was a fluke! A mistake!
— What if I disappoint?
— What if it doesn't happen?

— Maybe they saw something in me that I am in actuality not?
— What if I can't live up to their already high expectations
of me?

Besides all this negative thinking, fear, and doubt, I had a total
attachment to the result. This job, I believed, was the only possible
way for me to ever move forward—the only way for me to ever
make money and get to stay in Los Angeles.

I started practicing BEING a failure, even before I had the job.

A month later they called to say they could not hire me. It was just
too complicated because of my student visa and the paperwork and
the lawyers required to solve the situation.

In practicing my BEING power positively, I got my dream.
In practicing my BEING power negatively, I lost the dream.

What was my EGO trying to protect me from?

The pain of not BEING good enough.
The disappointment of not BEING good enough.

So at the time, I went back to my cave.

The beliefs our EGOs hold are like our passports giving or denying
us access to certain realities. To experience change, we need to get
out of the EGO's box and start believing something better. When
we do, so much is possible.

> One cannot succeed by
> trying not to fail.[16]
> — Darel Rutherford

Exercise #1: Getting in Touch With Our Negative Dialogues

Please take a moment to write down your own negative self-talk. Now that you have your list, it's time for the next exercise.

Get a photo of yourself as a little child anywhere between the ages of 2 and 10 years old.

Speak all of your sentences while looking directly at yourself when you were younger. Change all the negative sentences you have been saying in your head to "YOU" as you communicate to the little one in the photo . . .

— You are not smart enough.
— You are not good enough.
— You are a failure.
— Why should anyone care for you?
— Why should anyone love you?

. . . Doesn't feel good, right? It's worth your time to change this kind of self-talk.

Now, make a list of the words you believe you needed to hear but never did while going through challenging times growing up.

Tune in.

Understand what you yearned for and give yourself that love, support, courage, belief, celebration, reward, playtime, company, encouragement, and friendship.

Now talk to yourself, your inner child, with these new words instead, looking at the picture once again, with sincerity from your heart, to make a shift in how you are feeling.

Exercise #2: The Four Keys to Success

Take out a pen and paper and write down how the steps can apply to you personally for your business or dream.

1. Following one's bliss and inspiration
2. Commitment
3. Non-attachment
4. The Winner's Attitude

Write down why you are following your bliss.

— What does that look like for you?

— Why are you committed and what does that look like for you?

— How can you be free of the expected results?

At the same time, imagine the results but also try to find peace if the results don't happen in the way you expect. List the benefits of things going your way. List the benefits of things not going your way. How are you a winner, no matter how things turn out, before you even embark on your journey? How is it possible that you don't lose either way so that you set yourself free from the fear?

1 -

2 -

3 -

4 -

Everyone wants
the fairy tale,
but don't forget
there are dragons
in those stories.

— *Darkchylde*, R. Queen

HOW TO
TAME
YOUR
DRAGON

To some extent, this chapter is a brief summary of all the tactics and methods already discussed. By using these methods and exercises, you can better understand and discover your EGO and also get in the habit of learning to deal with its natural resistance.

When you're trying to get out of your cave and the EGO blocks you from stepping into a solution to create nothing less than a new reality, it means there's a dragon waiting to be faced inside and an illusion to be broken. A very clear vision of what you are choosing and moving toward is a must. You might not, say, know the specifics of the business you are going to create or otherwise what your next steps toward prosperity and change will look like exactly yet. But we always know the dynamics of what we truly want to belong to even if the specifics are not yet visible to us. You might not know exactly what business you are going to go into but that doesn't mean you don't know that working with children in some capacity excites you or that maybe teamwork is not something you like or whether you thrive in an environment of competition.

Again, think of it as going from point A to point B:

- I desire more intimate relationships
- I desire more prosperity
- I desire a life of fulfillment

- I desire happiness
- I desire to be more effective at work
- I desire to have my own business

It's important to have a clear vision of where you'll go when you get out of your cave. Otherwise, it's like getting into a cab:

— Where would you like to go?
— I don't know, wherever . . .

If you leave it to the cabdriver, you might not enjoy where you end up.

Can you imagine a world leader being like this?

— Mr. Gandhi, what is your vision for your country?
— I don't know, let's just go with the flow and see what happens.

1. HAVE A CRYSTAL-CLEAR VISION:
I really understood the importance of this principle when I did a ritual before I met my husband. After realizing I had never really been clear in this department, I sat down and wrote a long list of the kind of dynamics I wanted to experience in what would be my idea of an ideal relationship.

- A fun relationship in which we play like children, even at 40.
- A relationship of shared authority.
- A man who has the wisdom to honor women greatly.
- A relationship full of trust.

The list went on and on. The very last sentence was my favorite:

- A relationship in which we assist each other's growth and serve one another to reach our highest potential.

I didn't just write these sentences but spoke them out loud, getting into them energetically and feeling each word as if it were already a reality; I was like an artist painting her masterpiece. The entire exercise lasted for more than three hours.

Forty-eight hours later I met Ike. The list exactly as it was became a reality, along with so much more.

Initially I didn't tell him about this ritual (we pretty much started dating twenty-four hours after meeting one another). A week or two later, he told me he had done a ritual for a relationship as well.

— Honey, please don't think I'm weird. I did a ritual before I met you.
— I won't. What ritual?
— I threw all my superficial lists of what I wanted in a relationship into a fire pit at a coffeeshop in Santa Monica, and had just one single and simple clear vision.
— What was that?
— To meet a woman who inspires me to become a better man . . . I believe that is you.

You can imagine I almost fell down flat on my face in a swoon, not only because of the crazy romanticism of the situation, but also because we had literally called out to one another around the same time, if not on the exact day.

We met at a party in Los Angeles, a party we had at first both refused to go to. We each had said no four or five times before we finally agreed to show up because of the nonstop insistence of the hostess. It was love at first sight, and we were the last ones to leave the party because we could not stop talking to one another.

When there is clarity, inspiration, and a vision, the Universe can easily drive us to where we need to go, even in spite of ourselves.

One of the classic ways in which the EGO successfully blocks the exit from a cave is by convincing us we don't really know what we are looking for. To repeat, although we might not know the specifics, we always know the dynamics.

One way to bypass this resistance is to write down what you don't want to experience about a particular subject. Then, right across from each thing you don't want, write down the opposite, what you do want. This way you will see that you know so much more than what your EGO lets you realize.

In other words, go with the unwanted first. This will help you bypass the EGO's resistance. By converting the sentences to their opposite you will clearly see how your contrasting experience has already been serving you to clarify what you do prefer.

This exercise will also help you clarify your conflicting desires.

Sometimes, for example, a person might be searching for a corporate job, going to interviews but without any results.

If the person makes the list of what they don't want, maybe it reads:

- I no longer want to work nine to five
- I no longer want to take orders from a superior
- I don't want others deciding how many hours I need to work
- I don't like an inflexible schedule
- I don't like to work within the confines of too many rules

What is the opposite?

- I want a job that allows me to decide my own hours
- I want to decide how many clients to take on
- I want a super relaxed environment
- I want to set my own rules

Here the person is supposedly saying "YES" to a corporate job and perhaps even going on job interviews to get a position but in actuality the person is saying "NO" to everything about the corporate world.

There is a desire or a signal being sent out by the action of looking for a job but an immediate cancellation thereafter due to an internal rejection of the regular dynamics of the corporate world. The "I want to/I don't want to" game is going on. It's not going to yield actual results.

In such a case there are only two ways to go for results. Either find a perspective that will allow you to honestly get excited about what you don't want, or better yet go for whatever inspires you.

To arrive at our destinations, clarity is key.

2. SPARK THE DESIRE AND THE INSPIRATION:
Secondly, as you saw in previous chapters, the EGO's natural resistance and defenses can be rather powerful. To bypass this resistance, the desire to get out of the box has to be greater than the EGO's need to keep us securely tucked inside it. There has to be a willingness to rock the boat and shake the cage.

Going back to the cave example: If one of the prisoners in the cave is dragged out by force, they will freak out when the powerful sunshine hits their eyes and blinds them temporarily.

If the person was forced out, they will run screaming back to the cave at the first sign of discomfort. On the other hand, if the prisoner's desire to discover what's beyond the cave is super strong, if there is passion and willingness, he or she is going to accept the uncomfortable sunshine, deal with it successfully, adapt to the new light, and get to experience a new reality.

This is why it is nearly impossible for anyone to change or transform unless they have clearly chosen to do so. Real transformation and change can never be forced from the outside whether the pressure is from a loved one or society or the law. It has to be truly desired and inspired from the inside out to be real and long-lasting.

The way to activate that desire for the vision, goal, or next step is to write down twenty reasons why you want to experience it in the first place.

Darel Rutherford wouldn't even take on a coaching client if they could not come up with twenty reasons why they wanted a change.

I know I have given you this exercise before, but there's no harm in doing it again, and maybe different or more inspiring reasons will emerge from your heart this time around.

I used to think these types of exercises were just so boring, and I didn't believe they could be of much help, since I considered myself to be much smarter than that. When I started giving them a chance, however, I realized putting our thoughts onto a piece of paper can bring about much-needed clarity, and I found that doing so untangles confusion and unburdens energetic gridlocks.

It is so important to have a vision, a reason, and an inspiration behind anything that we do. It's like breathing life into our actions, which can otherwise remain very mechanical and dull.

If you have a financial goal, for example, the exercise might start something like this:

1. All the material stuff I want to buy (car, house, clothes).

Remember, the material usage of prosperity counts as only one reason. Now you need to come up with nineteen other reasons why you want prosperity. If you don't have good enough reasons for wanting prosperity, prosperity doesn't have good enough reasons to come and be with you.

It is the same for whatever else your goal might be.

There once was a man who really wanted enlightenment. He found the best guru and sought his help. The problem was that the guru, happily meditating in his cave, was not interested in having him as a student. Even so, the man did everything he could to get the guru to notice him and take him under his wing. He put food at the entrance of the cave every day for a month but the guru never ate it. He slept at the entrance of the cave every day for a month but was met with silence. He tried to enter the cave every day for a month but was chased away with stones and sticks.

Finally, the guru gave in:

— Come with me.
— Where are we going?
— Don't ask!

They arrived at a clearing in the forest and got into an old boat. The guru rowed the boat to the middle of the lake, where it was the deepest.

— Jump!
— What?
— Just jump into the water!

The man was so happy he was finally getting what he wanted that he jumped in with all his clothes on. As soon as he did, the guru put his hand on the man's head and started pushing it under the water. The man struggled until his very last breath and just a few seconds before he was about to drown the guru removed his hand. The man came up coughing and gasping for air.

— Are you utterly mad? Are you trying to kill me?
— When you desire enlightenment as much as you desired that last breath of life, then come and find me.

And the guru rowed off.

In the Western world, especially within yoga circles, the word "desire" is often given a bad name. Knowing that desire goes hand in hand with creation and expansion, it never made sense to me. Even creation has a desire to experience itself; that is why we exist.

Many years ago, to put the question to rest, I asked a very prominent yogi in India what he thought about the word *desire* and how it was seen in Western yoga circles as an emotion to be set aside. I loved his one-sentence reply:

— Do you think Buddha would have ever gotten enlightened had he no desire to be enlightened?

Desire and attachment are two vastly different vibrations, and are not to be mixed up with one another. Desire creates, and attachment blocks.

3. BYPASS THE EGO's PROTECTION:
Remember, the EGO is primarily there to protect you from something. This could be an unconscious fear or an unconscious pain as a natural result of the belief you are holding on to.

— What is it that I am so afraid of?
— What is the pain that I am trying to avoid?
— What is the pain and fear trying to warn me about?

If you really ask, you will really find out. Once you find the pain or fear, allow yourself to first experience it fully. Go full in, as if you are diving into a dark body of water. It's scary to do so, but it's also truly worth it. Once you have allowed yourself to experience and feel the pain or the fear fully, your EGO will no longer have such a strong need to protect you from stepping outside of the box. The EGO has just experienced the worst and has seen it's not the end of the world.

By allowing ourselves to experience the worst-case scenario in advance, we remove the protective mechanism of the EGO when it is not needed. In freeing ourselves from its hindrance, we befriend the dragon and fly out of the cave on its wings.

If you want to create prosperity and it is not happening, ask yourself:

— What pain and/or fear am I trying to avoid by resisting it?

If you want to achieve your next goal, such as opening your own business, and it is not happening, ask yourself:

— What pain and/or fear am I trying to avoid by resisting it?

If you are procrastinating on the next step, be it starting a new project or starting to write your book or having that talk with your partner, ask yourself:

— What is the pain and/or fear I am trying to avoid by resisting it?

- Find it.
- Feel it.
- Let it go.
- Move on.

4. HAVE THE WINNER'S ATTITUDE:
The fourth way to work with the EGO's natural resistance is to make the worst-case scenario okay. Again, ask your EGO:

— What are you so afraid of?

The EGO always has a worst-case scenario up its sleeve as it tries to protect us from something.

When I was an actress, a point came when I was no longer booking any projects, although I was getting a lot of auditions .... What was my worst-case scenario? . . . What was it that I was so afraid of?

I was afraid of failure.

What if they picked me for a real project and I was awful, being so out of practice? In terms of manifestation, my EGO was protecting me from being in a project so that I wouldn't experience my projected fear of failure. To be able to really say *So what?* to our worst-case scenario we need to shift it into something that looks pretty darn great. Being able to face the worst-case scenario in our heads as a winner instead of as a loser is key to success. It also helps the attachments go.

Here, the question to explore is:

— How would I come out as a winner, even if my worst-case scenario did happen?

I had just moved back to Turkey to bring Kundalini Yoga to my country. This was in itself so exciting, plus transformational coaching was just starting in my life and everything in these two departments was flowing effortlessly. The worst that could happen was I would just continue doing what I had already been doing. In this sense, there was nothing to lose whatsoever. If the acting wasn't happening anymore, that meant more time, more energy, and more love for all my other projects.

— Wow! I actually have nothing to lose!

The EGO, with all its attachments and identifications, is the part of us that believes in loss and tries to protect us from that. The Soul already knows there is nothing to lose. Our Souls know the closing of one door is the opening of another. In our capacity to embrace the worst-case scenario, the fear is removed.

One has to walk the journey emotionally to have the real shift; it cannot be done on just an intellectual level. I was no longer afraid to fail whatsoever because in my worst-case scenario I would have clarity about my life's direction.

Within forty-eight hours, three different auditions came along:

A big commercial campaign: TV and billboards
A TV series
A feature film

I booked all three projects, and people fought to make the scheduling work for me.

5. TALK TO YOUR EGO:
We have already talked about this as an exercise in another chapter, but we will go over it again, this time using an example. Remember the case study of Rebecca at the beginning of the book? Her belief was that more of anything, including prosperity, brought about unhappiness and loss.

Imagine you are the captain of a ship. The ship's regular route is from Los Angeles to Hawaii, but as the captain, you have decided the new destination is Tahiti. If you just think it, without informing the whole crew, meaning the team that physically operates the ship, you are going to find yourself in Hawaii although you intended to go to Tahiti.

In the same way, talk to your EGO and encourage it to come and hold the new reality in place. Remember, you have an EGO but you are not your EGO.

a) Let the EGO know you understand and acknowledge it.
— I know you believe money is the source of all unhappiness, but just because our parents fought about money does not mean money has that kind of power.

b) Give the EGO good arguments and examples from outside its box.
— There are many people who have abundance and are happy. We can be like those people. Our parents did not split because of money; they inherently did not get along and money was just an excuse as the final straw.

c) Let the EGO know who is the boss, but also give it a gift.
— Now, whatever you might choose to protect, just know I think it is time we allow abundance into our lives. And don't worry, I promise you I am not going to let us become

abundant at the expense of our happiness. Also, think of all the vacations we will get to go on once we allow the abundance in.

It's really like guiding a child, letting the unconditional love be known and felt but having the firmness to set new rules for the EGO.

Whether the EGO initially buys into the new reality is not the most important reason to talk with the EGO. The whole real trick with this exercise is:

> You cannot talk to your EGO
> and
> be your EGO
> at the same time.[17]
> — Darel Rutherford

d) Learn to smile at the EGO.
— It is simply an old tape playing, an old story playing itself out over and over again. When we fight with the EGO expressed as constant mind-chatter in our heads, we give it way too much power. Don't fight with the EGO; introduce it to a new story, and when it plays the old tape over again, just smile at it.

Remember the beautiful soul you are and that any negative and limiting story running inside is not who you truly are. If you don't give power to the story, it can't become real.

The wonderful thing about the above exercise is that through practicing it you get really clear about what your EGO's voice, language, and tactics sound like.

6. LEARN THE TACTICS OF YOUR EGO:
There are various tactics the EGO employs to keep us in the cave.

Here are a couple of examples:

- The "nonstop mind-chatter" game.
- The "I don't know" game
- The "forgetting" game
- The "making wrong" game
- The "keep changing your mind" game
- The "keep delaying" game
- The "it's impossible" game
- The "victim" game
- The "it's too late" game

These are just some of the many kinds of games the EGO plays.

For example, I know someone who is extremely talented and creative. Sarah is interested in living a different life and having a different job, but whenever she is excited about something, she never follows through. She doesn't commit to a new path. Her EGO keeps her busy and in the box by just constantly changing what she is excited about. This in turn keeps her in a consistent space of:

BEING the one who always *wants to.*

Successfully blocking her from: BEING the one who actually *chooses to.*

Sarah would first have to figure out what pain or fear her EGO is trying to protect her from, and then make the worst-case scenario okay and deal with it so that she can make a new committed BEING choice to belong to her preferred reality.

We have to first say no to the old way of BEING before we can say yes to a new way of BEING. After that it is about smiling and giving unconditional love to the EGO so that it too can transform. The irony is, transformation cannot happen if we are attached to the EGO changing. Our EGOs transform only in the space of unconditional love.

How does your EGO employ its control over you? What is your EGO's classic move to stop you from getting out of the cave? Discover the specific character, mode, and tactics of your EGO. Each of our EGOs has a specific character and method of functioning.

Even the need to interpret everything spiritually and the need to be better than and above our humanity is a very hidden and convoluted form of EGO, one that completely rejects and doesn't love the reality of being simply human.

As long as we don't take the EGO's story seriously, it has no control over us anymore.

You can look at your own EGO like one of those tiny Smurf characters or like one of the seven dwarfs of "Snow White." Smiling at the EGO is an important practice and act of self-love; judging it is a form of self-rejection.

If we don't resist the resistance, the resistance melts away.

7 . VISUALIZATION:
This is a great tool to rewire the brain out of negative expectations.

Let's say you are going for a job interview for the sixth time, and you are feeling rather rejected and hopeless. On your way to this sixth one, your mind could naturally already be spinning with "It's not going to happen."

STOP . . . Just STOP!

Close your eyes for a few minutes and visualize how you would like it to go. See it and feel it in detail. Make it okay if it doesn't go as you visualized. Then proceed. Learn to construct the vision powerfully but also to let go of it. Don't get attached to what you visualize; that is the key.

This is great training for the mind to begin having positive expectations. If you can see it, feel it, and BE it, you can have it.

8. FIND OUT YOUR EGO's GAIN:
We have already seen many examples of the EGO's gain. If we are not finding a solution to our so-called problem, it is not because the Universe is out of solutions for us; it's because a part of us wants the problem to remain in place.

The following exercise is not to be confused with the positive visualization exercise just above. It is very different and serves an entirely different purpose. It's more about putting ourselves in the picture of the goal, the vision, the point B in an exaggerated manner, and seeing and discovering what part of it we are resisting.

Think of the goal, the vision, the destination we claim we want as a blank canvas. If it's all pure and white, we can easily create it without even having to think about it. It will just happen. However, although we want to go there, if it has all these black marks on it—our limiting beliefs against it—we are not going to necessarily create it. This is what is meant by the EGO's gain.

Let's look at real-life examples.

One workshop participant, Leyla, was working on increasing her business. Leyla was about to sign on a new client that would double her monthly income. Yet, somehow the deal kept getting delayed.

We did the exercise and she closed her eyes and saw herself in the picture of the outcome with great detail. The contract was signed, the new client was added to the portfolio, the production line was working full time. Great! Right?

However, instead of smiling, she frowned.

— What was the problem when you went there?
— I saw myself working 24/7 because of the demand.
— Can't you delegate the workload?
— Yes.

She was hesitant in the way she said this. That is where the problem was.

— Okay! Close your eyes again. This time I want you to see yourself working only three to four hours a day and your very capable team taking care of the work as they are supposed to. You just make the decisions and monitor the outcome, and you have free time the rest of the day. What happens in this picture?

After a brief silence ...

— If I am not doing it ALL, I feel useless and unworthy.

Therefore, her new client wasn't coming through. She wanted the new client, yes, but she also did not want the client. She wanted income, yes, but because she also felt she had to do everything herself, she also didn't want all the extra hours of work that would be required for the job. Although it was her own business and she had a perfectly capable team in place, she couldn't delegate because of the gain of feeling worthy only when she was working like a dog.

For her business to expand, she had to give up:

BEING the one who does all the work herself, for . . .

BECOMING the one who delegates and trusts her team. (This would also mean she gives value to what her team has to offer.)

The beauty and the power of finding the GAIN is that in doing so, one automatically finds the belief as well.

Close your eyes and put yourself inside your vision, your goal, your desire. Live in that world for a bit. See what it is that you don't like. What aspect of it makes you automatically go

— Uuugghhh!!!

Now that you have found the resistance to your goal, what do you choose to do about it?

Are you ready to drop the GAIN and move on?
Are you ready for your next better version and reality?
Are you ready to update your operating system?

Now that you have found your hidden GAIN in not moving forward, go back to the visualization exercise #7 to practice your preferred outcome without any attachments to the results. See all that it can do for you. After you have figured out how your EGO specifically stops you from getting out of the box, talk to your EGO every day or whenever it offers you arguments of limitations and fear. Convince the EGO instead of being convinced by it. Let your clarity and inspiration keep you steady and committed on your path and most importantly, figure out in advance how to employ the Winner's Attitude. How can you position your perception so that no matter what the outcome is, you end up feeling like a winner? Let love, not fear, be your guide in whatever you choose, and practice this.

Ask yourself often:

— At this moment am I letting fear or love guide me?
— At this moment am I choosing limitation or freedom?

In your Soul's journey there is nothing to lose, only new experiences and understandings to be gained. The fear of loss is just the EGO's game to try to keep you in the box.

EXERCISE 1: NOTES _____

_____

_____

_____

_____

_____

_____

_____

_____

_____

_____

_____

_____

_____

_____

_____

_____

_____

_____

_____

_____

_____

_____

_____

_____

_____

_____

_____

_____

EXERCISE 2: NOTES _____

EXERCISE 3: NOTES _____

_____
_____
_____
_____
_____
_____
_____
_____
_____
_____
_____
_____
_____
_____
_____
_____
_____
_____
_____
_____
_____
_____
_____
_____
_____
_____
_____
_____

EXERCISE 4: NOTES _____

EXERCISE 5: NOTES _____

_____
_____
_____
_____
_____
_____
_____
_____
_____
_____
_____
_____
_____
_____
_____
_____
_____
_____
_____
_____
_____
_____
_____
_____
_____
_____
_____
_____

EXERCISE 6: NOTES _____

EXERCISE 7: NOTES _____

_____
_____
_____
_____
_____
_____
_____
_____
_____
_____
_____
_____
_____
_____
_____
_____
_____
_____
_____
_____
_____
_____
_____
_____
_____
_____
_____
_____

EXERCISE 8: NOTES

We are not
human beings having a
spiritual experience
but
spiritual beings
having a human one.

— Georges I. Gurdjieff

WHO
ON EARTH
ARE YOU,
ANYWAY?

I wonder why we have the tendency to think that intelligence is something that resides in the brain.

As if real intelligence has only to do with the size of our brains.

Honestly, have you ever watched bees or ants? How do worker bees know to obey the queen bee? How do bees know to create a honeycomb with out-of-this-world precise geometry?

Or the ants! Have you ever watched a group of ants on the move? They walk in such a way that we know for sure they are going about their lives with purpose. They are not confused or lost. They know exactly where they are going and what they are doing, and even if there are a hundred or more of them in one place moving simultaneously, they seem to be more organized than the regular traffic on our city highways, and they don't have the signposts to guide them.

What about salmon? Born in a river, they find their way out into the vast ocean only to return back not to any old river, but to the exact same one they were born in when it's time for the female to lay her eggs.

What a demonstration of finding one's way back home. Considering the brain size of the bee, ant, and salmon, I would have to argue that intelligence has to do with aspects beyond just the sheer mechanics of the brain.

What I am talking about is an innate capacity we have until it gets shut down by education systems or broader society. Learning ability is something entirely different, of course, as I doubt we can teach a bee to have proper table manners. But neither should intelligence be defined as narrowly as our capacity to become a trained monkey.

In our societies and educational systems everything learned from the outside is given value, and nothing is done to nurture the innate intelligence we are born with.

Just recently, a close friend who is an educator in the US told me that suicide rates in schools are alarmingly high and rising. What is wrong?

Education systems across the world are outdated, ineffective, and non-connective. Cramming endless amounts of information into memory is seen as education. While with the internet, knowledge is at the tip of one's fingers.

What about the creative aspect of intelligence?
What about inner guidance and intuition?
What about the intelligence of feelings?
What about learning to think for oneself instead of being trained only to follow guidelines?
What about trying to understand the Universe, the purpose of a human, our connection to nature, to life, to the overall system?

The medical world is the same.

You have a heart problem. They look at only one thing: your physical heart. What about the state of your liver? The liver affects the condition of the heart and the liver has everything to do with the overall digestive system as well. How about curing that too? All these systems are linked together as a whole.

Why is the heart having a problem in the first place? What happened to the person's heart? How and why was their heart broken? What emotion or life challenge was not handled or processed properly? Why were they stressed?

I remember learning biology at the university. A class I was most excited about taking ended up being painfully boring. We just memorized a whole bunch of chemical reactions, none of which were connected back to real and practical life. I simply memorized everything, only to forget it right after the exam.

It was much more exciting to learn in yoga, for example, how internal organs need to have a certain energetic balance and how a liver heating up too much can cause a rise in intense anger or an extreme and sudden release of sadness. One of the things that heats up the liver very fast is alcohol, blocking not only the body's capacity to physically detoxify but also to emotionally balance us. No wonder bars are fertile ground for fights or for crying on one another's shoulder: Drinking when feeling negative emotion is going to compound the problem. This is practical information that anyone can connect to and use to orchestrate their life for the better.

When you look at the Greek philosophers and mathematicians, you don't just find stale and compartmentalized theories, but an attempt to find connectivity across the various parts of life. Pythagoras looked at the mathematical ways in which the planets move and believed their movement created an inaudible sound like a symphony. He also believed the soul leaves the body and comes back again in a new body after death.

Connecting math to sound and the movement of the planets? Contemplating what happens to the soul after death?

It is grand, it is living, and it is connective.

All I learned in school about Pythagoras was the mathematics of a triangle. This is so limited, disconnected, boring, and lifeless, not to mention impractical unless one is going to become a mathematician.

If the youth are depressed and suicidal, this is not only alarming but also an indication that huge reforms are needed, in the educational systems worldwide and in many different systems across society.

We are, in essence, connected to Universal Intelligence, and this connectivity is inside, innate, not outside and definitely not just in our minds. Like the head of the octopus with its various arms extending out, different forms of existence—meaning the animal kingdom, the plant kingdom, the crystals, the earth we walk on—are all connected to the hub of that Universal Intelligence.

Even the crystals on our planet have a capacity. Let us not be fooled by the fact that they just sit there and look pretty. They amplify thought.

For example, Dr. Mitchell Gaynor writes in *The Healing Power of Sound:*

"Marcel Vogel, who worked as a senior scientist at IBM for nearly three decades and has spent many years researching quartz crystals, has concluded that the crystal emits a vibration which extends and amplifies the powers of the user's mind."[18]

Cleve Backster a plant biologist, was a student of Leonarde Keeler, co-inventor of the lie detector. That machine can detect very sublime stress levels by testing a person's physiology, which in turn is used as a basis to determine whether they are lying or telling the truth.

In February of 1966, something compelled Backster to test the leaf of a plant he had just gotten. So he hooked up the machine to the leaf of this plant. In his own words:

"The very moment the imagery of burning the leaf entered my mind, the polygraph recording pen moved to the top of the chart! No words were spoken, no touching the plant, no lighting of matches, just my clear intention to burn the leaf. The plant recording showed dramatic excitation. To me this was a powerful, high-quality observation. I must state that on February 2, 1966, at 13 minutes, 55 seconds into that chart recording, my whole consciousness changed."[19]

This indicates clearly the consciousness of the plant as it reacts to the threat being presented by Backster in his intention to burn the leaf. We are so interconnected in this manner.

Who on earth are we, anyway?

We are not only incredible beings born with Universal Intelligence, we are also connected to the rest of existence because of it.

How come as humans we can more resemble a chicken with its head cut off running around aimlessly, or a cat chasing its own tail around and around in circles, rolling with the same problem over and over again, sometimes never attaining a solution?

One reason out of many for that is because we are taught to disregard the importance of our feelings, or in other words our feelers. Even positive thinking can see negative emotions as a problem rather than as having their own purpose for being present.

Don't be angry.
Don't be sad.
Don't be judgmental.
Don't be unhappy.
Don't be depressed.

We are trained to avoid negative emotions like the plague. Again, this is a conditioning and a shutdown. The result is repression, denial, and a lack of understanding of ourselves. Avoiding negative emotions results in being arrested by them. When we don't have our intuition in place, and working and functioning properly, based on this kind of mistrust of feelings, it affects and limits us in business, relationships, and prosperity as well. Intuition is like our personal compass to find our own way home.

A distraught client came to a session. A business partner had embezzled funds from Cybill. She felt completely betrayed, and her trust in humanity was shaken to the core by the loss.

— What did you feel about this man when you first met him? Did you innately trust him?
— No!
— So why did you get into a business agreement with him?
— He hadn't done anything visibly wrong, so I had no reason to distrust him. I didn't want to be judgmental.

In an effort to play nice, Cybill had distrusted what she knew, and had betrayed herself.

This doesn't mean everything we feel is necessarily intuitive.

But when emotions and feelings have been belittled, judged, made wrong, and not really seen as portals of information coming our way—whether that be information about ourselves, other people, or situations—this intuitive capacity is shut down.

Discernment is like the ability to separate the stones from the rice or the thorns from the rose. Judgment is like the narrow borders of a certain belief that when projected onto a subject or person, blind us from truly seeing. It is important to know the difference.

When we judge judgment, however, discernment goes out the window too. The EGO will always be judging something or another outside of its box, whether silently or out loud, no matter what we pretend. When we use this capacity positively, it's called having good judgment. When we use it like a knee-jerk reaction, it can be bad judgment.

When there is a fear of being judgmental, which is a judgment within itself, we might deny what is staring at us blatantly as the truth, as Cybill did.

What belongs to us?
What is a match?
What is authentic?
What is toxic for us?
What is okay for us, what is not?

How many times have you experienced something and only after the fact exclaimed:

— I knew it! I just knew it.

But it's too late.

All feelings are like a biofeedback system, informational and useful in finding our own unique ways and paths. When something or someone is off kilter, we can feel negative about it.

What is off can be:

1. The person we are dancing with, as in Cybill's example.
2. A belief system that is limiting us or that we are projecting onto the other person.
3. A triggered painful memory that we have not processed yet.

Regardless of what is going on, the point is negative emotions have value and act as messengers of some kind. Don't shoot the messenger! What is the message trying to say?

In this sense there is nothing we should or shouldn't be feeling. If we are feeling it, it is no mistake at all and it has a purpose; it may be misplaced, but it is not to be repressed or overlooked.

One way to uncover the message is to be open to feeling a negative emotion deeply and then ask it a question:

— What are you trying to tell me?

And then listen deeply to what it has to say. This exercise can also train you to listen to the messages coming from your own body.

Fiona was experiencing paralyzing back pain when she came to a session. When we asked the pain what it was trying to say, she heard loud and clear:

— Just let the heaviness go!

At first she didn't understand what this meant, and her immediate response was to just stop instead of investigating further. But body messages or our intuition aren't going to converse with us like a regular human being, just eager to talk on and on. It is a one-sentence-at-a-time type of investigative conversation.

— The heaviness of what?
— The guilt!
— The guilt of what?

The pain's message and what it was referring to finally came online and the curtains opened.

The guilt had been about sexual abuse from a long time ago when she was a child. Fiona did the Inner Child work using a specific method we've created, which will be shared in the next chapter. During the moments she engaged with her inner child, she let the little one, her child self, know:

— It wasn't your fault!

Guess what?

Her back snapped into position and the paralyzing pain disappeared instantly. She had successfully let go of the guilt, which was not hers to have to carry anyway.

This is how connected mind, body, and emotion are.

A healing happened as she listened to the message of the pain coming from her body. We will come back to Fiona's example in more detail in the next chapter.

But for now, let's go back to the example of Cybill, who lost money in a business deal. Had she not betrayed her own intuition and instead listened to her negative emotions about her business partner, she would not have experienced betrayal.

In judging her own feelings, she missed understanding her own guidance.

With our intuition functioning properly, we feel safe. Luckily this is not something we need to learn but rather to simply reactivate and remember how to follow, as it is already built in.

Let's take a look at what potentially happens when we manage to kill the capacity to feel negative.

When I first started teaching Kundalini Yoga in Turkey in 2002, I met a super nice girl who seemed to benefit greatly from the classes. I was shocked to find out she was in her 30s. She was so sweet but completely lost, like a girl stuck in a woman's body. Her speech patterns and the kind of questions she asked and comments she made would have been plausible for a teenager.

After a couple of months she started looking much better. She told me she had quit her antidepressants and was feeling like herself for the first time in years. She had started taking the antidepressants at 17 and hadn't stopped for fifteen long years. Her capacity to feel negative feelings had been taken away by the drugs and replaced by a fake kind of feeling good. She had not found her way in life ever since, and it felt like she was emotionally still stuck at 17.

Whether we do this with antidepressants, drugs, alcohol, judgments against ourselves, or denial of our feelings, it's all the same thing and produces the same end results in varying degrees.

If a negative feeling is not intuitive guidance giving direction, what else can it be?

It could also be a wound inside that hasn't healed, just as in the example of Fiona with her back pain. In her case it was both a negative emotion, as she was really shut down, and also a physical pain, as the manifestation and therefore the messenger of the weight of the guilt she had been carrying around.

Another reason a negative emotion can arise is if we have a belief system that runs contrary to our goal. The conflict between the limiting belief and the expanded desire will also express itself as a negative emotion.

In this sense, it is a blessing to feel something negative if we are interested in discovery. We don't have to do this all the time, especially with the small stuff, but when major stuff comes up, it is very practical and solution-oriented to do so.

If we want to get married, for example, and we have a negative belief about marriage that we may not be aware of, we are going to get cold feet—perhaps shortly after the proposal, during the ceremony, or soon after the marriage.

The negative emotion could be intuition saying that our partner of choice is not the right person for us or we might be getting married for all the wrong reasons. But it could also be that we really want to get married to the person and are truly in love—yet have an unacknowledged limiting belief about marriage seething underneath.

Ike pretty much proposed in our first month. All I felt was intense panic. I didn't know why.

— Whoaa! Who says I want to get married? . . . I don't think I really believe in marriage.

— Okay. No problem.

Thankfully he did not take it personally.

After four years of living with Ike and having the time of our lives, one day my yoga teacher Gurmukh asked me after class:

— So, when are you two lovebirds getting married?
— I am still waiting to see . . .

She looked at me with her wise eyes, head tilted to the side, and went right to the core in the most gentle and innocent voice a human being could possibly muster:

— What is it exactly that you are waiting for?

There was no logical reason to be afraid, so I just suppressed the negative emotion that was there because I did not understand it. You see, we just assume that if there is no logical reason for an emotion, it should be discarded. Plus, everything else felt so good, I dismissed the fear. Swept it under the carpet. Gurmukh was right, there was no reason to wait, we were happy and in love.

I came home and told Ike:

— We can get married now!
— What happened to you, all of a sudden?
— Gurmukh happened!

We began the preparations, and Gurmukh and her husband Gurushabd graciously flew from Los Angeles to Istanbul for forty-eight hours just to marry us. She had gotten me into this. She was going to be there to hold my hand. The whole event was amazing, beyond a dream for us both. It was a forty-five-minute spiritual ceremony as the sun set in the background overlooking the Bosphorus Bridge, which connects the continents of Europe and Asia—beautiful and very symbolic for both of our lives. Gurmukh got all the guests up from their seats to bow down to the moon. It was quite a sight to behold.

We got our magical happy ending, riding off into the sunset . . . But soon after a problem arose.

Had we both not known by then how belief systems are picked up and how they create our realities, I probably would have destroyed a beautiful loving relationship just because we ended up getting married.

How many relationships have you known or heard about that lasted wonderfully until marriage? Doesn't that strike you as strange? Nine years the couple is happy but they get married and are divorced in nine days! What is going on might not even have anything to do with the two people in love but their beliefs and limitations about marriage might be what is getting in the way.

A couple of months into the marriage, I got into this incredible jealousy out of the blue.

A quick background before we proceed. I was known as the girl who never got jealous. Never! When we met, Ike was the one with jealousy issues. We worked on it together and he overcame his jealousy at the beginning of the relationship in six months.

— What on earth was going on with me now?

I couldn't understand myself and just cringed at the idea of now being the one who was jealous.

— Yuck! This was not me!. . . But then again, was it?

Why was I never a jealous person and now suddenly I was? What was the only thing that was different in my life?

— Marriage!

Marriage was the big change. This whole new strange me had come into play after the wedding. The belief had to be related to marriage and not necessarily to any beliefs about relationships.

This was the clue.

— What was it about marriage that I believed but I didn't know I believed?

Now it was Ike's turn to help me. He was so delighted and had so much fun with the idea that I had turned into him now. Together we found the memory.

I was going to my best friend's birthday party with the grown-ups when I was 9 or 10. Everybody was talking about a famous Italian surgeon and his beautiful wife. I was very curious about this couple since they were the subject of much conversation and I waited in excitement to meet them. They finally arrived, and I ended up sitting right across from them at the table. In awe, I stared at how vibrant and handsome he was with his even more beautiful and charismatic wife next to him. I decided in the future I wanted to be part of a couple just like them, vibrant and charismatic.

At one point, however, my napkin fell on the floor, and when I went under the table to get it, I witnessed the surgeon's hand stroking the leg not of his wife but of the woman sitting on his other side. I was shocked, as if someone had electrocuted me. My whole nervous system did a number on me. I hadn't had much awareness of the concept of couples cheating at that age, and it was news to me that this kind of stuff happened in the adult world.

My immediate conclusion about men and marriage became:

Successful married men cheat.

No wonder I had been resistant to marriage without knowing why.

I realized the jealousy had been activated shortly after Ike's book was published and became an overnight bestseller, eventually selling more than a million copies in Turkey. We got married and he reached a new level of success almost at the same time.

Now if the Universe doesn't have a good sense of humor, I don't know what does. The beast had been asleep and woke up as soon as the correct circumstances arose, triggering the belief that had been dormant.

Ike and I had a big laugh about this one.

But let's say I didn't resolve it and did end up becoming the classically jealous wife. What do you think in time I would have created? The funniest thing was that even my wedding invitations had been the poster of the movie *Runaway Bride* with our faces swapped in for Julia Roberts and Richard Gere. On the poster Julia Roberts is in a wedding dress already tying the laces of her running shoes in case she needs to bolt. Even an innocent choice like that for the wedding invitations had been representative of this unconscious belief hanging around.

Negative feelings have three different purposes.

1. Intuition.
2. An active wound becoming available for us to process, as someone or some event triggers it.
3. An indication there is a direct conflict between where we want to go and what our belief system holds about the destination we are trying to reach.

In all three cases, it is a message.

Both the negative feelings and the positive ones are like traffic lights guiding our journey. If all traffic lights were green, that would be a problem because we would crash into each other in chaos. If all of them were red lights, our cars wouldn't move and we would be stuck. Having both red and green lights moves the traffic and the journey forward.

If it feels good, go for it. (It's a green light.)
If it feels bad, stop. (It's a red light.)

If you're excited about a green light but are also seeing red ones, don't just run the red ones in pursuit of your goal. Always check to see what the red light might be about. Figure out what's going on before you proceed. Don't just pull out the weeds and throw them in the bin. Find out what is causing the weeds to grow in your garden to begin with. Each and every one of your feelings is a strength and a gift.

Who on earth are you?

A being infinitely connected to Universal Intelligence with a built-in self-navigation system to help you find your way on Earth.

If the salmon can find their way, so can you.

Exercise #1: Navigating the Negative

What emotion is underneath the negative feeling?

Anger?
Pain?
Sadness?

Make time for yourself. Find a private space where nobody can disturb or hear you. Feel the emotion or the physical pain completely. The point of the exercise is to open up to the emotion as much as you can. Give it complete permission. Be with it as you would with a friend going through a rough time. Don't rush it, don't resist, feel it totally.

— Pain, what are you trying to tell me?

Don't expect anything. Just listen and be receptive. Don't go after the answers; instead let the answers come to you.

If you manage to connect to your own wisdom, the answer will be profound and it will surprise you greatly. If you can't connect, try again until you do. Play with it a couple of times and write down the answers that come.

Be patient. Go slow. Don't push. Let it be revealed.

Purpose of the exercise: To realize negative emotions are messages waiting for us to hear them. (Use this exercise as needed, as stuff comes up.)

Exercise #2: Meditation Developing the Positive Mind

Sit in a comfortable position either cross-legged on the floor or in a chair, making sure your spine is straight. Curl both your pinky and ring fingers completely into your palms with the help of your thumbs to lock them in place and let the index and middle fingers remain straight. The palms are facing forward, the hands are in front of the shoulders, the elbows are bent and on the side of the body. The hands are placed at a thirty-degree angle to your chest. Sit straight.

Breath: Regular, normal deep and slow breathing from the nose.
Eyes: Close your eyes and put the focus between the eyebrows.
Time: 11 minutes; can also be practiced for 62 minutes.
Mantra: Silently and rhythmically chant as if singing from in between your eyebrows: SA (infinity)-TA (life)-NA (death)-MA (rebirth).

Practice: 40 or 90 days straight; 120 days in a row is ideal.
To finish: Inhale and exhale deeply 3 times. Then open and close your fists several times. Relax.

Effect: Activates the positive self, brings happiness and prosperity. This hand position can be seen in much of the religious art of the East. It is rumored that Buddha practiced this meditation in ancient times.[20]

The moment you doubt
whether you can fly,
you cease forever
to be able to do it.

— *Peter Pan*, J. M. Barrie

THE
HIGH MAGIC
OF
THE CHILD

The natural process of creation is easy for children simply because they haven't yet had the time to pick up many limiting beliefs along the way. Mostly these get compounded as we grow up. I think this is one of the reasons children learn languages so much faster than adults do. My little niece was speaking three languages by the time she was 5. Children don't have ideas about learning being hard or about things being impossible. They are wide open still because they are so innocent.

When the Sphinx told Socrates he was the wisest man in Greece, Socrates didn't believe it at first. Hence, he went to talk one by one with the wisest ones in the village. They all lived up to their reputation in wisdom, but they also all believed they knew everything. Socrates, on the other hand, knew he did not know. That is when he understood why the Sphinx had declared him the wisest man in Greece. Wisdom lacking innocence is incomplete.

In our sessions, Darel would say so very often:

— I don't know the answer to that question.

And that would immediately open up space for incredible exploration. To "know" is great and needed for the application of anything, but to "not know" is needed to get out of the box when the time comes. Otherwise, the "knowing" itself creates the boundaries preventing us from going outside of our most recent paradigms and understandings.

This is why when we are trying to manifest something:

— But, how is it going to happen?

Is simply not a good question.

When we try to know or dictate the how, we automatically limit the various possibilities with which the Universe can bring us what we are asking for; we predefine the path to being the only way we imagined it by trying to conjure up the how in advance. The Universal mind is like the eagle having a bird's eye view, a wider perception, aware of the various possibilities dancing simultaneously out there and therefore much better equipped to see the way than we are, in trying to figure out the how.

Are you going to figure out which is the better, shorter, or more scenic road to your destination by standing on the curb and looking at the streets, or when you are looking at a map and can see the total picture of the city from above in a single glance?

Figuring out the how in advance is not necessary. Becoming a match to what we are asking for, on the other hand, is essential.

Let go of the knowing and get cracking on BEING!

- Who would I be BEING if I were already successful?
- Who would I be BEING if I were already prosperous?
- Who would I be BEING if my problem were already resolved?
- Who would I be BEING if I were the solution to the problem?

Once we choose to BELONG to what we are asking for by making a new agreement with ourselves, the how will automatically show up and present itself.

We don't go to a restaurant and worry about how the food is cooked in the kitchen or how the waitress is going to bring it to us to eat. We naturally expect that the food will get delivered to our table.

A friend of my husband called him asking for his help with her daughter, who was no older than 6 and possibly even younger.

One day her daughter asked:

— Mommy, can we get a dog?
— No, love, we can't.
— But, why not?
— Because we live in an apartment and dogs aren't allowed here.
— If we had a house, could we get a dog then?
— Yes, love.
— Let's get a house then!
— We don't have the money to do that!

The little girl was so determined to have a dog she started to draw pictures of a house with a garden and a gate and a dog. When the mother asked her daughter what she was doing, she said she was creating a house, since it was a prerequisite for getting a dog. The mother was absolutely mortified and had called up Ike for some relief.

— I don't want her to continue with this pipe dream!
— Why not?
— She'll be disappointed when it doesn't happen.
— That's your fear, not hers.
— But . . . What'll I do when she's disappointed?
— Why are you trying to protect her?

— I don't want her to get hurt!

— You don't know she'll be disappointed. Sorry to inform you, but at one point or another she'll taste this feeling, as we all do. The sooner she knows disappointment, the better chance she has to learn to deal with it. Get out of her way. If she falls you can help her get up once again. But don't try to hold her back.

The mother decided to let her daughter be.

A couple of months later something happened in their lives and they had to leave their apartment. They still did not have enough money to buy a house of their own, so they started looking for an apartment about the same size.

One day as they were looking for a new place, they saw a house for sale with a garden. Something prompted the mother to go in and ask about it. The owner happened to open the door. She was an older lady living on her own in the house next door and they connected so well that the afternoon was spent having cakes and tea and sharing stories about life.

In the US, due to the nature of the real estate business, this may be hard to imagine. But in Turkey the whole process works rather differently and not so formally.

— You know, I really like your family. I'd love for you to buy the house.

— Oh! That'd be a dream, but it's way beyond our budget.

— I'm ailing and I don't have any family to leave the house to when I am gone. I'm willing to do whatever it takes to make it work with your current budget. You can even pay me monthly, small amounts, like rent.

— What?????????

They moved into the house with a garden and the little girl finally got her dog. What she envisioned, drew, felt, entertained, believed, and dreamed simply happened, regardless of their monetary limitations.

Whose regular intelligence or logic could figure out in a million years that this event could possibly unfold in such a manner?

The Universe is a much better orchestrator of events than we ever could be. It is wise not to grasp for the *how* and to get out of the way and dare to be innocent enough to trust existence.

Some of you still might be thinking the little girl's story was just a coincidence. It took me a long time to trust these kinds of things as well, wondering and questioning whether they were all just happy coincidences. After hundreds and hundreds of examples, however, there came a point when even my EGO couldn't deny the very precise correlations between asking and receiving.

Children carry the gift and power of innocence. Their relationship to the Universe is much simpler, much more open and trusting than that of adults, and they are a thousand times more intuitive and intelligent, as they have access to the quantum field while adults lose this in the process of growing up.

On the other hand, also due to their innocence, in the same way that they learn things quickly and download information instantly, they also can get conditioned very quickly.

Although we grow up, we still have access to our inner child.

I cannot emphasize enough the importance of reconnecting to our inner child's innocence and intuition once again, while at the same time setting free the conditioning and shutdowns we experienced growing up.

The inner child work not only helps us access the setups, beliefs, and conclusions about life that may still be limiting us in the present, but also helps us transform them, creating dramatic changes in our lives. Not only that, but since children are so much more closely connected to the quantum field, a healthy connection with the inner child means renewed access to the quantum field, which in return invokes our creativity, spontaneity, and ability to think and perceive outside of the box.

This is an important step—maybe the most important step—in letting success, prosperity, health, and better relationships back into our lives and returning to a level of soaking in pleasure, satisfaction, beauty, and fun day in and day out.

When we've created so many defensive barriers, how can we expect to let the good stuff come in? It is important to melt away those limitations and reopen what was shut down.

In forgetting to be present and living disconnected from the moment, with the mind consistently locked in the past or the future, the whole magic of the moment is missed. The inner child helps us heal this disconnection when we go back and really reconnect to him or her, giving our child self permission, unconditional love, encouragement, support, and the feelings of safety, acceptance, and admiration the child may not have received while growing up.

In the quantum field, time doesn't have a beginning, middle, or end. In this field, all time is just one time. If we can change the response of the inner child to a past event by going back in time, the current timeline is also affected and changed as a result. Once the child is resurrected in this manner, by receiving acknowledgement, respect, admiration, power, protection, or unconditional love, in return the child gives us the quantum wisdom, the innocence, the creativity, the joy, the bliss, and all that may have been lost growing up.

Let us look at some examples of how the shutdown begins, and also at some examples of how incredibly intuitive and connected to the quantum field children naturally are.

As we proceed, make an intention right now to remember as you are reading how incredibly intuitive you were as a child. Also remember a moment when you too were severely shut down and think about how this may still be overshadowing your life to this very day.

Let's invite both the innocence and the shadow to the table now for some new conversations.

We created our company and got married in 2008. We decided to come up with a combination of syllables from our first names for the company name. Ike's other name is Aykut, and so we took the two first letters, AY, which means the moon. We took the last two letters of my name, RA, which is the name of the ancient Egyptian sun god, resulting in our company name AY-RA, the sun and the moon being symbolic of the masculine and feminine energy and the two together forming a perfect balance.

Maybe two or three times before Ike and I got married and before we started our company, our beloved cleaning lady in Istanbul brought her granddaughter to our home. Derya was a very shy, quiet 7-year-old girl and did not speak even when spoken to. We honored that and tried to make her feel as comfortable as possible when she did come.

When she heard from her grandmother that we were getting married, she wanted to gift us with a painting she created. Her grandmother took one look at the drawing and asked:

— What is this?
— The sun and the moon!
— Why are they purple and green?
— One represents her and the other him.

Her grandmother told the little one this was not a good gift and that the colors of the moon and the sun were all wrong.

— They won't like this gift, you should just throw it away.

Can you believe she was connecting to the symbols of our company in such a way? So precisely and at the exact time we were creating them? Our cleaning lady told me this story herself as if it was the most normal happening. Derya had demonstrated an incredible sensitivity, but she had only been made wrong for it, however well-meaning her grandmother's intentions had been.

In her silence and from a distance, the little girl's heart had connected to us, and with her gift she was teaching me on what kinds of levels communication was possible. I doubt, however, she will ever get into art. Perhaps a great talent is lost, just from an incident such as this.

I would have loved to receive that painting and would have prized it over any others.

Another powerful story belongs to my father. His mother and father were divorced and no longer on speaking terms. Since this was a long time ago and divorcing was kind of taboo back then, they did not explain to him what was really going on, perhaps believing he could not understand any of it.

They told him instead that his father was the captain of a ship and out at sea on a long journey. This was the only explanation, not to mention a total lie, as to why he was not getting to see his father. My father longed for his father, and my grandfather for his son, but due to certain complications they were blocked from seeing one another, at least until my father was a bit older.

One day when he was only 4 years old and bouncing a red ball off the walls of the house, he suddenly held onto it tightly and swiveled around to my grandmother:

— I guess my father's ship has sunk now.

My grandmother had no idea what he was talking about, but a couple of hours later the sad news arrived that my grandfather had passed away from a sudden heart attack.

Children know things without seeing or hearing. They know without knowing, and this for me is the definition of intuition. It comes from the doors of the heart still being wide open to existence and easy access to the quantum field.

Certain things happen to us early on. Sometimes they're too painful to digest, too much to understand or to process, or things we are not able to cope with in a healthy way, and so we shut down, perhaps our creativity, positivity, intelligence, intuition, trust, or many other things. The shutdown is a defense mechanism, but with it our intuition and inner guidance may be dimmed as well.

At the end of this chapter, you will find our technique of connecting to the inner child summarized step by step. You don't have to adhere to it exactly. Make it up or change it as you go if you like, but at least it is a basic outline to begin practicing.

Try it and see what happens for you.

The technique was born from a mixture of a couple of different things.

Ike and I had been practicing Darel Rutherford's concept of talking to the EGO for years, and we both had really reaped the benefits of it. Around 2012, I started attending the Matrix Energetics courses created and taught by Dr. Richard Bartlett.[21]

He spoke about, and demonstrated on stage, the benefits of going back in time, literally counting back down to before a disease or an accident took place, shifting it as if it never occurred and consequently changing the result in the now. It was crazy. I didn't think I could do it, but I knew it was possible, and I saw many changes in his workshops.

Soon after my first course, I spilled a whole cup of boiling hot tea onto my hand.

— Ouch!

I was in shock, and because of the pain and shock my logical mind had no time to think or negotiate, or my EGO the luxury of protecting the idea that such a healing can't happen. I just counted myself back in time, pretending I was going back to just before the tea spilled, to unhook myself from what had just happened as I had been taught.

There was no thought, and I did not have time to doubt in this emergency situation.

— Five, four, three, two, one . . .

A great ball of heat left my hand. I had no signs of a burn after that, and my hand didn't even turn red or swell. This is not a very uncommon phenomenon, as mentioned before in Charlotte

Heffelmire's story: When shock shakes one out of the box, something totally new and different becomes possible.

One day, Ike, having witnessed what happened to my hand and other similar incidents, had the fantastic idea of combining traveling back in time with the talking to the EGO exercise. Eventually it changed into talking to our child self, just before an unpleasant event took place, to give the child self a chance to make a new choice and/or set free a limiting belief that might have formed as a result of the event. We started practicing on ourselves immediately and had some fantastic results. As I mentioned before this is not only about freeing the various child versions of ourselves stuck and arrested in time due to our shutdowns, but also a way to discover the source of our limiting belief systems so we can transform them if we choose to.

The more we find our different child selves and communicate, connect, and heal, the more the quantum qualities of the child begin to effortlessly cross over to our adult lives, bringing back our magic and ability to fly.

Let us look at a couple more examples of what is possible through this work:

A client came to me for inner child work. Milena had been a successful lawyer for ten years but now was feeling empty inside and wanted to get out of the corporate world. She was done with being a lawyer.

— I don't know what I want next. I have no clue about what to do. What do you think I should do?
— Well, if you don't know, I don't know either. What excites you?
— If we talk enough, maybe you can figure it out?
— Nope! Even if I knew the answer, it's not my place to tell you. It's a discovery that you need to make.

Milena told me briefly she was upset with her career because she felt she had been wasting her life doing something she did not really want to be doing. She also reported feeling totally out of touch with her own creativity.

— I'm sick of my success being judged, measured, seen, and rewarded through the eyes of other people. It makes me feel down and unworthy, as if I'm missing the purpose of my life.
— How does being a lawyer make you feel? Don't tell me what you think about it! Tell me the feeling of it; give me an image for it.
— Like in a prison; I don't feel free.

When ready for the process, it's important to close our eyes.

— Where do you feel that feeling in your body?
— My heart; I literally see an image of prison bars around my heart!
— Okay! Stay connected to the feeling. What memory or timeline of your childhood does this feeling take you to?

In this technique, we are using the physical body and a feeling of restriction in the body to enter the realm of the unconscious mind, where everything we have experienced can be found. It is different from just trying to sit down and remember things in a linear fashion.

— I find myself as a 9-year-old standing outside of the new school I'm about to start. There are iron gates surrounding it, which look exactly like the image I just saw around my heart!

Bam! We were there and went right in.

— What's going on at that time?
— I'm being placed in a new school. My old school was really easy. I loved it, and we did a lot of creative projects.
— Why did you have to change schools?

— My parents didn't feel like the old school was good enough. I
had to go to this new prestigious school and everybody had been
telling me how hard, how tough, how impossible it was to do well
there.
— How does the little girl version of you standing outside this new
school feel?
— I think I am afraid.
— Don't assume; let's ask her. Tell her that you are a future version
of her coming back to the past to revisit. Introduce yourself and
connect with her first.

Not rushing this part is important.

— Now, ask her how she feels and let her answer you. Let the
information come from her. Is she mad at her parents for moving
her? Does she want to go to this new school? Is she devastated
about having to leave the old one?

In this method it is important not to interpret the information
from an adult's perspective, but to ask the inner child what is going
on. We are trying to understand the child's perspective.

— Oh my god! Yes, she is afraid, yes, but also . . . she is kind of
excited about the new school. How interesting!!! It's like a part
of her wants to take the challenge on. No, she isn't mad at her
parents. She wants this new school just as much as they do. WOW!
I didn't remember this before.
— Okay. So, what belief system has she constructed about success,
life, and/or about herself in this scene?
— Hmmm! I can see now how I decided back then that what I
want doesn't matter, and what others value matters more. What
society considers valuable is the train I want to get on. My little self
really wants to go to this new school but she is just afraid she might
not succeed. The fear of failure is the prison, but she is okay and
excited about following what "others" think is more prestigious.

257

— So, can we say she adopted what her parents think as her own belief system? And was she okay and aligned with that choice, at that time?

— Yes, totally!!!

— So why did you become a lawyer again?

— Hah! It was the most "prestigious" career.

— And were you successful at it? Did you "make it" in the eyes of other people?

— Yes, yes I did.

— So, how come it's a waste?

— The past isn't feeling like such a mistake now. I got and lived exactly what I chose.

This is so empowering.

— Now what?

Here she paused a little bit. In essence she was feeling into what she wanted to create next after being empowered by the knowledge that she had created her reality exactly as she had chosen. Now it was about weaving a new one.

— I want something different for my future, something that belongs to me and is entirely a choice from within. Now I want to live my life free from the eyes and opinions of others.

— Let's go back and give that little girl permission to choose something different. The thing is, you know her future because you have lived it, but she doesn't know her future yet.

— I'm ready.

— First, tell her about her future so she can relax a little about the new school. Tell her she doesn't need to be afraid and she'll achieve the success she's looking for.

— I can see her relaxing. I also feel more relaxed.

— Great! Now, re-parent her in your own words by giving her

permission to continue her life the way she wants to as opposed to living a life based on the expectations of others.

Ask her, in her heart, what she would love to be doing. Tell her that what she values, even if others don't, is really important, really valuable, and you're willing to support her on this.

We coached the child by giving her permission to be herself, encouraging her to follow her own heart and give value to what was important to her instead of what she "should" value. We completely reversed the belief she had arrived at back then. Now it was important to run the memory forward and just observe whether the child or the memory changed in anyway. Not by pushing or trying to make it happen but simply letting go and observing to see whether anything was different.

— Hug her, love her, give her permission. Give her a new passport so she can travel with ease to another reality.
— Okay.
— Now the important part! Run the memory forward.
— What do you mean?
— Run the memory forward and see if the memory plays out differently, or if she behaves differently in any way after this conversation.
— She's dancing in front of me! She feels happy, free, and light . . . That prison-like feeling and imagery is gone from my heart. Hold on a minute . . .
— Take your time. No need to rush. Just keep on watching her. I think she's trying to tell you something.
— Oh my god! Oh my god! Wait a minute! She's changing again. She's showing me something. Wow! She's vigorously writing!!! Just writing and writing. She's clearly telling me to write!

The interesting thing was that when she had started the session and asked me what she should be doing next (though obviously it was not my place to answer such a question), I had heard inside myself the word:

— Writing!

Her inner child had shown us both the exact same thing. This was obviously an important message for her whether it meant she would become a writer or not. Who knows? But it was important for her to begin writing even if it started off as a diary initially.

Our quantum intelligence knows the next best step for us, and the inner child is very connected to this field. Everything that we need to know can be accessed from it as long as our hearts are still open, as in my father's example as a child or the quiet girl with her drawing of the sun and the moon.

There is no such thing as not knowing what we want or what makes our heart sing. We know deep inside, although our limiting belief systems may be shielding us from seeing it.

Another example is a client whose changes I got to observe more closely and longer term after the inner child work, as she was an ongoing coaching client.

Deniz's underlying problem was feeling unwanted. This was affecting her relationship with her daughter and her advancement at work as well. She was shut down, closed off, and unsocial because she felt nobody really wanted to be around her.

This is how she had felt for sixty years, and she believed this attitude had been a barrier to her advancement at work.

Deniz's parents had divorced soon after her birth. She had never seen her father after that and had always missed his presence. Her mother brought her up, telling her awful things about him. When Deniz was 6, a relative secretly took her to meet her father at a park.

This was the memory that came up after we went through the beginning steps of the technique.

— Nobody wants me!
— Where do you feel it in your body when you focus on the sadness you have about people not wanting you?
— In my heart. It hurts my chest.
— Go there and take a while to feel it, until it's activated and expands. Go deep into your heart as if you are descending in an elevator. What memory comes up OR at what age does the child show up in front of you?

It's helpful to think of the pain and its physical location here as the entryway into an old cave. Once we get inside the cave, we can find the source of the belief system and break the illusion.

When this happens:

- We realize the innocence of the decision
- We connect back with our inner child
- We can love, heal, and open a new door for them
- We can reactivate what was shut down
- We can realize how ridiculous the limiting belief is that we have been holding on to

When Deniz met her father, without meaning to she parroted what her mother had said about him all those years. The words automatically came flying out of her mouth when she met this stranger who was the father she had so longed for.

— You are a bad man!

Deniz was only 6 years old and had not meant any harm. The father, more childish than a 6-year-old, had been triggered and reacted:

— I don't ever want to see you again!

He turned around and left. Traumatized beyond consoling, she decided right then and there:

If even my father doesn't want me,
nobody will ever want me!

Since then, this story ruled most of her life and her relationships with family and colleagues at work.

We had to re-parent and coach the 6-year-old girl by letting her know there was nothing wrong with her. The little girl had triggered her father, who was an insecure man. She was just imitating her mother, like little ducklings do. It was normal behavior for a child. It wasn't her fault. We gave her lots of love and lots of hugs. She was darling and there was no reason for people not to want her. Just because her father had acted like a child didn't mean Deniz was unlovable.

After coaching her child, now it was time to run the memory forward to see whether anything changed.

The above is a guide for how we can consciously dissolve a belief. Her adult self could obviously have come to this reasoning and logic on her own, perhaps with coaching, but just because our adult self knows and can reason with the past, that still:

Does NOT mean our inner child knows.

This is why we can know things logically and be an adult but still act like a child under certain circumstances when the inner child is triggered or activated.

Being angry, when logically there is nothing to be angry about. Being jealous, when logically there is nothing to be jealous of. Being afraid, when logically there is nothing to be afraid of.

In the original memory she had come home crying in the arms of her relative who had secretly taken her to the meeting. After the reparenting when we re-ran the memory forward, something entirely different showed up.

This time as a child she met him cordially. This time, Deniz did not put him down as her mother had taught her to. And after giving him a brief hug and playing with the balloon he had brought for her, they said their goodbyes and she did not mind him leaving at all.

The drama and trauma of the event had been erased; she wasn't left on the floor to bleed. The feelings of abandonment were gone.

To Deniz's great surprise, the past had been reframed by the inner child. The new memory formation shifted her and she felt very different after the session. This doesn't mean she forgot how things actually happened, but let's just say an alternative memory had also been formed.

There has to be zero manipulation when we rerun the memory forward.

After we have done all the steps, we just sit back and watch as we rerun the memory from the beginning and just observe what is different and what changes organically. Maybe nothing is different but that doesn't mean there has been no benefit. Even just going back to a memory to connect with our child self just to give him or her love is a benefit. Actually, when I work with clients, I don't even explain any of the steps, so that they have zero expectations and preconceived ideas about the process.

Changing the past changes the present.

The following week when we met for our session, she was amazed at what was happening in her life. Her daughter, who always seemed to avoid her, had called and said she wanted to spend more time with her and heal their relationship.

A colleague at a conference she routinely attended came up and gave her a hug:

— I'm so glad you're here!

This colleague had never done something like that before, and in fact Deniz swore that the person used to avoid her like the plague and look right past her as if she were invisible. She reported other incidents in which people she had felt hadn't wanted her had behaved 180 degrees differently that week.

— It feels as if I was asleep all my life and just woke up.

Do you remember Fiona from the past chapter?

When we asked her back pain what message it had for Fiona, the message had been about letting go of the guilt she was carrying. The guilt and self-blame had been about sexual abuse from a family member when she was just a child. After she found the memory, we let the inner child know that she wasn't to be blamed and that she deserved all the love, valuing, and protection in the world. However, I also specifically asked Fiona to give her child the permission to behave in any way she might want to, now that she knew what was about to happen to her.

— Tell little Fiona she has the right to do anything at all to this man now that she knows what he is about. Allow the little one to take her power back but don't tell her what to do. Just give her your unconditional love, support, and permission.

After Fiona was done speaking to her child self in the memory, we reran the memory.

The child decided to kick and spit on the abusive man, then turned on her heels and walked away before she entered the room.

Now, Fiona didn't imagine this; I would like to underline that again and again. After she talked to the child, she just got out of the way and simply observed the child's behavior. Fiona herself was very surprised and shrieked in awe at how the child behaved in the replay of that memory.

Remember the example with the train? When the train jumps onto a new track, both the past and the future change. The entire timeline is different now. Fiona got her power back from the past, and something amazing happened in the present moment too.

Her back healed instantly.

Let's look at another example that has to do with money.

Reyhan, a student in our program, wanted to pay for the third level. The whole program is priced so that the fee gets higher at each of the four levels we offer. The reason we make the first level the cheapest is so people can sign up even if they don't have funds for the entire program. Once they start creating prosperity and start to manifest they continue the course if they choose to.

Reyhan had enough money for only level one originally but was able to continue once she began making more money. For level three, she was eager to pay as soon as possible and was really happy she had manifested the money.

But when her payment did not go through, maybe due to the wiring process at her bank, and she found the money still sitting in her account, she got really upset, even though all she had to do was just rewire it. These kinds of emotional overreactions to things or to people are great clues that some limiting belief is getting activated.

Having learned the technique, she immediately started looking at what all the emotional sizzling was about.

Reyhan realized her belief was:

Money feels like a burden.

But why?

When she was only 3 or 4 years old, her father had given her some money and sent her to the store across the street to buy some bread. Reyhan was afraid, as it was her first time doing something alone. She was aware that her father was secretly watching her from behind a wall. He was watching her to make sure Reyhan was okay, but as a child she had assumed it was because he cared a lot more about the money and did not want her to drop it.

The pressure of being watched secretly by her father made her feel as if money was a weight, too much of a responsibility, and she didn't want it.

Money is a burden.

No drama, no trauma. Just a simple, very innocent, very young decision about money based on a simple misinterpretation of what was actually going on.

Once she re-parented her inner child with awareness that her father's only intention was to protect her, and that he did not care about the money, she saw a huge jump in her finances soon after.

There are some beliefs that hold us back from manifesting and then there are other beliefs that hold us back from keeping what we have manifested. As long as money felt like a burden to her, it would have been hard for her to be able to save enough to start making investments.

As she took her foot off the hose of prosperity, abundance started pouring in. In less than a year, she started being able to invest, whereas before she had hardly even the money to come to the course.

Let us look at another monetary example.

While in our course, Beth started saving money. This was a big improvement on her path; however, she also noticed how attached she was becoming to her savings. When she looked a little deeper, she realized the subject of money made her feel insecure in general.

— If I don't have lots of savings, I am not safe!
— What if you do have a lot of savings?
— Again, I am not safe!

Now this may look like a contradiction that doesn't make any sense, but it makes perfect sense. Money doesn't have any more meaning than what we give it in the matrix of our own minds.

Although it may look like:

- The government did such and such and it's because of that . . .
- The economy is doing something and it's because of that . . .
- My business partner did this and that and it's because of that . . .
- The laws changed and it's because of that . . .
- The market crashed and it's because of that . . .

Do we get into the fear?
Do we get into a panic?
Do we believe the source of prosperity is our job, our career, our father, or mother, partner, or boss?

OR

Do we believe the source of prosperity is simply our own relationship to it? How much do we trust the Universe to mirror that?

When our best friend, soul partner, and publisher in Turkey died, we were distraught. It was as if a light had gone out of this world, and it took us a while to get over the grief. With his death, we also lost a rather huge amount of money we were owed from books sold, as we had let him keep a large part of our share to help support his company—a company we really believed in and felt was well worth the support. His publishing firm had been one of the oldest companies in Turkey, publishing books of a spiritual and self-help nature. The various people who took over the company for a while before it eventually dissolved not only didn't pay their debt to us, they also sold thousands more copies of our books left in storage without paying for those either.

Was it unfair? . . . Yes.

Did it have to matter?

Both my husband and I knew the money belonged to us. We had done a wonderful deed by supporting our friend and publisher who deserved the help one hundred percent.

In my eyes it was inevitable this money would come back to us in one way or another. Having internalized this helped both of us easily keep a positive focus and expectation in regard to prosperity. We mourned our friend in peace, instead of needing to go into a legal battle.

In less than three months, another company came along. They wanted to publish my husband's famous book and asked him to write a new one as well. They came to the meeting ready with an offer. The amount?

The exact amount the first publisher owed us. Not one dollar less, and not one dollar more.

Instead of worrying about what had happened, we focused on a response that felt good and aligned with trusting prosperity, which then paved the way for the next happening.

Going back to Beth's example:

We focused on her feelings of insecurity about money and where those feelings were coming from.

—What kind of an emotion is it?

— It feels like desperation! Just the subject of money in general makes me feel weak and scared, whether I have too little or too much.

It turns out, at a time when a huge construction project was going on in her childhood home, her father had left in the middle of it all. Her mother, being a housewife, had not been able to pay the debt her father had left them with. Her mother felt very embarrassed and desperate, and reluctantly had to ask for help from family and friends, which made her feel small. Beth had never before experienced her mother feeling so desperate, and she arrived at a specific conclusion about money because of it.

Money makes people weak and desperate.

Whether she thought of having a lot of money or too little of it, her relationship to money was the same; it simply did not feel safe either way.

We sometimes derive different choices from the dynamics going on in our environment, or sometimes we directly take on the patterns around us and wear them like clothes. In her case she had soaked in her mother's emotions and relationship to money and had made them her own. When we did the inner child work, she let go of the meanings she had uploaded onto money. Her inner child felt relaxed and powerful and free of anxiety.

After that, the real magic happened.

Once she got out of the pattern that was causing her so much insecurity and anxiety about money, she remembered something that had never before been a part of her conscious awareness.

Another experience that had happened later on in the story began to reveal itself to her. It was something her EGO had completely blocked out until that moment. She began to remember that her mother had started making lace and selling her work and had collected enough money to pay off the debt after all. She was distraught and weakened initially, but her mother rose above the problem and became the solution.

(Her eyes were still closed.)

— I can so clearly see, in great detail, all the different patterns of the laces she wove now. They were beautiful!

The new light in which she saw and remembered her own mother was added as an additional layer of richness as she took her power back from that memory.

I believe this example is a great one for showing how the EGO functions. Once a person makes a decision about anything, like about money in this case, it is frozen in time, and any other occurrence or evidence contrary to the already crystallized belief is totally erased from perception. This is how the EGO is able to protect our beliefs.

One last example involves a self-concept. In this specific case, it is about self-image.

Sinem, a successful self-made businesswoman who is extremely beautiful, felt ugly. This is a rather common pattern for women. To make matters worse, Sinem had just gotten a nose job to help her breathe more comfortably, but her nose had ended up slightly crooked after the operation. She was devastated and planned to get it fixed with another surgery.

As we went into her memory, we found the moment she had made up her mind about her looks. As a little girl, she had always been compared to her slightly older sister, who apparently was even more beautiful than she was. Although she was a gorgeous child herself, this constant comparison was very damaging and wounding to her, as is the case for most children.

One specific day, she had gone with her family to a neighbor's home for a visit, and her sister happened to walk in first. The hostess of the house just praised and praised the older sister's beauty and didn't even acknowledge the younger sister who followed.

Sinem, as a little girl, had stepped out onto the balcony, feeling terribly left out and sorry for herself. She concluded:

I am ugly.

As an adult, she had boyfriends who complimented her looks often, but of course her EGO, protecting the old belief, would wave it all off and assume they were just giving compliments to appease her.

We went into the memory and talked to her inner child, telling her how beautiful the little girl actually was. We also explained that just because her sister was found to be more beautiful, this did not mean she herself was not absolutely gorgeous.

There was no need to play the damaging game of comparison, as there would always be someone more beautiful, more this or more that, somewhere in the world. She felt fantastic when we were done.

The real magic happened the following morning, though, when she woke up and went to wash her face. She looked up at the mirror.

— What's this? What? Oh my god!

Her nose, which had remained slightly crooked from the operation, had completely aligned itself back to normal.

> Mirror, mirror, on the wall,
> who in this land is the fairest of all?
> — Snow White, *Grimm's Fairy Tales*

Warning: Please practice this exercise ONLY on yourself. Do not try to guide others without proper training and experience.

An Introduction to the Inner Child Work
as Taught by Esra and Ike Ogut:
(Remember, the technique can be applied to any subject.)

When you focus on the problem you are working on, whether this is about prosperity or something else:

What happens?

- Does it make you angry?
- Does the subject itself frustrate you?
- Make you feel vulnerable?
- Make you feel unworthy?
- Make you feel small?
- Does it make you feel unsuccessful?
- Does it make you feel like there is not enough?

What does the subject make you feel? After you are aware of the feeling, feel the feeling and find out where in your physical body it creates a constriction.

Heart? Shoulders? Stomach? Throat? Back?

The heart area usually signifies a moment when our heart was broken and/or we decided to dim our own light and hide.

The shoulders or back are more about the past, a burden we carry, and sometimes even those patterns we brought down from our own ancestors. What is the heaviness you carry?

The stomach area is often about issues around lack of power, lack of boundaries, or something or someone we can't emotionally digest.

The throat area is about authentic self-expression. Not giving permission to express our truth or abusive speech toward others or ourselves may cause a constriction here.

Problems around the womb or genital area are about the misuse and/or suppression of sexual energy or problems in relationships or gender identity.

Knowing these correlations might assist you further as you go into self-discovery, but don't take them as rules set in stone.

Get into the matrix of your own self to solve the puzzle. The answers are inside you waiting patiently to be found.

Your own consciousness is the best guide.

STEP ONE:
Set an intention before you begin. What would you like to achieve? Freedom? Trust? Self-worth? Prosperity? More intimate and close relationships? Better health? Success? Creativity? Peace?

Speak out loud whatever your intention is.

After you have learned the steps, close your eyes to practice. Or, record the steps out loud on your phone and just follow step by step.

STEP TWO: (Optional)
Imagine you write your intention on a balloon. What color does the balloon show up as for you? Write down the sentence of your intention and let it go. Watch as the balloon rises up to the sky and disappears from sight. Make this a ritual as you set your intention and send it to the Universe. Trust you have been heard.

STEP THREE:

Focus on the problem until you activate the feeling associated with it. Feel the feeling. Where is it located in your physical body? Does it feel like a pressure? Like a prison? Like a knot? How does it physically feel? Connect to that physical part of your body and stay with the feeling.

STEP FOUR:

Ask the physical constriction the following questions:

— When did I first meet you?
— What memory or time are you coming from?
— What message do you have for me?
— What time in my life are you related to?

If no memory is coming, do not worry!

Either watch the memory that comes, OR if you see just a child at a certain age pop up, be aware of how they are coming to you. Just go with whatever comes up.

Sad? Worried? Shut down? Observe first.

Now introduce yourself. Let the inner child know you have come from the future to give and to receive help.

STEP FIVE:

Ask the inner child to tell you about what is going on. How are they feeling? Why? What is the story? What is the memory? What is the conclusion the child has drawn? Do not answer on behalf of the child; let them tell you what is going on. This is the discovery phase. Find out all the information directly from the child. After you have all the information, you can go to the next step.

STEP SIX:
Go to the beginning of the memory formation. As an example, if the child fell off the stairs and decided *I am dumb,* go to the point just before the child falls. Go to the beginning of the happening and pause everything, as if you are putting a movie on pause. First inform the child what is about to happen. (Since you have rewound time, the child hasn't had the experience yet.) Secondly, re-parent them about what is going to happen. What do they need to know about the situation that could heal or open a new door in the inner child's perception? What did they take personally? How can this not be about limitation? How can they look at the situation with a new pair of eyes?

If no memory has come up and only a version of your child is showing up, see how they are showing up and after you have collected enough information you can re-parent according to the needs of your child.

Just make suggestions. NEVER dictate. Don't be attached to them getting it or agreeing with you. Simply suggest a new angle, a new perception, or explain things in a new light and give the inner child your unconditional love.

STEP SEVEN:
After re-parenting, give them loving words. Honor the inner child. Hug the child. Make them feel worthy. Let the child know they are not alone anymore and that you will be there to take care of them whenever there is a need from this point on. Make that connection; show that friendship.

STEP EIGHT:
Now become the observer and rerun the memory forward. If no memory came, simply watch what the child does after your connection to them. What is different? How are they different? What are they telling you, showing you, wanting to do with you?

Pay attention to the inner child's need or message for you, or be aware of how the memory is changing by itself and morphing into a new scenario.

If you have done the steps sincerely and haven't tried to control anything, what shows up will come as a surprise. It will be unexpected.

Even if nothing changes, just the fact that you are connecting to your inner child and talking in a loving and soothing manner will eventually start creating shifts.

STEP NINE:
Open your eyes and write it down. Answer the questions below and also be aware how your week might be showing up differently.

Write down your observations in a personal diary . . .

Don't allow your EGO to make you forget what is different.

How do you feel?
What is different?
How does your body feel?
Does the room look different?
Is the room looking brighter to you?
Do you feel like there is more space?

. . . Write it down.

Otherwise the EGO will make you forget.

The difference between
success and failure
is simple:
Are you solution-oriented
or
problem-oriented?

— Darel Rutherford

THE
WINNER'S
ATTITUDE

Darel Rutherford was truly unlike any other teacher or human being I have ever met. He was kind but also at times compassionately brutal. He made me realize it is not the words that teach, but the choices we make about who we are BEING that transmits the information more clearly.

This alone was one of his biggest gifts to me, which I realized more and more deeply as time went on.

I finished this book on the 21st of March 2020, and on March 23rd, our beloved mentor, Darel Rutherford, left his body to continue his journey in other realms. I can say it was his dream that I write a book, and through his coaching over the years, it ended up becoming mine as well. I wish I could have put the book in his hands before he left, as writing it was in so many ways my tribute to him.

After a week of grief, I don't know exactly why, but I came back to this specific chapter and without even taking a look at what I had originally written, erased it all and started again. My grief was short as I knew he continued on to another journey but I was sad as we would miss our weekly coaching sesions that had been a part of our lives for more than sixteen years. Darel was an enlightened being who had figured out how to have a wonderful human experience and he was a father, a best friend, an inspiration, and a mentor all in one.

Perhaps I wanted to rewrite it because as I said my goodbye to him, sitting on one of my favorite beaches in Kauai, letting the ocean receive my tears, I remembered very specific coaching sessions with him and certain sentences echoed in my ears. While on the beach, sitting with my eyes closed, I saw his smiling face as clearly as a photograph over my head. All of a sudden, a single word wrote itself above his picture, like a title of sorts, as if to commemorate his amazing life and his peaceful death.

— Celebrate!

As soon as I opened my eyes, they happened to land on a lighthouse standing tall on a cliff jutting out into the ocean in the morning mist. I smiled to myself, not only because he had been a lighthouse in this life for me, but also because it had been the symbol and logo of his company. He was reminding me to celebrate life in all its facets, including death, which for the one who is leaving is actually a rebirth.

The Winner's Attitude was extremely important for Darel, and indeed in employing it, a lot changed for me. Although I knew about it, Darel was the person who taught me to live by it.

There are countless stories I could write about how success seems to stick to you when you choose to detach yourself from the end results of your quest. It does not mean we can't visualize what we choose, it does not mean we can't be clear about the outcome, but the golden key is to simply let the outcome go and not be attached to the specific results. It is okay to dream but let it go as well.

Imagine it is like playing basketball. The player practices, is disciplined, dribbles the ball, strategizes, focuses, knows what the intended goal is, but if he doesn't let go of the ball at one point he cannot ever score.

One way to be able to do that is to decide to employ the Winner's Attitude in life.

Simply put, the Winner's Attitude is the readiness in advance to celebrate in life every single possible outcome, as is. This was one of my mentor's last reminders to me as he left.

There is a magic about this approach that, when done sincerely, is so beyond this world it is hard to put into words. Perhaps only specific examples of choosing to BE the one who has the Winner's Attitude in life can do it justice.

To many, the attitude can seem too much like a Pollyanna approach, but let's face it—Pollyanna lived and died very happy. The definition of "Pollyanna" in the dictionary is an excessively optimistic and cheerful person. The word is also used to indicate one who pretends and kids themselves in denial of the real facts.

The Winner's Attitude is not at all about a denial of anything. On the contrary, it is about daring to have unwavering trust in existence. It is about remembering our own power to create and how in the way we respond to something, anything at all, the energy of the response itself paves the way for the next happening in our life.

Remember the four simple keys to success?

1. Inspiration
2. Commitment
3. Non-attachment
4. The Winner's Attitude

It is not so much what happens to us that matters but how we respond to what happens to us that paves the way for the next creation. Therefore:

Do we respond as a Winner or a Loser?

This last step determines the rest of the way, and it also helps us to cultivate the third step, which can be briefly summarized as:

— Just let it go!

With celebration.

We were coaching Ozlem in our program about this specific understanding. I gave her a ritualistic way to make a clear intention and told her about this golden key of just letting it go, the brief exercise at the start of the chapter "The Journey of Consciousness."

Ozlem decided to practice this principle with commitment. A manager for actors and actresses, she was very attached to placing one of her people into a specific project. When it didn't happen, instead of becoming miserable and upset, she just decided to let it go. Prosperity could come in other ways, and maybe there was an even a better project waiting for her client. She didn't have to know, dictate, or control the how. Ozlem just needed to BE a vibrational match to what she wanted.

When we employ the Winner's Attitude, immediately we become a closer and closer match to what we are asking for. The Winner's Attitude is developing the mental state in which everything is seen as a win and not as a loss.

That same company called her a couple of days later. They hadn't picked her client for the project, but they wanted to shoot the entire project at her house.

Guess what the company was called?

"Let Go" Productions.

Let us first look at what the opposite attitude is:

The Loser's Attitude: The victim psychology, a state of BEING that Darel never had the time, energy, or much sympathy for.

> The world will never become a better place
> as long as
> the victim attitude is rewarded.[22]
> — Darel Rutherford

If I showed up to a session with my victim attitude in place, he would usually hang up.

First, he would say:

— Let me get out my violin and play it for you.

If that did not work:

— You're not coachable today. Let's see if you are next week.

I knew that if I wanted coaching I couldn't show up in victim mode, because he simply would not hold space for it. This was the best training of my entire life, and it is what got me into developing the Winner's Attitude for myself.

The difference between a victim approach and a Winner's Attitude is very simple. The victim mode focuses on the problem. The Winner's Attitude focuses on the solution.

How can you figure out if you are BEING a victim?

- If you are complaining
- If you are blaming
- If you are defending the problem

If you are doing any one or all of the above, you are in a victim mode and employing the Loser's Attitude toward your problem. It is really that straightforward without any exceptions whatsoever. In this state, if the entire world tried to help you, you would still not be able to experience what you prefer, as your state of BEING wouldn't be a match to the solution.

As long as we are BEING in the victim mode, at least we can do ourselves a great favor and not have the ridiculous expectation of receiving any solutions anytime soon until we are out of that mode.

A Loser's Attitude is a match to problems.
A Winner's Attitude is a match to solutions.

That right there is the simple difference between failure and success.

If we are walking our dog through the journey of life, and we throw it a ball to retrieve and bring back to us, it is going to fetch the ball from whichever direction we throw it. If we throw the ball to the right, naturally the dog is not going to go left. In the same manner, if we throw our mind's focus into the quantum field to fetch more problems, it will. If we throw it to fetch solutions, it will.

If we are focused on problems, more will come . . .
If we are focused on solutions, more will come . . .

Darel was such an absolutely relentless master at teaching this that

I must share this story about him that was shared by one of his students in the memorial we had for him online.

He was giving a workshop and had said something or other about not being a victim.

A woman in the crowd dramatically got up from the very last row, took off her shoes, walked up to him with everybody wondering what it was she was doing, and laid her shoes in front of him.

— Go ahead, walk in my shoes before you talk about finding the solution.

Unfazed, he responded in that voice of his that was neither judging nor compromising.

— Go ahead and stay in your limitation, if that is what you want and choose.

What is it that keeps us in this type of victim mode? What is it that keeps the feeling in place that unless circumstances change, unless people change, unless the world changes, we cannot be who we want to BE or reach a solution?

It is always about attachment to something or other that we are not willing to give up. It could be:

- Our fears
- An ideology
- A self-concept
- The need for sympathy
- The need to be acknowledged
- Our stories, myths, and beliefs
- The need for the world to change first

But whatever it is, ask:

— What attachment do I need to give up to BE who I really am?

Darel pushed me to become a coach beginning in 2006, about two years after I started working with him on a weekly basis.

The way Ike and I danced through our limitations together to create a very magical relationship was a source of inspiration for him. Financially, too, Ike and I were already doing much better compared to before and Darel applauded, appreciated, and enjoyed witnessing our rapid movement one step at a time.

In one session that changed my life, Darel and Ike conspired to trick me into thinking that the specific phone session I am about to share was going to cost us five hundred dollars. It was a joke, but I didn't know this at the time. I broke into a sweat when they told me. Yes, we were doing much better financially, but two thousand dollars a month for coaching would have still been very tricky.

But I remember thinking very quickly on my feet before I proceeded with the call:

I won't eat
I won't go out
I'll get another job

Whatever it takes, I WILL afford this.

— What are you waiting for to become a coach? You'll be very good at it!
— I don't know, Darel; I don't know all there is to know yet. How can I truly and sincerely help people, for real, if I haven't solved all of my own problems yet?

— Cut the crap! What is the real story that's holding you back?

— I'm not good enough!

— Don't you understand? There is no journey left when you know all there is to know.

You'd have no inspiration or even desire to teach if you'd already solved ALL your problems!! Let it go!

As he was talking to me, I realized I was chasing after an imaginary perfect version of myself that kept eluding me; it was just an illusionary attachment to the need to BE perfect before I allowed myself to deserve, honor, and put on the table what I already did know and had in me to give to the world.

I realized that while we look for acknowledgment in all the wrong places, we forget the one that really matters: the acknowledgment we can give to ourselves. When I could let go of my need to be on a high horse, the fear of falling off left with it. There was no possible way to lose, and that was the Winner's Attitude.

Darel also wanted to make a point about how when people pay for things, a space gets created for them to be ready to receive more—and I got that too. Out of the many sessions we had over the years, that single one was the richest for me. That was the session during which I decided to become a transformational coach and change my whole life.

The next day a friend, Yasemin, who was also my acting agent, showed up. She went out of her way to convince me to become her coach!

— Go to Darel!

— No, I want to learn from you. What'll you charge me?

(Without a beat.)

— It's $150 per session.

— Done!

We started a couple of days later. Eventually, she recommended me to a client of hers; that client recommended me to another, and before I knew it, in less than two months, I was fully booked. The yoga classes started filling up like crazy too. That was the year when I increased my income by fifteen times over the year before, and in 2008, when the economic crisis was shaking the world, even more financial expansion took place.

My limiting beliefs around money had been set free, but also further limitations around self-concept and self-worth had dissolved too.

A year after I started coaching, Ike decided to become a coach as well. He made a new BEING choice about himself too. He let go of becoming a big-shot actor in Hollywood, a path he had dedicated ten years to. He had left his family to come to America to pursue acting, learned English from scratch and worked at restaurants as a waiter to support this dream. Yes, he had done movies and commercials in the US, but it's not like he had won an Oscar or could pay his way in life with acting.

His decision to follow me to Turkey at the time was a very big way of letting go of his attachment to huge success, something he had dreamt of for ten years. He let go of his attachment to success and decided to BE happy with what is, still dreaming but no longer holding on to the dream.

The way to let attachment go is to figure out a way to be happy and fullfilled even if that *thing* never happens.

Soon after, in an almost identical way, it happened to me. At a large dinner gathering, a young woman neither one of us knew said she wanted to take sessions with Ike.

— I'm not the coach, my wife is!
— But I want to work with you!

We'd both had big dreams and a time came when we just let them go at about the same time. Not in sadness or with the perspective of having lost anything, but in the way of being willing to explore other doors.

When all this was happening, there was no Instagram, no Facebook; we did not have a proper website, an office, or even a real business card. For both of us, having come back to Turkey after a decade of living in the US, we did not really have any networking capacity or even many friends. Really, we had nothing!

However, we both had a new BEING choice in place, and the rest of it was taken care of by word of mouth. First individually then by combining our efforts, our business flourished like crazy at an incredible speed.

Our number one priority and principle in business became: Only do what you do if it is enjoyable and inspirational, and let everything else go.

There were many offers and projects that offered us a high income, but we turned them down when they did not fit the above principle and eventually we ended up creating incomes way beyond those original offers. An aligned state of BEING is a faster, cheaper, and more powerful way of getting your business to succeed than any sort of marketing available out there. Joy and inspiration are indicators that you are in that state.

Eventually, Ike decided to write a book—the one that became a national bestseller. Before this, our coaching schedules were already fully booked, without any marketing or book.

His book was not just about the teachings, but also about how and why he failed while trying to succeed.

— My love, what do you hope to achieve with the book?
— Well, it would be cool if it sells a lot.
— And if it doesn't?
— Even if it sells just one or two thousand copies, I'd be thrilled! When people keep asking us questions in our social life about what we teach, it'll be such a relief to say, "Here you go, here is the book, leave me alone and let me enjoy my dinner now"!

That is the Winner's Attitude right there. The Winner's Attitude is knowing there is nothing to lose by employing a perspective of BEING a winner no matter what. It's been more than a decade, and the book is still selling . . . We may tend to forget ourselves many times over, but the Universe never forgets our dreams. It's all about knowing how to get out of the way and to stop stepping on the hose with attachments.

Who would you be BEING if you could employ the Winner's Attitude right now?

Dream big, let it go, and enjoy the ride!

Thank you, Darel, for this precious gift. As you open a new door, closing this one behind you, we are in remembrance of you and grateful for everything you have shared. You live through us and with us, all because you followed your dreams.

And it is my promise to you that I will celebrate, even more . . .

NOTES _____

You cannot succeed
while
trying not to fail.

— Darel Rutherford

MAKING
FAILURE
OUR
FRIEND

Unfortunately in many cultures failure is a big, ingrained taboo.

From the time we are in school, a lack of performance leads to punishment. Children are brought up in a manner where love and approval—the two things children need most to construct a healthy identity—are under threat of being withdrawn unless they are successful, which is often equated with performing well and fitting expectations.

If somehow, before you embark on the journey, you can find a way to win even if you were to lose, the focus will be removed from failure, as you are no longer resisting the worst-case scenario but instead embracing it.

When a child is learning to walk, how many of us get disappointed when they fall in their initial attempts? Unless we are crazy, we know the fall is unavoidable, a necessary part of learning to walk. When learning tennis, getting the ball caught in the net is a necessary part of understanding how to control the ball to play successfully.

Failure is an inevitable necessity for success. When failure is avoided, so is success. The two are part and parcel of the same thing.

As an exercise, count to twenty, and while you're counting, please, whatever you do:

Do NOT think of a pink elephant.

Go!

. . . What happened?

Were you able to count to twenty without imagining a pink elephant?

I am willing to bet you thought about a pink elephant at least several times, if not almost all the way through, even while trying your best not to. We create and manifest whatever we powerfully focus on, whether it is wanted or unwanted. When we resist something, and say:

— No . . . No . . . No!

Just by the sheer fact of resisting it, we end up creating it, because our focus is so strongly wrapped around the unwanted. This is true of the big things in our lives as well as the small, practical everyday stuff.

On a rainy day, it can be challenging to find a taxi in a big city like Istanbul. On one of those days, I waited in the rain for twenty minutes. Finally, a cab stopped in front of me. I opened the door and was about to get in, but the cab smelled awful from the driver's body odor. I just couldn't get in and my stomach churned.

— Thank you, but no thank you!

I just kept walking in the hope of finding another cab, but I couldn't get my mind off the subject of people not using deodorant.

Complaining under my breath while imaging that specific cabdriver in my mind:

— Why was this the case?
— At least he could use soap or shower more often or something.
— Why wasn't he aware he smelled so unpleasant?
— Didn't he have friends who warned him?
— Could a seminar be held about the importance of smelling good for business?

Finally, another cab came after another thirty-minute walk on my part, and at this point I was completely soaked down to my toes. Wet and cold, I dove into the car and looked forward to some warmth.

Guess what?

It was the exact same cabdriver. I rolled down all the windows and just laughed out loud at myself and at how precisely my focus had manifested.

— No, no, no.

Is translated by the Universe as:

— Yes!

Sometimes people will say: I'm so unlucky!!

Why do you say that?

— Whatever I think might go wrong ends up finding me.

This is so funny. Feeling unlucky is nothing other than using the power of focus to magnify the unwanted. The power of focus is like a magnifying glass. If you take a piece of paper and put a magnifying glass on top of it, letting the sun's rays focus on the paper, you can create a fire. Our thoughts are as powerful as the sun's rays, and our focus is exactly like that magnifying glass.

This does not mean we shouldn't have negative thoughts or should avoid them at all cost. On the contrary, in resisting negative thoughts, we give them more power and food, just as in the pink elephant example.

Understand instead:

What is the fear about?
What is the anger about?
What is the resistance about?

As we understand what those thoughts and emotions are about, we release our judgments toward them and consequently about ourselves. Through understanding, the so-called negative thoughts or emotions are free to lift off. But first they have a message to convey, and without our understanding the message, they don't truly lift off. Instead they get buried and scream because they have not been heard, like the ghosts of the dead.

Where there is judgment, there can be no understanding. Where there is understanding, there can be no judgment.

Now let's do the opposite exercise. Count again to twenty and this time allow yourself completely and totally to have the pink elephant image in your mind as much as you want.

Go!

What happened this time? How was it different?

Probably there were fewer pink elephants in the picture, if any, than when the pink elephant wasn't allowed. When you stop resisting the thought, feeling, situation, person, ache, or worst-case scenario in your reality, it will stop persisting.

When resistance is replaced with acceptance and allowance, the pink elephant has to fly away.

What does all this have to do with success?

If you are dead-afraid of failure, trying so hard not to fail, doing everything you can not to fail and really, really resisting any possibility of failing:

Where is your focus?
In which direction are you traveling?
Toward failure or success?

What would it be like if you made failure completely fine in advance?

What kind of a nightmare is the EGO putting in front of you as your worst-case scenario? Remember, the EGO is there to protect a belief, and to protect you because of that belief. It is naturally going to bring to your attention all kinds of fears, doubts, and dangers about the big bad wolf outside of its box.

Listen to the EGO.

What is it telling you to be careful about?

— What is my EGO afraid of?
— What is the worst-case scenario being presented to me?
— What is my EGO trying to protect me from?

— Can I look at my worst-case scenario and figure out a way to make it okay?

— In fact, how far can I go in falling in love with my worst-case scenario?

Just recently we were working with a client, Tricia, on her goals. I noticed that whenever she set a goal for herself, it would become a major stressor for her. She would get so attached to achieving it that playfulness would go out the window and she would get extremely serious about things.

Failure was a big taboo for Tricia. We had to go into this taboo and find out what was keeping her there.

— So, what if you can't achieve your goals?

— I guess it's okay.

— That's not true. If that were the case, you wouldn't be trying so hard to achieve them.

You have to first make it okay not to achieve before you can achieve; otherwise, you'll be stuck! Why can't you make it okay? What's the big deal? If you are not successful, so what?

A flood of tears like Niagara Falls opened a pain so old and so deep.

— Nobody will see me if I don't deliver results.

— Who's watching you? Who's the observer?

— The whole world is watching me!

(Actually, the whole world is busy with their own journey. Nobody talks or thinks about us more than five minutes if we fail.)

— What happens then? If you don't show up in the world with success and everybody is watching?

— It's as if I don't even really exist unless I succeed.
— Do you see your incredible attachment to success here?

It was like a matter of life or death for her.

— If I mess up, nobody will see me and I won't matter.

Eventually, we found the memory . . .

Her father died when she was young. Her mother did not have
much energy to take care of things. Tricia took on the role of being
a problem-solver at a young age. She solved everyone's problems
and took care of others before herself, including her mother and
brother. When she took on this role, it was the first time she
actually felt she mattered to anyone; before, she felt invisible to
her family. It was the first time the grown-ups related to her like
a person, as an individual who mattered, instead of like a vase of
pretty flowers in the corner somewhere.

Failure for her meant being like a ghost.

— Can you let this story go? Now that you know where the source
comes from?

She saw her own setup, her own programming, and was able to let
most of its heaviness go. She looked like a different person at the
end of the session.

— I am going to make my mistakes okay!

First thing the next morning, in her pajamas and slippers, she went
down to her building's storage area. When she got to the storage
area she realized she had not grabbed the keys to her apartment.
She had a lot of work to do and was locked out of her home. But
instead of just idly waiting hours for the locksmith to show up, she

decided to go to breakfast in her pajamas because she was hungry
and did not mind showing up in them.

— Usually I would be kicking myself for the mistake instead.

Everybody at the restaurant stared at her in her funny pajamas and
slippers. To make matters worse, she chose an upscale breakfast
place, where everybody else was dressed up first thing in the
morning as if going to a gala.

She told the waiters:

— I'm locked out of my house! I have no money! No place to go!

They offered her a coffee, on the house. One of the waiters even ran
across the street to buy her favorite cigarette brand, on the house.
Some complete strangers invited her to their table to have breakfast
with them. There she was having a perfectly fun day, only to stop
in the middle of laughing to take a mental note:

— Everybody in the restaurant has turned around and looked at
me in my pajamas and slippers. I am seen. I am being taken care
of by total strangers, and I did not have to take care of others to
deserve it. All this is thanks to my mistake this morning.

Some more laughter rises from the cafe as the curtains close on this
chapter.

NOTES _____

A man is but the product
of his thoughts.
What he thinks,
he becomes.

— Mahatma Gandhi

WHAT'S LOVE GOT
TO DO WITH IT?

An upgrade, an upleveling in one's sense of self-worth and self-love, is essential to play the game of life at the next level. The degree to which we tell ourselves we deserve something is the degree to which we can have it. This is not as easy as it sounds. It really takes a lot of self-reflection and discovery, as we can have so many limitations and perceptions of being undeserving that we are not even aware of.

Self-love dissolves these patterns of limitation like fire does ice. As the melting takes place we let in more love, more prosperity, more energy, more vitality, more peace, more possibilities, more of everything that is worth experiencing.

Without self-love, we unconsciously push away prosperity, solutions, growth, expansion, love, and peace.

Let's look at an example from a client, Cynthia, who owned her own business.

— I finally got what I wanted! But I'm in so much fear and stress, I can't sleep at night. I almost didn't sign the deal. I almost turned it down!!

Her company's highest paying job from a single project had been $70,000. Her goal was to double that. The project she had just signed paid $170,000. Cynthia had surpassed her mark and had manifested her goal, but she was not happy about it.

First, we looked at the regular and natural resistance of her EGO to stepping outside the box, which meant more expansion and prosperity.

What was her EGO trying to protect her from?
What was her EGO trying to avoid?

— If I don't succeed, I'll feel so ashamed. I feel like I won't be able to look anybody in the face if I don't perform after getting paid so much money.

This was a new reality for her and her EGO was naturally freaking out.

Her income had risen but her sense of self-worth had not made the same jump to match the new reality. This is one example of how people manifest something only to de-manifest it shortly after. The amount of money Cynthia manifested made her feel so uncomfortable that she had trouble allowing herself to receive it, and therefore she almost destroyed the manifestation by refusing what she had been asking for.

However, this is not self-sabotage. When a video we are trying to watch in our computer won't play because the flash player needs to be updated, we don't sit back in our seat in frustration and say:

— The video player is trying to sabotage me!!

No, we go and download a new version of the flash player so we can watch our video.We just need to update for things to start playing on our own screen. Whenever we want to play the game on a new level, we need an internal upgrade of self-worth if the new movie is going to play without a glitch.

In such cases of fear, the first thing to figure out, before embarking on the journey, is how to cope with the worst-case scenario should it happen. Again, we don't want to walk the path hoping, wishing, and praying the worst won't happen. If we do, we have our powerful focus locked toward the direction we don't want to go.

If we are trying really hard not to fail, we will. Of course, detaching from success doesn't mean not doing our absolute best. On the contrary, commitment, excellence, expertise, and discipline are the very words that belong to the vibration of success.

In a case like Cynthia's where the fear of failure is high, a second step could be to apply the inner child work to rescue the internal child who was educated to be ashamed of failure. It's very useful to find out when the decision to make failure a taboo happened and introduce a different perspective followed by making sure the inner child knows she is loved unconditionally whether she succeeds or fails.

An important step when we want to change a pattern is to talk to the EGO every single time it comes up to defend its story. For Cynthia her EGO was defending the fear of failure by whispering to her how shameful it would be. Then it's time to introduce the EGO to solutions and dialogues in which shame is not a part of the equation anymore.

Another useful step for Cynthia could be to raise her self-worth by making a list of everything she has to give to the client.

For example:

My company will give: Good quality . . . Transparency . . . Honesty . . . Easy delivery . . . No charge for delivery . . .

I will give: Great expertise . . . Creative solutions . . . Real care . . .

At the end of the day, it isn't really about making lists, but such exercises get the ball rolling to help oneself eventually make a new BEING choice to become a true giver in life. When we focus on what we have to give and are truly ready to give it from our hearts, a tremendous surge of self-worth happens automatically.

In giving to another, if sincerely executed, we give to ourselves tenfold.

I learned about this principle at a time when I felt I had nothing to give. I was depressed, broke, working on movie sets for free, and feeling like my life was going nowhere. The situation made me feel worthless.

One day I decided that instead of sitting on my couch and feeling sorry for myself I was going to do something useful, no matter what.

— What could I give? . . . My time!

That was in fact something I had plenty of and I could give it away in service.

That weekend I found an organization that fed the homeless and needed volunteers to serve meals and distribute food. It was the most amazing experience. I came home emotionally balanced. Giving my time away completely jump-started my sense of self-worth.

In giving we receive, but the giving has to be genuine.

It wasn't by chance they selected me for the new position at the Millennium Live TV project even though I had no prior experience and asked for double the amount they had in mind to pay. I showed up as a giver with my intention. This is why it is not a good idea to give anything to anyone for free unless you want to rob them of this surge of self-worth by blocking their chance to give in return.

When Ike desperately needed money because rent was due, he asked Darel, who was very wealthy, for a $5,000 loan. Darel, being a master of prosperity, knew that just lending the money to Ike would have been of no true value long term.

Because Darel knew how good Ike is with technical stuff and websites:

— I won't loan you the money, Ike, but I sure could use two new websites; it's been on my mind for some time. Would you like to do it? I had around $5,000 in mind to pay for it.

Shortly after this incident, Ike's prosperity got a jump-start because his sense of self-worth went up when he was paid for the valuable service he provided in return for the money he received. In refusing to see a victim in Ike, Darel gave him so much more than just $5,000.

What do you have to give?

Now, in Cynthia's case, there was another layer going on that was once again tied to her self-worth. When there are holes in our self-worth we try to find fulfillment from the outside world. One way this can manifest is by finding ourselves in the Spender's Law, which is finally the subject of the next chapter. As mentioned, the law involves trying to feel better by spending lots of money and living beyond one's means.

Cynthia wasn't overspending money but she was overspending her energy. She slept only a few hours a night and worried about the project the rest of her waking hours.

— I feel like I'm going to have a heart attack before this project's over!

She went on and on, advertising her problem.

When a person has a GAIN from the problem, it has to be dealt with before the steps and exercises above can work. Otherwise, there you are trying to help someone get out of the box while they want to remain in the problem.

— What is your real GAIN from making this journey so hard on yourself?
— What? Say that again, I didn't hear you.

Yup. We were on the right track for sure.

The EGO hates that question, and therefore often it doesn't even allow the person to hear the question as the answer enables one to step outside of the box and look at the self from another perspective.

I got Cynthia to visualize:

As the boss, you are like the eagle who can see the bigger picture from above with sharp eyes and wisdom. You know what needs to get done; you also know who in the company can get each piece done the best. You delegate and you trust it gets done; you oversee but you don't work so hard. What is the point of having your own business if you are working double the amount you would work as an employee for somebody else doing the exact same thing?

We ended with:

— It's so easy for you to operate your business effectively that four hours a day is enough to take care of everything. Then you can go take a walk, spend time with your family, get a massage, and chill.

(Pause)

— How does that feel?
— Ughh! Not good.

Bingo.

— Why?
— I don't see anybody appreciating me or anyone applauding me if things go too smoothly.

It's got to be difficult and hard for me to feel worthy.

This belief was the reason Cynthia was creating her success with such a headache.

Now it's time for the final and most important step.

— Who would you be BEING if you already felt more worthy?
— The image of my child self comes up.
— What does that mean for you?
— Just like my child self, who knew she was worthy just because she existed, I'd know my worth without needing to prove it.
— Wonderful! Open that up a bit more and describe how you would be BEING in your business, as a boss?
— Each project I'd take on would be exciting and fun, and I could enjoy every step of the way without having to create the stress or the various hoops to jump through for myself.

How beautiful is that? Her inner child reframed self-worth so simply, showing her a new and beautiful way of feeling truly more confident.

— Wow! I see now this is a consistent pattern with me. I've never let anything come easily to me. Ever!

Life is like a game we have forgotten to play with.

Cynthia is already on a path of manifesting more and more. She finally gained the courage to head the family business, and she took back a certain level of authority from her father to run the business on her own terms. She has come a long way in increasing company profits, but as always, there is yet another level and another level to discover and grow into. The company income had doubled from a single deal because of her, but her sense of self-worth and self-love had not doubled to match the new game. Now that she had located the belief, she could choose to live a different way and manifest with more fun, grace, and ease.

It is one thing to become good and conscious at manifesting but quite another to feel worthy of accepting the goodies when they arrive. If no one is home to open the door, the delivery person is going to leave and take the package back with them, as your signature is required to receive it.

Continuous increases in our sense of self-worth and self-love are essential components of being able to continue the game of life with a sense of celebratory expansion.

The goals, cars, prosperity, and great relationships are wonderful and well deserved, but they are also like carrots in front of a donkey: They help get us back to what truly matters.

The more we truly love, the wealthier we feel, the more we can allow to show up for us, and I don't just mean money.

Prosperity is receptivity.

Does the tree shy away from receiving all the sunlight?

Love of self has everything to do with it.

Exercise #1: Meditation for a Calm Heart

Sit as always either with your legs crossed on the floor or
normally in a chair, making sure your spine is straight. Since
we are working with energy, the energy should be able to flow
unobstructed.

Left hand is on the heart center, in the middle of the chest, with
the fingers pointed to the right. Right hand is in GYAN mudra,
meaning the thumb and the index finger touch at the tips, forming
a circle, while all other fingers are straight. The right palm faces out
by your right shoulder as if you are taking an oath.

Breath: You inhale and hold the breath for as long as you can
without straining yourself; exhale all the breath and hold it out
as long as you can without gasping, and continue regulating the
breath consciously in this manner.

Neck position: Apply a light Jalandhar band; tuck your chin back and slightly in to have a light neck lock.

Eyes: Closed and focused on the point between the brows, or eyes are 1/10th open looking straight ahead. Either is fine. I prefer the first eye position.

Time: Start with 3 minutes only. Can be practiced for up to 11 or 31 minutes daily.

Practice: 40 or 90 days straight; 120 days in a row is ideal.

End: Taking a big breath, inhale and exhale 3 times. Relax.

Effects: It physically strengthens the heart and lungs. It brings calmness to one's feelings and focuses the prana at the heart center. Use it whenever you are upset and need to calm down. This meditation brings clarity and calm to your relationships as well, both to yourself and others. See how every time you return to your heart and your breath, you are in the ecstasy of being taken care of by you.

A stronger heart center and a conscious connection to the heart mean more receptivity and more self-allowance, leading to prosperity of all kinds.[23]

WHAT'S LOVE GOT TO DO WITH IT?

NOTES _____

_____

_____

_____

_____

_____

_____

_____

_____

_____

_____

_____

_____

_____

_____

_____

_____

_____

_____

_____

_____

_____

_____

_____

_____

_____

_____

_____

_____

_____

_____

_____

_____

The poverty consciousness
thinks about
what to buy with money,
while the prosperity
consciousness
focuses on
how to earn with it.

— Darel Rutherford

UNDER
THE INFLUENCE
OF THE
SPENDER'S LAW

What prosperity train track are you on?

Do you have the: I have, I have, I have . . .
Or the: I don't have, I don't have, it's never enough . . .

. . . story going on?

Your manifestation of prosperity is dependent on the following steps:

A new and committed BEING choice to BE wealthy (the ability to feel and perceive abundance before it manifests). Discovering and choosing out of your limiting beliefs about money. An utter rejection of living under the influence of the Spender's Law.

The amount of income I earned increased three and a half times when I got the TV job, but regardless, I held on to my reality of:

— It is never enough!

Although my income increased, it did not solve my habitual difficulty making ends meet. The scenario remained the same, as my personal story around prosperity hadn't shifted yet. This is a perfect example of how just a doing solution alone doesn't work.

Prosperity is a state of BEING.

I was under the influence of the Spender's Law. When people have a bad relationship with money, or limiting beliefs around the subject, the outcome is manifested under this exact influence.

We are under the influence of the Spender's Law as long as our spending is surpassing our income or we spend as much as we make. Since there is no surplus, there is also no positive cash flow.

Just as alcoholism can affect anyone regardless of age, sex, education, or background, the Spender's Law can affect anyone regardless of their income amounts. Just because a person is making millions doesn't mean they are automatically free from the influence of the Spender's Law.

For example, what is your response if I tell you a celebrity who makes, let's say, twenty million dollars a year or more has just gone bankrupt? (We hear about this kind of stuff all the time.)

Is your response:

— Sure! It's quite possible!

Or is it more like:

— No way! That's total craziness!

People who don't understand prosperity consciousness are shocked and ask (shaking their heads in disapproval):

— How can people who make so much money manage to spend it all? Rich people are seriously nuts!

Yet, often those people shaking their heads are doing the exact same thing themselves (just as I was), with the only difference being that their actions don't make the headlines.

Let me put it a little more bluntly: **The Spender's Law is the cancer of prosperity.**

Being able to attract a lot of money doesn't necessarily mean you have a prosperity consciousness. When someone is under the influence of the Spender's Law, as income grows, so do expenses. The person automatically creates more expenses; therefore the difference between incoming and outgoing amounts remains the same. No matter how much the income is growing, the expenses are following in equal or sometimes in surpassing amounts.

For example, when I started manifesting more money initially, I started to get into debt more often. A larger chunk than usual coming in would excite me, and I would go off and spend more than what was coming in before the money even had a chance to hit the bank.

The fact that more was coming in would be the exact trigger to get me to spend more than usual. I would justify the expenses by saying I was spending only on basic essentials. In a way it was true—I was spending on essentials mostly. But nevertheless, all at once my essentials list would quadruple due to the extra income being on the way. My EGO would start listing a lot more items as essential. That right there, in a nutshell, is the mentality of someone under this influence.

If you were to confront someone under the influence of the Spender's Law, which is unfortunately a large part of the population, this is how the conversation would go:

— What is all this spending about?
— I'm not spending except for the essentials. Really!

Since people under the influence don't like to make a budget, they are not even aware this is the problem, and it is the basis for why they don't feel richer no matter what the size of their income is.

This is why prosperity is not about how much we make or don't make but rather about our individual relationship to money.

Who are you BEING in relationship to money?

To the outside world, people with huge incomes may seem very prosperous; they have a five-million-dollar home and a Jaguar parked right in front of it. But, in reality, they might not be prosperous at all.

A glossy package does not show what is going on inside.

If I make $3,600 a month and all of a sudden I eat out all the time (as now I can) and take a cab to work instead of the bus (as now I can) and my expenses become $4,000 a month, I am running short by $400.

This is exactly what happened to me when my income went up and my reality did not change.

If I make $20,000,000 a year in income and my expenses are $2,000,000 a month, I am short by $4,000,000 at the end of the year.

In higher earning people, the Spender's Law habit can create even bigger disasters due to the financial amounts they are playing with.

It is easier to borrow $400 to make up the difference as opposed to coming up with $4,000,000 on the spot to close a debt.

The above is common sense, yet it is overlooked so often.

I did not get this for a while. Not that I didn't understand the principle, but being under the Spender's Law is like being under a spell. One is so under the illusion that the denials and justifications delay waking up to and breaking this pattern.

Just like alcoholics can't quit drinking until they admit they have a problem, you can't get out of the grasp of the Spender's Law until you admit to being under its influence.

If you don't have savings, you are under this influence, and it has nothing to do with how much you make. That right there is the test and a very tangible one.

I have seen so many people's lives hit catastrophe because they didn't understand and apply this simple understanding. It can be especially problematic in retirement, once income sources are finished and there are no investments to supply any more income since everything has been sold or spent along the way. It is tragic, but the remedy is simple.

Now you might still be thinking . . .

— But wait! How can someone who has a five-million-dollar home and a Jaguar parked in front of it not be prosperous? How?

Once again, prosperity doesn't specifically dwell in the having state but in the BEING state.

When we were moving out of our rental home, we had the movers come, pack, and take everything away to be shipped. Ike and I spent our last days in our pool saying goodbye to our beautiful rental home with the magnificent views of a deep canyon all around. On one of those days, I was watching the dance of an eagle high above and feeling grateful to be bathing in a limitless sense of freedom, which I had so longed for in the past. I lingered lazily in the moment and smiled in anticipation of the move to Hawaii we had planned.

My landlord interrupted my basking. He came into our garden carrying his living room couch with one other person helping, as they were living next door on the same property. They had rented out the home they were in and were going to move into ours when we left, so he had already started to bring over some of the furniture.

They owned this beautiful expansive land with two wonderful homes in a very prominent neighborhood. They had more than we did yet they were experiencing financial limitations.

My landlord was so cute. He came in sweating, huffing and puffing, breaking his back, and there we were in the pool with some music, sipping our cold ice teas. We all kind of froze looking at each other for a second, until he broke the silence:

— Wait a minute! . . . There is just something so wrong with this picture!

A unified laughter echoed in the canyon.

I have yet to meet a person who is under the Spender's Law and yet has a positive expectation and relationship to prosperity. The habit of the Spender's Law automatically colors our relationship to finances with:

- Limitation
- Fear of loss
- Not enough
- Frustration

The feeling one is rowing the boat for no reason.

When this is who we are BEING, how are we going to BE a match with prosperity? We are not vibrationally anywhere near prosperity.

The above is true whether we are talking about:

- A salesperson
- An Oscar winner
- A business
- A country

Sooner or later, the Spender's Law ends up creating financial disaster.

The remedy is to do or die, and get out of this habit.

When Mustafa Kemal Ataturk inherited Turkey, the "sick man of Europe" (as foreigners called the Ottoman Empire at the time), with it came an economy in shambles. Not only was the Ottoman Empire crumbling but it had also entered World War I and lost. In the meantime, minorities rose up and the countries on the winning side of the war were not going to stay out of it. Some foreign countries supported the uprisings to further divide the country (which became the Turkish Republic in 1923) into pieces.

However, Ataturk, named by the nation as the "Father of Turks," revived her spirit when the victors of World War I were already preparing to divide the land amongst themselves. Turkey got up, resurrected herself, and fought an incredible war of independence at a time when it was already depleted of all kinds of resources, in terms of both manpower and materials. The children made ammunition and women carried it to the battleground. The men were outnumbered by the enemy but nevertheless fought for Turkey's independence in the name of freedom or death.

The creation of the Turkish Republic herself is an amazing story of victory under the most impossible conditions. Ataturk's vision, love, and commitment helped give birth to the nation by injecting self-worth and by reconnecting the Turks with the power of their spirit. Turkey's birth was a miracle and nothing less than a testament to the power of will and the power of love to create.

The English, Greeks, French, you name it, everybody wanted to feast on the pieces of this once mighty but long-dead Ottoman Empire. Under the exemplary leadership of Ataturk, with his extraordinary military genius and capacity to unite people with a true love for the country, and the sacrifice of so many brave men, women, and children, Turkey's freedom, her republic, and therefore her democracy were born. The Turkish nation flew to her political independence like a phoenix rising from its own ashes.

Despite Ataturk having inherited an economy riddled with debt, crippled by war, Turkey became a healthy, fast-growing economy shortly thereafter.

> The Ataturk period was the most successful period of Turkish economy with zero inflation and a steady growth rate.[24]
> — Sabahattin Özel

How was this achieved?

For Ataturk, national debt was unacceptable. His policy stated that a balanced budget and surplus were a must. If Turkey was going to maintain her independence politically, she could not be dependent on other countries economically. In contrast, the Ottoman Empire had sold everything it had to foreign countries; even the railroads were not operated locally at that time. This leaning on other countries would create dependency, fear, and a lack of authority and invite foreign control, which is exactly what had caused the Ottoman Empire to collapse.

How could she be powerful without her self-reliance in place?

Ataturk saw to it that the country put in place many policies, laws, and reforms, not to mention the education needed to create the know-how, to bring production back to the mother country instead of importing everything from other countries. This idea of bringing production back home was also the policy Gandhi used to bring India out of her dependence on British rule, which in return broke the chains of control.

Ataturk himself would not wear imported clothes. Nor would he allow tea or coffee services in his governmental meetings, underlining the importance of saving money. His close circle of officials followed his example, some even using their personal cars instead of government vehicles while on the job to make a point of living in a manner that would help bring the deficit down on every possible front. Ataturk got the country and her people out of the Spender's Law and the result was an influx of prosperity.

Ike's great-grandfather was a high-level government official back then, and one day when she was a child his daughter (Ike's grandma) visited her father's office. She wanted to draw a picture on a piece of paper. She reached out for the pen on her father's desk. Her father gently stopped her from using the pen.

— No, darling! That pen belongs to the government. Please don't use it.

He pulled out a pen from his own pocket.

— Let me give you mine.

Desperate times call for desperate measures. Getting out of the Spender's Law doesn't mean we can't spend money. We can spend as much as we like as long as we are creating a positive monthly cash flow, putting at least ten to fifteen if not thirty percent of our earnings aside and living with what is left until we create more flow.

Whether we are speaking of a nation or an individual, self-sufficiency and living without debt are musts for independence and self-authority and not living in a state of neediness.

A state of neediness is indeed the biggest poverty.

When I was in debt, I would beg for credit card increases that would naturally never happen. Now that I am in prosperity, banks beg me to take loans, sending me one offer after another with very low interest rates.

> When you need it, you can't have it.
> When you don't need it,
> you can have all you want and more.[25]
> — Darel Rutherford

A successful product and business, and good sales, don't necessarily add up to financial success if one is under the influence of the Spender's Law.

I had a client, Beatrice, whose products became extremely popular and her business grew into a total success, which was wonderful. But she refused to understand prosperity consciousness and continued to spend money like crazy and never made a budget.

She kept on experiencing financial problems and limitations, and the success of her incredible business that spread worldwide didn't remedy this situation.

Whether you get someone to do it for you or you figure it out yourself, making a budget—along with committing to BEING a person who achieves positive cash flow—no matter what, on a monthly basis, is one of the main pillars of prosperity.

Ike and I didn't understand the importance of this principle for a long time ourselves. Darel would tell us over and over again and we would both nod in agreement like two puppets on a string. And the next thing you knew we were back on the never-ending spending wheel.

Are you on the wheel of fortune or the wheel of spending?

One day, Ike was complaining about this to Darel.

— How much money do you have in your wallet, Ike?
— I don't know.
— Do you know where Esra is?
— Yes, she went to lunch with her mom.
— How come you know where she is but you have no idea where your money is?
— Mmmmm!
— You value her, but you don't value your money. That's the problem right there.

(Lightbulbs.)

If we don't care about money, why should it want to come to us? Even if it does, why should it stay? The Spender's Law is exactly like being an alcoholic because people can so easily deny that the law applies to them.

When Darel first confronted me about having this problem:

— Is he crazy? What am I to save? . . . How can I save when I don't have? . . . I get what it is but it most definitely doesn't apply to me!!

It didn't even occur to me that what he was talking about had already been my experience, proven and sealed in the past. I had already experienced how earning more hadn't necessarily gotten me anywhere different.

When it doesn't click, it just doesn't click.

When I finally started to save $100 a month, however, it really changed everything. Only then I realized it wasn't about the $100 a month being put aside, it was the changed attitude and relationship with money that made the real difference.

Simply defined, positive cash flow is:

Making sure that every month there is a surplus, a predecided percentage of the income goes into a savings account and is not to be touched. One has to budget one's life accordingly to achieve this. Don't spend and then see what is left over to save. There has to be a dedicated, committed decision to save a certain percentage in advance and then the organizing of one's life to fit that choice. Even if your income fluctuates you can still commit to a certain percentage of it every month.

Anybody can do this. If you have a zillion excuses as to why you personally can't, just like I did, you can be sure your EGO is blocking you from getting out of the cave of financial limitation.

Getting into a positive cash flow, no matter what, is important for three reasons:

1. The ability to start saving (not from a place of "I have to" but from a place of "I want to") is exciting. It is an indication of a shifted relationship to finances.
2. Positive cash flow naturally keeps our focus on money in alignment with abundance instead of lack.
3. The ability to save allows us to eventually invest, creating a reality in which instead of us working for money, money begins to work for us.

Not to mention, it also shields us from panic and makes it easier to keep focused on prosperity when faced with the unexpected, such as the coronavirus pandemic.

Let's take a look:

1. The ability to start saving:
It's kind of like a test to see if we have really made a new BEING choice toward prosperity or not.

The reason people overspend is they feel good temporarily during the act of spending.

The capacity to make a budget, have a positive cash flow, and spend only what is available after you have already saved ten to thirty percent of your income is an indication that the alcoholism of spending and the wound behind it has been healed.

Let's look at an example . . .

Sally came to one of our courses. She was supposedly making a budget but was basically just kidding herself by writing stuff down on a piece of paper as if writing down a recipe. Looking at what you spend and just keeping track of it is not the same as making sure you are living in positive cash flow and managing your budget. The truth was, she was in debt.

One cannot be in a positive cash flow and in debt at the same time. She had to first figure out why she was keeping herself in debt in the first place.

What was her GAIN?

She had to first choose out from BEING the one who lives in debt before she could choose for real BEING the one who lives in positive cash flow.

It turns out that when she was a child her father lived in debt, and therefore resources were always limited. Whatever came in went out, and there was nothing left over for more. She was not allowed to have stuff other kids had, and this made her feel awful and less than others.

When she asked for something:

— We can't. It's not possible.

As an adult, she was still trying to prove to herself the opposite:

— I can have whatever I want!

To have all the things she couldn't have in the past, she spent and spent, putting everything on credit cards and/or taking out loans from banks. She was reliving the feeling of lack coming from her past, trying to remedy it with "doing" solutions such as purchasing beyond her current limits. This was her specific pattern of keeping herself the prisoner of the Spender's Law.

Poverty consciousness is a pattern of hunger—a hunger that never gets satisfied unless perception shifts, meaning the stories we have been carrying around about money change. The wounded inner child might also need help if decisions about money have been made because of certain family dynamics.

— What is it that I am trying to prove in my need to always spend?

A good place to start is to see what is missing inside. Once what's missing is identified, fulfill the need, without spending money to do so.

Ask yourself the following question:

— How rich do I feel?

1 = I am about to kill myself.
10 = I feel like the king or queen of the jungle.

Let's just say it's a 4 or 5.

Why? . . . What are you choosing to believe? . . . What story is running your game?

Additionally, ask yourself:

How can I change the way I feel and get myself to a prosperity feeling state that is within a range of 7–10?

How can I get myself to feel abundant just for the sake of it and before the prosperity arrives?

The habitual practice of gratitude, the subject of the final chapter, is key for this. But for the time being, another way to sustain a state of abundance is having a consistent positive cash flow.

2. Positive cash flow naturally keeps our focus about money in the positive direction.
It is much harder to play the "I have and I have" game if you are in negative cash flow or in debt.

Imagine you have six months to a year's worth of expenses saved for your busines and personally, to stay afloat in case of emergency.

As I mentioned before and would like to underline again, if something crazy happens in the world like the coronavirus or a huge global economic crash or for whatever reason you lose your job, you have time to turn it all around because you already have enough sustenance for six months to a year. If you don't get into a focus of lack you will keep attracting abundance under all circumstances whether in the form of money, help, new ideas, or new opportunities.

Savings not only buy time to figure out a solution, but even more importantly, savings completely cut out any negative focus on fear, lack, or stress, at least economically speaking, which enables us to automatically take the next step with so much more ease and grace and without losing the golden focus of:

— I have.

3. The ability to save allows us to eventually invest.
Saving, once again, eventually changes your relationship to money.

Are you working for money or is money working for you?

As long as we need to keep working and working hard to make money, we can never become wealthy. We didn't come onto the earth to work endlessly for money. We all deserve a good life and it is possible to achieve.

When we can create residual income, enough to have a comfortable life, we no longer need to work for money. This doesn't mean we won't work and be productive, it just means we are no longer bound to work. This habit can start one step at a time, until one reaches that point.

- Buying a house or commercial real estate and renting it.
- Renting an extra room in your apartment.
- Writing a book that keeps selling long after you are done writing it.
- Creating a product that keeps selling on your website.
- Investing in a project or a business you believe will grow.

The point is to start getting into a reality in which you no longer have to trade your hours for money. If even as you sleep money flows into your bank accounts, now money has begun to work for you, instead of the other way around.

Doesn't that make the idea of saving look like so much fun? Before your EGO comes up with a:

— Yes, but . . .

Just a quick reminder: I started the journey with just $100 of savings a month.

No matter what your level of income is, a positive cash flow habit is a must for a healthy and sustained growth of prosperity and for eventually reaching the space in which money begins to work for you.

To achieve positive cash flow:

1. Downsize and reduce your expenses.
2. Increase your income.
3. Do both at the same time.
4. Find out what belief keeps you in the Spender's Law.

Make a new BEING commitment today!

Who won the race?
The tortoise or the hare?

THE
PYRAMID
OF
PROSPERITY

Imagine there is a long staircase and you want to climb to the top. The natural way to proceed would be to take one step at a time to get there, knowing that without a doubt, as long as you can walk, you will eventually get to the top. You wouldn't be on the first step and immediately just jump to the very top like a ninja. Yet when it comes to abundance goals, this is what I see people try to do all the time. Then they get disappointed when they come crashing down because they tried to jump too far too early from where they were to begin with.

One step at a time!

— How much do you make?
— $1,000 a month.
— What is your financial goal?
— $1,000,000 dollars a year.

This is like saying:

— When did you get pregnant?
— Two months ago!
— Awwww, in seven more months you'll have a baby!
— No, no! My baby is coming tomorrow!

Hopefully not!

Like anything else, prosperity consciousness will need to grow and expand over time. Yes, quantum jumps are always possible as the Universe has no limits, but if your container has not grown in equal amount, it is not going to be able to hold what comes. Steady baby steps will get you into a faster and steadier growth pattern than quantum jumps, which are not necessarily easy to hold.

The first step:
Get out of debt.

The goal here is to just focus on paying off your debt and never again operating from a debt-oriented mindset. Mortgages and business loans for investment purposes can't be considered debt. Those are debt literally speaking, but in essence they are not, at least not within the context of what we are talking about here.

If you are spending more just to have more stuff and this puts you into a negative cash flow in your budget, that is debt.

If you are spending more but it doesn't put you into a negative cash flow and is intended to make you more money or to provide education on how to become more effective at something, that is an investment.

If an Uber driver buys a car with credit, that is an investment, since they will generate business and income because of it.

If you buy a car for yourself with credit, that is debt.

I had a friend who was experiencing dire financial problems, but she still went out and leased a Mercedes just because it made her feel better to drive an upscale car. That is nothing other than being purely under the influence of the Spender's Law.

Not being able to do with less, when necessary, is an indication of how much you are giving up your power to needing and having things. This is the mentality that keeps one in debt ongoingly.

When you need to spend more than what you have to feel better about yourself, you are in the Spender's Law. When a steady positive monthly cash flow is what starts to make you feel better about yourself, you are out of the Spender's Law and that means you are on your way to attracting more prosperity.

It is important to get out of the Spender's Law before actualizing the next step.

There is a great saying in Turkish: "Extend your legs out according to the size of your blanket."

This is a must approach if you want to eventually increase the size of that blanket too.

Even in paying back debt, make a doable plan. Start with baby steps and pay off the smallest debt, then go to the next larger debt. Start with the smallest debt and pay the largest one last. The point is to surround yourself with the emotional encouragement of moving forward, not taking for granted the importance and the power of baby steps. The more you can stay in the perspective of "it's happening, it's easy, it's doable" the more it will happen quickly and easily, and you will be done with it sooner than you think.

Remember, when you make a real BEING commitment to live debt-free, the Universe will have to support you in matching the new reality.

The second step:
Work hard to achieve positive cash flow. Do whatever it takes to be in the song of:

— I have, I have, I have, I have . . .

Cut down expenses and get a second job if necessary.

When Ike had been a waiter/bartender for ten years to support his acting career, he was barely making ends meet. Darel suggested he take a second job in another restaurant to help him reach his dreams.

We were both like:

— What?

However, the increase in positive cash flow was going to increase Ike's positive feelings in his relationship to money and Darel knew this.

We really didn't get it back then.

Although we didn't like the idea, Ike went and found a second job. His income doubled and more cash started to flow into his life. Sure enough, after four months of him feeling better about his money situation, out of the blue he got offered a voice-over job.

It wasn't out of the blue, of course. It was right on target as his next natural step, which came into being as soon as he started feeling better about his finances. It took four months because a momentum of feeling good had to be built up a little bit before the next shift could happen. Feeling better about your financial situation due to positive cash flow is a huge leverage into prosperity.

The more financially feeling good momentum has been acquired, the faster the financial change will come. Just like a snow slide gains momentum and speed while cascading down the mountain, turning into an avalanche.

Although he was getting paid at the voice-over job the same as the two restaurant jobs combined, his work hours decreased by fifty percent and he was doing something he loved. When his per hour income was calculated, in the first scenario it was $15 per hour. In the second scenario it was $30 an hour.

What happened?

His income actually doubled.

If the opposite happens and you make twenty-five percent more income a month by increasing your work hours fifty percent, then your actual income has decreased.

How much time are you spending to make how much money?

It is very important to understand how much you make per hour to see the real picture of what is actually going on financially in your life. It also helps you assess whether you are using your efforts effectively.

Time is precious. More time means either more investment in creating abundance such as starting a new side business, or investment in yourself such as an education or polishing up your skills with a course and gaining more expertise in what you do.

By being willing to work more hours even in a job he did not like to achieve a positive cash flow, Ike was able to be in the song of:

— I have, I have . . .

Which got him not only a job he loved for the same amount of money but also spending way fewer hours working for the same amount. By being willing to work more initially, he was able to achieve working less eventually.

This is how crucial it is to activate a sense of feeling more abundant because of positive cash flow.

The third step:
Work fewer hours to make the same amount of income or possibly make even more income.

At this stage, it is about increasing your self-worth per work hour.

If you previously made $10,000 a month working forty hours a week, now try to manifest the same amount or more working perhaps only twenty hours a week. Or it could be that you still work forty hours a week but now make $20,000 a month instead of $10,000 because you have achieved a real and perceptual shift around your own self-worth.

This shift can happen as you actually get better at what you do. This requires time, experience, know-how, additional knowledge, and polishing yourself to a new level of expertise, and it can also happen as a result of a realization about owning your self-worth in a way that you were blind to previously.

But if you have done the same job for twenty years and you are still getting paid the same amount, whether you work for yourself or somebody else, please do realize there is a big problem there. Either you haven't expanded at all or you are not owning your self-worth.

An increase in income is an indication that your sense of worth and value has increased, and life's magic mirror is now able to reflect this back to you. Every time you want to play the game on a new level, your sense of worth and value needs to go up as well to match the new reality.

A great example of this was Darel running his company.

Darel used to work sixteen hours a day in his business. After his wife dragged him to Hawaii on a holiday and he spent time watching the beautiful sunsets, sunrises, and rainbows, he realized he was missing out on life. He decided right then and there that he was going to run his company working only four hours a day but also double his profits.

Notice that this was a decision of increased deservedness and hence a direct increase in self-worth.

When he got back home, he rearranged his company, realizing that to make his new dream come true,

He had to STOP—BEING the one who finds all the solutions and answers for his employees.

And START—BEING the one who expects the employees to come up with the solutions themselves and just bring those to Darel for a yes or no.

Some employees left, others changed who they were BEING to match Darel's new vision and the company hired new employees to replace the ones who had left. In no time, he was working only four hours a day running his business, and his profits surpassed even what he had intended in just one year.

But to achieve this, he had to step out of the box and belief:

I have to work hard to deserve.

AND

I can make money only by trading my hours for money.

The fourth step:
Once your positive cash flow has yielded enough savings, start, even if in small ways and amounts, to invest.

Make a BEING choice to experience residual income.

When I was at this stage, I kept asking Darel:

— But what will I invest in? I don't know anything about investments! I hate the stock market and I don't have enough to buy property! What should I do?
— Just make a BEING choice to be the one who BELONGS to residual income and it will manifest!
— Oh! That again . . . Grrrr!

I think we went back and forth like this for two months. Every phone call I would ask the same question and every time he would give me basically the same answer.

Sometime within that year, I woke up to realize Ike and I had created multiple sources of residual income. The books were one source; our website products were another; my yoga DVD was another. Once we had created these initial products, we were well on our way to experiencing what it was like to make money without having to work for it in an ongoing manner.

In one of those sessions with Darel, I finally felt I belonged to prosperity flowing without having to trade my valuable time for it every step of the way.

The fifth step:
The richer you feel by:

- Getting the limiting belief systems out of the way
- Focusing on and feeling the abundance you already have
- Understanding abundance is not just money and learning to focus on its other forms
- BEING in and staying in gratitude
- Steadily growing positive cash flow

The more you attract easily.

These practices can begin at any level of income. It is the same whether you make a thousand dollars a month or a million dollars a month.

Start growing your investments more and more.

At this point, the goal is to be able to have a standard of living that is pleasing to you and that your residual income alone provides for.

The sixth step:
Welcome to wealth!

Your money works for you entirely and you no longer have to work for pay.

Now is the time to save the dolphins, to create incredible projects, travel the world, perhaps work for a cause, follow your hobbies, invent something, or just spend quality time with your family and take care of yourself in every way imaginable.

The above is just a loose basic map to point out that prosperity is a step-by-step journey. So many people get disappointed and give up somewhere along the path, when sometimes the only mistake they are making is setting too high of a goal way too early on.

You don't need to be a ninja!

Each of these steps requires a growth in consciousness so that you come to know that like the birds and bees you are supported and abundance is all around you. When you expect abundance because it has naturalized itself in your consciousness, more comes to you without much effort. The best help is not to give someone the fish they need but rather to teach them how to fish for themselves. It is terrible advice when people who have achieved true prosperity consciousness at a very high level try to tell others:

— None of it matters.

No! This is not entirely true.

It really does matter—until it doesn't anymore.

A real sadhu, an ascetic having renounced all worldly goods, who walks around with nothing because he or she has truly come to believe everything will be provided by the Universe, and who actually experiences this as a day-to-day reality, not lacking anything, is not the same as someone begging, because that person believes in essence that they can't have.

They may look very similar from the outside in terms of the way they dress or they may have a similar demeanor, but in actuality they are on opposite ends of the journey of prosperity.

When true prosperity consciousness is achieved, one doesn't experience financial problems anymore, no matter what is going on in the world. Rather, one lives in the reality in which the fountain of prosperity is constantly flowing.

I invite you to take a look at psychologist Abraham Maslow's pyramid on the following page.[26] He suggests that the basic needs of an individual must be not only met but also mastered before true self-actualization and transcendence can happen.

Whether he is right or wrong is a discussion for psychologists, but I want to point out one thing about his pyramid. Some believe spirituality and prosperity must be exclusive of one another. I also believed this at one point in my life.

Early on, I used my yoga mat or meditations as a form of escape from facing certain things or solving real problems in my life.

I don't think spirituality should become a tool of our refusal to grow up and become an adult, which at a minimum level means becoming self-sufficient.

Mastery of self-sufficiency not only graduates us from the childish psychology of dependency on other people and social and governmental systems but also serves as the rainbow bridge to deepening our individual, unique, and spiritual potentials up life's pyramid.

There is nothing spiritual about separating ourselves from the endless possibilities that existence has to offer us. Existence doesn't hold anything back, but we can be limiting ourselves through what it is we have chosen to believe.

If the fountain of prosperity is in continuous flow, the real question becomes:

What is the size of your container?

Maslow's Pyramid

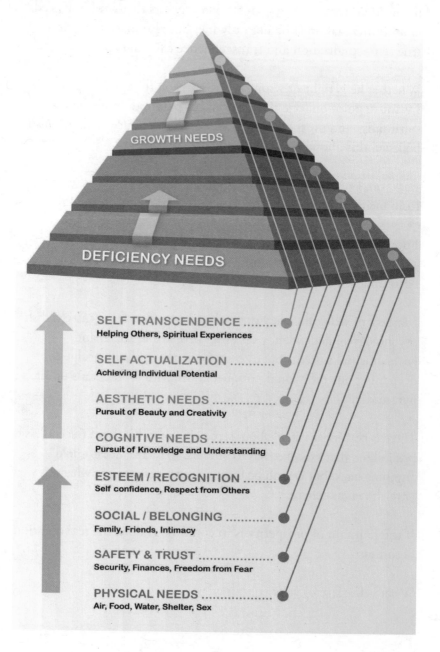

NOTES _____

ABRACADABRA
(I Create As I Speak)

ABRACADABRA

ABRACADABRA means: I create as I speak.

I have always enjoyed this word and used it often as a child when playing magician, so I loved recently learning its meaning.

Getting ourselves into a state of gratitude is a very direct, simple, and effective tool for manifesting directly what we prefer. It is rather amazing how such a simple tool can change your reality entirely, yet I feel its value is so little known and understood.

Making a habit of a state of gratitude is not only useful for attracting prosperity but also for resolving problems, as it raises our vibration quickly and makes it easier for us to BE the solution. The practice causes us to feel energized, healthy, and joyful without a reason, and brings in the awareness of our own spirit as alive and thriving.

For some reason, tap dancing imagery comes to my mind. The kind where one partner taps as the other watches and then they switch, as the observer begins to dance and the dancer observes. In this same manner, when I practice my gratefulness exercises, it is as if the Universe begins to dance as I watch in awe. Then I tap some more, then it does some more, and it is just such a synchronized dance.

After fifteen years of practicing almost on a daily basis, I consider myself quite the queen of gratefulness. It still surprises me, though, when I realize it is not necessarily an easy thing for other people to latch on to, probably because they don't trust that something so simple can make a real difference.

It does take practice, momentum, and understanding. It is not just about paying lip service to gratitude; rather it's more about practicing to actually attain the state of gratitude itself. We cannot be in a true state of gratitude and a state of lack at the same time. We cannot be truly grateful and unhappy at the same time. It is impossible.

I am not just talking about a mental gratitude here. People will sometimes claim they are very positive and grateful when really they are focusing heavily on lack as a habit. In essence their gratitude is more of a concept than an actual state of being.

It took me a couple of months of practicing gratitude as an exercise every day and experimenting with the idea to begin finding momentum on truly feeling grateful. I developed my own way that worked for me, which I will share at the end of this chapter. In the first couple of months of trying to create the method that worked for me, all I discovered was how negative and lack-oriented my mind was. It seemed I couldn't get a sentence out of my mouth without my mind automatically dropping back into lack.

My mouth would say: I am grateful I have a roof over my head . . . But my mind would think: Poor me! I just have a roof over my head to be grateful for.

(Oops.)

— I am so grateful I came to the US to follow my dreams.

But really, I would be focusing on:

— I'm distributing free movie tickets for a company on the streets of Santa Monica, and the people are waving me away as if I'm an annoying mosquito . . . Damn those free movie tickets and so much for following my dreams!

(Ouch.)

My brain felt as if it were glued to an endless spiral of lack about prosperity and about believing in myself. I was shocked and it was a wake-up call. Little by little, though, with patience, I was able to shift from consistently dropping into a focus on lack and instead found myself increasingly able to get into the states of BEING that were a match to what I had been asking for. Once you get the hang of it, gratitude is such a powerful method to help rise above problems and manifest things very quickly.

When our clients who come to the course do this exercise for three to six months nonstop, they change in incredible ways. Besides prosperity flow, they start opening up and becoming more relaxed and humorous. But what never ceases to delight me is that they also start looking ten or fifteen years younger. It is quite a sight to behold.

Now, let me try to demonstrate what I mean about raising the vibration with a quick exercise so that it can be felt rather than just understood.

Think of a very unpleasant memory from the past or focus on a current problem that might really be bothering you in your life. The more dramatic it is, the better. Activate it by thinking about it and dwelling on it; let the unpleasant feelings come up.

With your eyes closed, relive every single detail and focus on it. Be especially aware of how your body feels and reacts as the emotions come up.

Please don't play the "I'm holier than thou; I don't ever feel negative" game. Unless you are a robot, you have feelings you don't prefer and it might be a good idea to learn to get in touch with them.

Remember that the word "negative" is also just another label.

Stay here for at least three minutes.

Go ahead and open your eyes when the three minutes are up.

How did you feel?

- Small?
- Angry?
- Frustrated?
- Anxious?

How did your body feel?

- Was your breathing heavier or shallower?
- Did your heart rate increase?
- Did your shoulders slump?
- Was there a knot in your core?

If you aren't repressed, you will be able to reactivate a negative state rather quickly, because you have easy access to your feelings. You will notice that even your body reacted quickly to the unwanted state you chose to go into.

Now, please memorize the following steps first and then practice with your eyes closed.

Step #1: Speak out loud and be grateful for at least three different subjects in your life (three to five minutes or so). Really dwell on each subject and just go on and on for a while. For example, if your subject is your relationship, here are some examples:

— I am grateful we laugh so much together.

— I am grateful I trust my partner.

— I am grateful my partner is an excellent cook and makes delicious food for us, and I love our conversations at dinner.

— I am grateful we both love to travel and we have an upcoming exotic place to visit together that we are both so excited about.

Pick three different subjects and dwell on them using at least ten spontaneous grateful sentences for each.

Step #2: Visualize something pleasant for you, either a past memory when you felt great or a location that brings you much peace and joy (two minutes or so).

Step #3: Speak out loud loving sentences about yourself (two minutes or so).

Summarized, the simple three-step process is:

- Gratefulness
- Visualization
- Loving sentences about yourself

Go back to the problem or memory that you picked at the beginning of the exercise, close your eyes, and try to refocus on it again for about thirty seconds.

Once you are done, please open your eyes and answer the questions below.

What happened?
How was it different?
How did your body react this time?
Were you able to focus at all on the problem?

Did you feel the difference between how you related to the problem at first and what happened differently when you consciously took a few minutes to raise your vibration?

Some of you will not be able to refocus back on the emotions of the unwanted state at all, although you were really trying to. It is as if the problem cannot be recalled. It ceases to be so important and begins to look so small.

When we raise our frequency through a conscious focus, our way of relating to the problem changes because of the shift in our state of BEING.

It's kind of like going up in an elevator: The problem or what was visible on the ground floor gets smaller and smaller as we keep going up. Think of each floor in the building as a different reality. The floor below the ground floor sees nothing, maybe because it is the parking lot. A view is nonexistent. It looks like there is no solution to the problem.

The ground floor sees perhaps just the entrance to the building and the gates surrounding the premises. So maybe there is a sliver of hope about the problem, but that's about it.

- The first floor sees the whole backyard.
- The second floor sees the backyard and the road behind it.
- The third floor sees the tall mountains beyond the road.
- The fourth floor sees a glimpse of the ocean.
- The fifth floor sees a full ocean view.

The top floor sees the unlimited blue sky and a view of everything.

Think of raising your vibration through your conscious focus as the elevator going up and the floor you decide to get off and live on as your BEING choice. Just as in real estate, the top floors have more value, more unlimited views, but in this case the only currency to afford the top floors is your focus and state of consciousness. Yes, we will go up and down in the elevator, meaning our energy will sometimes drop and sometimes rise. This is normal, but what floor do we choose to habitually live on?

In the exercise at the end of this chapter, I will share my own way of raising my vibration. Either use it, modify it, or create your own way. At least, the first part will be about raising your vibration. The second part is about the ABRACADABRA: the art of literally speaking your reality into existence.

Before you begin to practice the exercise, ask yourself the following question.

— What is the difference between a bad actor and a good one?

The bad actor just imitates and says the words; they just pretend.

The good actor begins to feel and think and behave like the character so that when we watch them on the stage or screen, we cry with them, laugh with them, feel and understand things through them. Wow!

— Why wow?

Because if they are good, they are not just imitating but becoming the state of BEING of the character for that period of time, and as the audience, we get pulled into the experience as if it's real.

Pete, after he had increased his prosperity and was sharing about it in our program, moved me to tears. The description of how his state of BEING changed, through a realization and due to the gratitude exercise, was so incredibly beautiful.

This was after months and months of practicing gratitude—using the specific exercise formatted at the end of the chapter.

— There was a moment one morning when it all came together for me. As if all the gratitude practice I had done culminated in that moment of understanding. I was having my morning coffee and looking out into my garden and for the first time I noticed a blossoming cherry tree. It was so beautiful! It produced yearly but I had never noticed it before in all the years it sat quietly blossoming in my own backyard. All of a sudden it dawned on me that abundance is the same. It is always there but we don't notice it. From that moment on, my income started increasing.

Money *DOES* grow on trees.

As we come to the end of this book, I would like to share the story of how it got into your hands. It has a lot to do with the exercise that I hope you will begin practicing.

Also before I share, I want to give credit to the Teachings of Abraham-Hicks for awakening me in 2001 to the importance of gratitude.[27] Understanding the importance of gratitude in those days is what activated the commitment to practice it in a way that I like to.

I hadn't even started to write this book but I knew I had to find an agent, which is not an easy task in the US. I just didn't want to deal with the whole ordeal of finding one, therefore I turned to my gratitude exercise, which is always in my magical hat as a manifestation tool.

Usually after first raising myself vibrationally by being grateful for what is already in my life, I begin speaking of the reality I want to experience as if it has already happened.

On one of my favorite beaches on Kauai, walking up and down, talking out loud in excitement, feeling grateful for having found an agent, I listed all the qualities and dynamics I wanted to experience as if I were already experiencing them, trying in the meantime to remain oblivious to the people staring at me. On the eleventh day or so of this focused ritual, I went to a massage session deep in the hills of Kauai. Diane, a friend living on the island, insisted that I go, convincing me of the healing potency of Hezar's massage. She just kept badgering me until I finally made an appointment.

After a glorious heavenly massage, during which I flew to another dimension and came back, I was stuck at the massage therapist's house for forty minutes because there wasn't an Uber close enough to pick me up immediately. As I waited for the Uber to arrive, having found one to drive all the way across from the other side of the island, Hezar and I got into a wonderful conversation over a cup of tea. One thing led to another and the next thing I knew she had scribbled an email address on a piece of paper and put it into the palm of my hand just as I was heading out the door.

— I feel the two of you have to connect.
— Who is it?
— A friend of mine, a literary agent.
— What?

I emailed and called when I returned to Los Angeles. I hit it off immediately with this agent and decided to meet him, but his office was two hours away from LA. Ike and I got stuck in awful traffic and were late, so the meeting ended up happening over an amazing, delicious dinner at sunset with his lovely wife instead of at his office.

Not only was this dinner scenario in my gratitude ritual but so was the desire for him to have represented a writer I admired. He turned out to have been the agent for two of my favorite bestselling authors in the US, way back when I had started my journey. We shook hands.

BINGO!

Never in a million years could I have personally imagined or orchestrated finding my literary agent, of all the possible places on earth, in the deep and forgotten jungles of Kauai.

Thanks to him, I began to write.

Such is the magic of ABRACADABRA.

Exercise #1: The Daily Gratitude Exercise

First, be grateful for at least five minutes for what already truly exists in your life. Go from subject to subject, but make sure you dwell on each subject for a while. Think of more than just a couple of sentences for each subject. The point is to stay long enough on a subject that you begin to feel differently about it and you honestly begin to conjure feelings of appreciation. Don't be a robot and be grateful for the same subjects with the same sentences day in and day out. The purpose of the exercise, just like a physical exercise, is to stretch your feelings to a fresh level of expansion. Instead of being grateful for the same subjects every day, think about what happened that day or that week and find very specific, organic things that you can be personally and specifically grateful for.

Once you achieve and only IF you achieve a different feeling space, go on into the second phase of the exercise. Start by being grateful for what you would like to experience, AS IF it has already happened. As you are being grateful at this stage, use the present tense AS IF it is your experience already. Spend at least five minutes minimum.

At the beginning, I would advise you to choose subjects for this second phase that you are not too attached to achieving. Think of something simple like a parking space, or a good laugh, or a trip somewhere—subjects that are not a big deal for you and you know you will be fine whether they happen or not.

Once you begin to experience the ABRACADABRA, meaning you are seeing clear correlations between what you speak and what happens, then you can begin to apply it to the more important subjects as the believability momentum forms.

Remember that you cannot create on behalf of others. You can hold space for them, but ultimately everyone creates their own realities. Make sure your gratefulness sentences are not dependent on specific people, companies, or groups. Just speak of the dynamics you would like to experience and let the Universe take care of the who, what, where, and when.

For example if you are being grateful for a relationship as if it is in your experience already, be grateful for the dynamics you are experiencing and don't make it about John specifically. John may or may not be the right match, plus whatever it is you prefer, you specifically might not be who John is asking for.

Play with the exercise in various ways and see what happens for you.

Exercise #2: The Water Experiment

Take a regular glass of drinking water and be aware of how it tastes, feels, and goes down your throat as you take a couple of sips.

Now take that same glass of water and talk to it and be grateful for it as if you are talking to a lover or a friend. Just keep pouring heartfelt sentences of gratitude toward it and bombard it with true appreciation.

Drink it! How does it feel? How does it taste? How is it different? Is it sweeter? Softer in texture going down your throat? Fuller?

Dr. Masaru Emoto, an independent scientist, conducted some very interesting experiments with water. He wrote loving words or sentences of appreciation and stuck them onto containers of water. He froze the containers and looked at the crystals that formed in the frozen water. The containers of water treated in this manner created beautiful, harmonious, perfectly geometrical crystals that were like pieces of art to look at.

He also did the opposite, writing swear words and foul language that he placed on other containers of water coming from the same source. The containers of water treated in this manner when frozen formed jagged, distorted, and unharmonious patterns.

Reading his book *The Hidden Messages of Water* inspired the above exercise.[28]

Dr. Emoto concluded that positive or negative words change the actual molecular structure of water.

In remembering you are mostly made of water, what does that say to you about the power of your words?

A client of ours, Senay, was very impressed by how different the water felt and tasted after she did the exercise above. However, she decided to test the process herself.

Senay, who was working at a water company, took a bottle of totally sealed water and did the "I am grateful" exercise with it. Afterward she had the lab at the company test it. The tester at the lab just couldn't make sense of it.

— This has to be our water since it is bottled and already sealed, but I don't get it. It's not registering as even close to being our company water.

Scratching his head . . .

— How could another water source have possibly gotten into our sealed bottles? It just doesn't make any sense at all!

You can change the world by the power of your word.

NOTES _____

_____

_____

_____

_____

_____

_____

_____

_____

_____

_____

_____

_____

_____

_____

_____

_____

_____

_____

_____

_____

_____

_____

_____

_____

_____

_____

_____

_____

_____

A Personal Story

THE SONG
OF
THE TREES

On my birthday in June of 2012, I decided to take a shamanic journey with a Peruvian shaman. The entire process lasted for 24 hours and included ingesting some sort of hallucinogenic plant. I hadn't touched anything of the sort since my early 20s. After I started practicing yoga, drug experiences of any kind went out of my life entirely. The breathing, moving, and meditating were more than enough to lead me on inner journeys that were much richer and healthier than drug experiences. However, in the summer of 2012, my inner guidance called me to experience this specific shamanic journey.

The whole thing was really a trip of another kind, and the entire experience would take days and days to write about. However, there was a small section within the entire experience that I want to share as the end of this book.

After we ingested the plant, I left the group to be in the forest by myself. I had an incredible urge just to be alone.

The same memory of the 5-year-old, the one I mentioned at the beginning of this book, came to visit me once again.

— Why are you coming up again? I thought we were complete.

Without a warning it had popped up in front of me like a scene from a movie. I sat in the forest and watched it again from beginning to end—all the colors, details, feelings, heartbreak, smells, and grayish sky, all of it so vivid in my head.

My mother tells me the memory I speak of didn't happen exactly on my birthday, but who knows whose remembrance is the true one, and what matters is the way it kept showing up for me still from my past. Without getting into other layers of that memory, it is sufficient to say here it was again as the uninvited guest at my birthday.

Before the shamanic journey, I had been revisited by this sense of not feeling free. Was this imagery and memory the reason for it again? I did not try to figure it out with my mind.

I just asked the empty space in front of me:

— Why now? What is the message? Why this again?

I posed the question to the forest and the trees, the empty space in front of me, the Universe, the quantum field, the void, or whatever one chooses to call it.

I heard the answer loud and clear:

— Remember, my child, you have been eternally free!

I jumped to my feet.

Where was this answer coming from? I could have sworn I was in the forest all alone. I got up to look around, almost expecting to find someone. I looked back at the forest, knowing it was telling me the truth. It seemed to come through the whispers of the trees, huddled together, swaying from the slight wind that was beginning to pick up some speed. The sun was up but rain seemed to be moving in.

I was surprised, a little scared, shocked, and inspired and promised the forest that I would remember this message. I knew it was not a song for my ears only.

— Should I go back and join the rest of the group?
— Where the shaman was, where the comfort was?
— Where perhaps, relatively speaking, the more normal was?
— Or should I dare to go deeper?
— But where was it that I would be going exactly?

The forest spoke and the trees watched me.

— Get up and walk!
— Don't return back!
— Come this way, deeper toward me . . .

I got up, scared and slightly trembling, but intuitively walked even further away, deeper into the forest, until I came upon a clearing. I couldn't believe my eyes.

It looked exactly like the garden in Bulgaria from all those years ago and it was the birthday of my 5-year-old self all over again, in the now. The sky was divided, half of it in the sun and the other half in grey.

— Dance!

The forest commanded. At the exact same moment, the shaman far away started to play his drums and they echoed loudly across the distance and through the corridor of trees, reaching me from the lonely house in the mountains.

The sounds caught my feet like dancing shoes as I stepped into the clearing. Simultaneously, within the first two steps, the skies opened and it started raining, soaking me and washing me all the way through.

It was the 13th of June 2012, and the child of 5 was dancing freely exactly as she had envisioned so many years before. The whole of nature was celebrating with her now. I burst into tears in joining the rain, this time not in sadness but in celebration of the perfection life had been.

I lifted my head up to the sky in ecstasy and caught a rainbow in its actual formation. It came out from the sky above and landed on the mountains in front me, as if forming a bridge between this world and what is beyond the veil.

- Everything was perfect.
- Everything was whole.
- Everything was a reflection.
- Everything was one.
- Everything was now.

But I knew by the next morning all of it would be forgotten.

The reality would fall into a dream.

AND

The dream would fall into reality.

- That was the adventure
- This was the point
- The forgetting and the remembering
- The hide and seek

So I just kept on dancing . . .

ODE TO A TREE

By Esra Banguoglu Ogut

Dedicated to Mother Nature in memory of Darel Rutherford, who lives on through the millions he touched.

I leaned against a tree and asked:
Tell me, what secrets of yours can you whisper to me?

You and I are connected, more than you know,
I am everywhere you go.
If I disappeared, you could not breathe,
If I were to go, you would not live.

Yet you hurt me and I let it go,
As a mother would with a child who doesn't understand.

Talk to me and I will tell you all my wisdom that I know.
Hold! Be in silence and you will hear me,
Not just in the rustle of my leaves, when I dance in the wind,
But in the movement of your soul as it awakens from its sleep.

Remember the wisdom planted on this earth long ago?
All but forgotten, except perhaps in a dream now!

Do not just learn from the words in the books,
Made of my body when I am dead,
Learn from me, as I am alive and here for you.
Understand that you and I are connected more than you know.

What I bear becomes your body,
My sway your shade,
My body your shelter,
These you know.

But my voice you don't know,
As you think only words can speak.

Come to the forest and embrace me,
As you would your ancient family,
Ask me a question and be silent.
You will find your roots in listening deeply.

I was never gone,
You were never lost.
Look around you,
Bow down to the abundance
That surrounds you.

When you die your spirit will fly back to the stars,
But your body will return to me.

**Find me not then,
But now!**

Have a Wonderful Journey

Notes on Quotes:

Page xxvi. George Orwell, *The Complete Works of George Orwell, vol. 16: I have tried to tell the truth, 1943-1944*. Peter Hobley Davison, ed. (London: Secker & Warburg, 1998), p. 204.

Page 26. Abraham-Hicks workshops, copyrighted by Esther Hicks. © Copyright 1997–2021, Abraham-Hicks Publications. www.abraham-hicks.com.

Page 120. Though this quote is frequently attributed to Anaïs Nin, no cited source links it to any of her work. In March 2013, a former director of public relations at California's John F. Kennedy University in Orinda, Elizabeth Appell, claimed she had authored the quote in 1979 as an inspirational header on a class schedule. See Paul Herron, "Who wrote 'Risk'? Is the mystery solved?" *The Official Anaïs Nin Blog*, March 5, 2013. http://anaisninblog.skybluepress.com/2013/03/who-wrote-risk-is-the-mystery-solved

Page 158. Darel Rutherford, private sessions, 2004–2020.

Page 196. R. Queen, *Darkchylde: The Ariel Chylde Saga*, Curiosity Quills Press, 2016.

Page 224. This quote is attributed to Pierre Teilhard de Chardin in *The Joy of Kindness*, by Robert J. Furey (Chestnut Ridge, NY: Crossroad Books, 1993), p.138, and in the essay "The Phenomenon of Man," by de Chardin, 1955, but it is attributed to G. I. Gurdjieff in *Beyond Prophecies and Predictions: Everyone's Guide to the Coming Changes* by Moira Timms (New York: Random House, 1993), p. 62; neither cites a source. It was widely popularized by Wayne Dyer, who often quoted it in his presentations, crediting it to Chardin.

Page 278. Darel Rutherford, ibid.

Page 292. Darel Rutherford, ibid.

Page 302. M.K. Gandhi, *Ethical Religion* (Madras: S. Ganesan, 1922), p.61.

Page 314. Darel Rutherford, ibid.

Page 346. Lawrence Kushner, *The Book of Words: Talking Spiritual Life, Living Spiritual Talk* (Nashville, TN: Jewish Lights Publishing, 1998), p. 11.

References:

1. Darel Rutherford, private sessions, 2004–2020.
2. Although generally attributed to Henry Ford, this quote has never been successfully linked to him. https://www.thehenryford.org/collections-and-research/digital-resources/popular-topics/henry-ford-quotes/, accessed 2021.
3. Terry Turner, "Teen Girl Lifts Truck Off Her Father, Saves Family From Fire," Good News Network, Jan. 12, 2016. https://www.goodnewsnetwork.org/teen-girl-lifts-truck-off-his-father-saves-family-from-fire/, accessed 2021.
4. Philip Ball, "Two Slits and One Hell of a Quantum Conundrum," *Nature*, August 7, 2018. https://www.nature.com/articles/d41586-018-05892-6.
5. Abraham-Hicks workshops, copyrighted by Esther Hicks. © Copyright 1997–2021, Abraham-Hicks Publications. www.abraham-hicks.com.
6. Darel Rutherford, ibid.
7. "Clearing the Subconscious," 3HO. https://www.3ho.org/clearingsubconscious.

8. "Meditation for the Negative Mind," 3HO. https://www.3ho.org/kundaliniyoga/meditation/featured-meditations/meditation-negative-mind.
9. Also generally attributed to Henry Ford, though never successfully linked to him. Ibid.
10. Rumi (translated by Esra Banguoglu Ogut), in Joseph Campbell, *The Hero With a Thousand Faces* (Princeton, NJ: Princeton University Press, 1949). Copyright, Bollingen Foundation Inc., New York, N.Y. 1949.
11. "Soothing Left Nostril Breathing," 3HO. https://www.3ho.org/kundaliniyoga/pranayam/pranayam-techniques/soothing-left-nostril-breathing.
12. Rumi, ibid.
13. "Stress Relief and Clearing the Emotions of the Past," 3HO. https://www.3ho.org/3ho-lifestyle/authentic-relationships/stress-relief-and-clearingemotions-past.
14. *The Matrix*, dir. Andy Wachowski and Larry Wachowski. Warner Bros. Pictures, 1999. DVD.
15. "Sat Kriya," 3HO. https://www.3ho.org/sat-kriya.
16. Darel Rutherford, ibid.
17. Darel Rutherford, ibid.
18. Mitchell L. Gaynor, M.D., *The Healing Power of Sound* (Boulder, CO: Shambhala Publications, 1999), p. 115.
19. Cleve Backster, *Primary Perception: Biocommunication with Plants, Living Foods, and Human Cells* (Anza, CA: White Rose Millennium Press, 2003), page 25.
20. "Meditation for the Positive Mind," 3HO. https://www.3ho.org/kundaliniyoga/meditation/featuredmeditations/meditation-positive-mind.
21. Richard Bartlett, N.D., D.C., Matrix Energetics Workshops. http://www.matrixenergetics.com.
22. Darel Rutherford, ibid.
23. "Meditation for a Calm Heart," 3HO. https://www.3ho.org/kundalini-yoga/pranayam/pranayam-techniques/meditation-calm-heart.
24. Sabahattin Özel, "Atatürk Dönemi Türkiye Ekonomisi," *İstanbul Üniversitesi Yakın Dönem Türkiye Araştırmaları Dergisi*, no: 2, 2002, p. 248.
25. Darel Rutherford, ibid.
26. A. H. Maslow, Maslow's Hierarchy of Needs, from "A Theory of Human Motivation," *Psychological Review*, 50 (4): 370-96, 1943.
27. Abraham-Hicks workshops, ibid.
28. Masaru Emoto, *The Hidden Messages in Water* (New York: Atria Books, 2011).

We but mirror the world.
All the tendencies present
in the outer world are
to be found in the world
of our body.
If we could change
ourselves, the tendencies
in the world would
also change.
As a man changes his own
nature, so does